An Administrative Bureau
during the Old Regime

An Administrative Bureau during the Old Regime

The Bureau of Commerce
and Its Relations
to French Industry
from May 1781 to November 1783

Harold T. Parker

Newark: University of Delaware Press
London and Toronto: Associated University Presses

© 1993 by Associated University Presses, Inc.

All rights reserved. Authorization to photocopy items for internal or personal use, or the internal or personal use of specific clients, is granted by the copyright owner, provided that a base fee of $10.00, plus eight cents per page, per copy is paid directly to the Copyright Clearance Center, 27 Congress Street, Salem, Massachusetts 01970.
[ISBN 0-87413-467- 6/93 $10.00 + 8¢ pp, pc.]

Associated University Presses
440 Forsgate Drive
Cranbury, NJ 08512

Associated University Presses
25 Sicilian Avenue
London WC1A 2QH, England

Associated University Presses
P.O. Box 338, Port Credit
Mississauga, Ontario
Canada L5G 4L8

The paper used in this publication meets the requirements
of the American National Standard for Permanence of Paper
for Printed Library Materials Z39.48-1984.

Library of Congress Cataloging-in-Publication Data

Parker, Harold Talbot, 1907–
    An administrative bureau during the old regime : the Bureau of Commerce and its relations to French industry from May 1781 to November 1783 / Harold T. Parker.
    p.   cm.
    Includes bibliographical references and index.
    ISBN 0-87413-467-6 (alk. paper)
    1. France. Bureau du commerce—History. 2. Industry and state—France—History—18th century. I. Title.
HF73.F7P36 1993
354.440082—dc20   92-50634
                                                        CIP

To Louise

Contents

Preface	9
1. The Administrative Context	13
2. The Story	24
3. The Yield in Conclusions and Reflections	88
Appendix: A Partial List of Outgoing Dispatches on the Subject of the New Regulations Sent out by the Four Intendants of Commerce during the Early Months of 1782	99
Notes	106
Bibliography	122
Index	151

Preface

This book is a second probe into the operations of an administrative bureau of the Old Regime. The first probe, *the Bureau of Commerce in 1781 and Its Policies with Respect to French Industry* (1979), analytically described the organization, personnel, procedures, and strategic industrial policies of the operating administrators, the four intendants of commerce, of the Bureau of Commerce. This second probe watches them in action (or sometimes inaction) as they moved from case to case, from problem to problem, through twenty-nine months of historical time, from May 1781 to November 1783.

The period chosen has two advantages. One: since the two controllers general in charge during these months, Joly de Fleury and d'Ormesson, were nearly ciphers in economic matters, we have the opportunity to observe the Bureau as it *essentially* was, undisturbed by any intruding, abrasive superior. Two: we have the opportunity to watch the four intendants of the Bureau not only in routine performance but also as they managed (or attempted to manage) two major crises: the mass mutiny of most French textile artisans against the Bureau's new textile regulations and the developing surge of British inventions, productivity, and competitiveness, especially in textiles and iron and steel.

The structure of the book is simple. The first chapter ("The Administrative Context") places the Bureau within the context of the administrative monarchy of Louis XVI and discusses problems of historical method. The second ("The Story") presents the data as a flow-of-activity narrative. The third ("The Yield") reflects on the meaning and significance of the data thus presented. Together the chapters are intended to convey a sense of what it was like to be a civil servant amid the often frustrating complexities of the Old Regime economy, society, and government. The chapters thus throw light on the qualities of the royal administration, which was one of the most enduring legacies of the French monarchy to later regimes, and on the relations of that administration to the French economy and people.

In the preparation of the book my primary obligation is to the staff of the Archives Nationales, without whose courteous cooperation the volume could not have been written. Along the way many others have aided me. Once the topic was defined, the late Jacques Godechot, with his unfailing kindness, encouraged me to persist. William Reddy, a colleague at Duke University, read an early, experimental draft and liked the way the project was "set up." He is not responsible, of course, for its later development. Four distinguished specialists in the field, Richard J. Barker (Montclair State College), Marie Donaghay (Villanova University), J. R. Harris (University of Birmingham, England), and Robert D. Harris (University of Idaho), generously gave their time and energy to read in second draft the chapters entitled "The Story" and "The Yield." Their intense scrutiny saved me from many compromising errors of detail. Throughout the years J. R. Harris has unstintingly shared with me his vast knowledge of the industrial technology of eighteenth-century Great Britain and France. The introductory chapter, "The Administrative Context," prepared upon the recommendation of the four readers, was perused by J. F. Bosher (York University), a specialist in administrative history. His perspicacious emendations sharpened both my vision of the Bourbon monarchy and my expression. I am immeasurably indebted to the anonymous scholarly reader for the University of Delaware Press, who helped me clarify the presentation while maintaining the integrity of my vision. Finally, Laura Oaks, my copyeditor for many years, clarified and strengthened the manuscript at every point. The volume would have been much weaker without the work of these readers. I am solely responsible for whatever deficiencies remain.

An Administrative Bureau during the Old Regime

1
The Administrative Context

The Bureau of Commerce and its four intendants were parts of a royal administration that had been developing over the centuries within a society and a government that were still incompletely unified. Since Hugh Capet (987–996) a chief problem of the French kings had been to get themselves obeyed. As we shall see, even the administrative monarchy of Louis XVI could not always secure obedience. The king's authority was "absolute," but not his power. In the interests of assuring obedience the French kings had negotiated bargains, contracts, and understandings with the towns, the provinces, and the leading privileged classes of clergy, nobles, merchants, and manufacturers. These agreements gradually covered the kingdom with a crazy-quilt maze of local laws, local tolls and tariffs, local weights and measures, privileged exemptions from taxation and quarterings of troops, and privileged monopolies of manufacture and trade. The individual privileges of exemption and monopoly were so numerous and so ancient that not even the royal lawyers knew them all. The king might learn of a privilege accorded by a predecessor only when he inadvertently generated another privilege that infringed it.

Within this complexity the kings had elaborated over the centuries several hierarchies through which they controlled the population. These included the ecclesiastical hierarchy of the Roman Catholic Church from the vicars and priests to the bishops and archbishops; the military hierarchy of the army and navy from the private soldier and sailor to the marshals and admirals of France; the judicial hierarchy of courts from the humble *juge des manufactures* to the highest court, the Parlement of Paris; and the bureaucratic hierarchies of the several ministerial departments.

In 1781, from the standpoint of the king, there were six such departments: Foreign Affairs, War (the army), Navy, the Royal Household, the Controller General's Department, and the office of the Keeper of the Seals, the chief judicial officer of the crown. Each of the first four departments was assigned to a secretary of state, and each had a core major function, as indicated by its title. By contrast, in the Controller General's Department the title of its head varied—Controller General of Finances (Turgot), Director General of Finances (Necker), Minister of State and Finances (Joly de Fleury), and Controller General again (d'Ormesson and

Calonne)—and its functions were multifarious. Indeed, the controller general "was hampered a great deal by the extraordinarily wide range of his responsibilities." As Tocqueville remarked, "he acted in turn as Minister of Finance, Minister of the Interior, Minister of Commerce, and, we might now add, Minister of Health and Welfare, Minister of Supply, Minister of Economic Development and others."[1]

The king met regularly on an individual basis with each of the six department heads, heard their reports, and rendered decisions on the items of business they each brought to him. Questions of salient importance he considered with his major advisors assembled regularly in two councils—questions of foreign affairs in the *Conseil d'en haut*, which met nearly every Sunday and Wednesday, and internal matters in the *Conseil des dépêches*, which was scheduled for every Saturday. There in the privacy of his council chamber he listened to discussion of the issues and then, in the presence of his councilors, gave his measured decision. There were also a *Conseil royal des finances*, on paper meeting every Tuesday, and a *Conseil royal de commerce*, scheduled for fortnightly sessions. In fact during Louis XVI's reign they rarely assembled, perhaps once or twice a year or not at all.[2]

From the meetings in council and with the department heads the royal decisions flowed down through the transmitting administrative bureaus in Paris to the executant officials—perhaps to an ambassador, to a general, a captain of a naval vessel, a *procureur-général* of a parlement, or to the intendant of a *généralité* and through him to his subdelegates, who carried the decisions into the forty thousand parishes and villages.

Each ministerial department had its own set of executive bureaus in Paris/Versailles. The staff of each bureau was a rather intimate group. It was composed of a *garçon de bureau*, who trimmed the pens, fed the fire in the stove and took out the ashes, and tended the lamps and the chandeliers of candles; two or three *expéditionnaires*, who copied in a clear secretarial hand the outgoing correspondence and reports and doubled as file clerks as well; two or three *rédacteurs*, who drafted the letters; and a dependable bureau chief, who was generally a model senior civil servant, hard-working, exact, and a master of the business of his office—in brief, a total of six to seven persons who often worked together in a single room. In another room would be shelved boxes holding the past dispatches and reports.

In a homogeneous department, such as that of war, the specialized division of labor and arrangement of bureaus was logical, functional, and simple. In the War Department, for example, there were five bureaus: Finances, Movement and Provisioning of Troops, Artillery and Engineering, the Etat-Major, and the administrative supervision of the frontier provinces, including Corsica, for which the department was responsible. The secretary of state for war regularly met with each bureau chief to go over his reports and to render a series of decisions, just as he (the secretary) met with the king.[3]

The organization of the Controller General's Department was more complex, because of the multiplicity and variety of its functions.[4] There were intendants of finance and their bureaus, intendants of commerce and their bureau chiefs, and so on, arranged in a variety of ways. Nevertheless, whatever their number and arrangement, the bureaus of each department performed the same function of transmission and communication: they received from below petitions and reports, responded to them, sometimes by reference to higher authorities, and then received from above orders and requests for additional information, to be transmitted down the line, frequently to the intendant of a *généralité*.

The intendant, in turn, was the king's man within his jurisdiction. In the words of a royal instruction, he was to "watch over the enforcement of edicts, the administration of civil and criminal justice and economic legislation, and in general over all the affairs concerning the well-being and repose of our subjects." The intendant of a *généralité* was further charged to keep an eye on "all those whose dignity, office, or fortune assured them a personal influence, which they might abuse: the ecclesiastics, the nobles, the royal officers. He was to seek out abuses which were being committed . . . and propose the remedy."[5] He was to watch the parlement, preside if he wished over lesser courts, and judge certain cases himself; verify the accounts of the collectors of taxes, correct the distribution of taxes among parishes and individuals, and issue fiscal regulations; supervise inspectors of manufactures; direct the levy and victualing of troops and provide for the payment of garrisons; deliver an opening address to the provincial estates (where these existed), propose the amount of money they should grant, and manage and menace them until he got it; appoint the mayors and other officials of the town and village communities, verify their accounts, approve their expenditures, and liquidate their debts. To aid him in the performance of his duties, he too had in the capital of the *généralité* a *premier commis* to supervise an executive bureau of clerks. Throughout his jurisdiction he had subdelegates (*subdélégués*), each responsible for a group of parishes. The subdelegate brought the royal administration right into the parish and into the life of each individual. The subdelegate might supervise the assessment of certain taxes, encourage local industry, and even select the town and village officials. Since the subdelegates corresponded with the intendant and often referred problems to him for decision, and the intendants corresponded with the controller general and the relevant secretaries of state and often referred to them for decision, nearly all the administrative business of the kingdom was supervised from Paris/Versailles and all important decisions (and some that were unimportant) might come before the king in some form for consideration.

Thus far, on paper this seems schematically a pyramidal, formal administrative organization, with reports and petitions passing upward along well-established channels of communication, and orders passing down along well-defined channels of communication and command. In practice, the system was not so simple. It was subject to personal influences not recorded in the *Almanach Royal* or anywhere else. The question arises: Where were the decisions being made, and who was making them? That depended *at a given moment of time* on who was king and who was influencing him; on who was keeper of the seals, secretary of state for foreign affairs, for war, for the navy, for the royal household, and who was controller general and what were their relations with one another; on who was the chief of the bureau most involved and what were his relations with his superiors, his chief clerk or *premier commis*, and with other sectors of the administration; on who was the intendant of the *généralité* in question and who were his subaltern clerks and subdelegates; and who was requesting a decision.

Who in the Bureau of Commerce, for example, was making the decisions with respect to French industry, the subject of this probe? The answers to that question are neither simple nor uniform, nor with the available evidence are they always clear and definitive. Nevertheless, we can say the decisions were being made within the following context.

Within the sprawling Controller General's Department incoming queries and petitions respecting the relation of the royal government to the French economy were referred to a nonexecutive "Bureau pour les affaires du Commerce," which met twice a week. Its members included five "conseillers d'état" and five "maîtres des requêtes, intendants du commerce." Also attending the meetings but without a vote were thirteen consultative deputies of commerce, each of whom represented an important French commercial or industrial town or an overseas colony.

Four of the five *conseillers* were elderly members of the nobility of the robe who served on other royal deliberative bodies: Jean-Baptiste Paulin d'Aguesseau de Fresnes (1701–1784) was *doyen* of the royal council and member of the Conseil des dépêches and the moribund Conseil royal de commerce; Louis Jean Bertier de Sauvigny (1709–1788) was member of the Conseil des dépêches; Antoine Martin Chaumont de la Galaizière (1697–1783), member of the royal council and the Conseil royal de commerce; and Claude Henry Feydeau de Marville (1705–1787), member of the royal council. They had had long careers in the royal government, as presidents of the Parlement of Paris or as intendants of a *généralité* and councilors of the king. They brought experience and judgment to the affairs before the Bureau but no special competence in its business. The case of the fifth *conseiller*, Jules François de Cotte (1721–1810), was somewhat different. A younger member of the nobility of the robe, he had served as a president of the Parlement of Paris (1745–1758) and, most important, he had been an active intendant of commerce for nearly twenty years (1758–1777). From experience and from the insights gained therefrom he could be a valuable and valued member of the Bureau.[6]

Of the five intendants of commerce four were the working members of the Bureau. They prepared the dossiers of the cases that were brought to the attention of the Bureau and the controller general. They were paid civil servants who were each responsible for supervising and thinking about a single major industry (silk, linen, knitted goods, or paper and leather together) and one of the four economic regions into which France was administratively divided.

Of these four intendants the dean, both in age and length of service, was Jacques Marie Jérôme Michau de Montaran. Born in 1701, he had been appointed intendant of commerce in 1744. His division included the *généralités* of Paris (except the city itself, which was under the supervision of the lieutenant general of police), Roussillon, Languedoc, Provence, Dauphiny, Auvergne, Montauban, Auch, and Béarn, and throughout the kingdom the manufacture of linen. He was assisted by his son Jean Jacques Mauville Michau de Montaran (1735–1816), who upon the elder Montaran's death on August 5, 1782 succeeded him in his functions. Two other intendants, Jean François Tolozan (1722–1802) and Antoine Louis Blondel (1737–?), had been commissioned in the same year, 1776. Tolozan's division embraced the *généralités* of Lower, Middle, and Upper Normandy (Caen, Alençon, and Rouen), Brittany, Bourges, Orléans, and Moulins as well as the manufacture of stockings and other knitted goods throughout France. When Jean Charles Philibert Trudaine de Montigny, the son of the economic statesman-bureaucrat Daniel Charles Trudaine, died in 1777, Necker had entrusted his suite of offices, his inherited accumulation of official papers, and his *premier commis*, Etienne Pierre Valioud Dormenville (1728–?), to Tolozan. Necker also gave Tolozan the supervision of the *Caisse du commerce*, the Bureau of Commerce's treasury, which paid out subsidies to favored manufacturers upon the collegial decision of the four intendants and the controller general.[7] The division of Blondel comprised the *généralités* of Soissons, Picardy, Flanders and Artois, Hainaut and Cambrésis, Champagne, the Three Bishoprics (Metz, Toul, Verdun), Lorraine and Barrois, and Alsace, and throughout France the manufacture of paper and leather. The fourth intendant was Pierre Joseph Colonia (1746–1823), whose division was the *généralités* of the Lyonnais, Burgundy (duchy and county), Limousin, Touraine, Poitou, La Rochelle, and Bordeaux, and in France the manufacture of silk.[8]

Each of the four intendants of commerce had his own office, in his town house in Paris. Each had his own small executive bureau: that is, his own *premier commis* or chief clerk who coordinated the work of the office, two or three *rédacteurs* who drafted dispatches and memoranda, an *expéditionnaire* or copyist, a keeper of the registers and files, and an office boy.[9] Each intendant was a person, a running function in time. The intendants were neither devils nor demigods,[10] but men facing succeeding situations and seeking, usually, to do something about them. They received petitions, they read reports, they gave audiences, they consulted with their *premiers commis* and with each other, and they made decisions.

The four intendants conferred with Louis Guillaume de Vilevault (1716–1786), the fifth intendant of commerce, when they considered questions involving maritime foreign commerce or the Farmers General, the semipublic agency that collected the indirect taxes. The four intendants also conferred on occasion with a consultative body known as the deputies of commerce. Since the beginning of the eighteenth century the chambers of commerce of the leading French commercial and industrial towns had each nominated and paid a deputy to represent and defend in Paris their towns' special interests.[11] By 1781 these deputies served as advisors to the Bureau of Commerce on questions, usually concerning tariffs, that were referred to them. They met each Tuesday and Friday morning to prepare their formal written opinions (*avis*) for presentation to the four intendants of commerce and to the full Bureau. Their loyalties were divided. As counselors to the king, the controller general, and the Bureau they were asked to think in terms of *le bien public*, the economic welfare of the kingdom. But as agents of elitist chambers of commerce in prominent towns, they were expected to defend the privileges and localized policies of their respective towns even when these ran contrary to the royal and national interest. As tenured officials who served and lived in the Paris/Versailles environment for decades, they tended over the years to take the national viewpoint, to the increasing dissatisfaction of their original municipal constituents. Although the deputies of commerce could not vote in the meetings of the full Bureau of Commerce, their *avis*, thoroughly researched, intelligently thought through, and usually objective and dispassionate, carried considerable weight with the full Bureau, including the four intendants of commerce. The deputies of commerce, though having only a consultative voice, possessed the authority of informed and rational opinion. That their views were listened to and often accepted tells us something of the quality and tone of this segment of the royal administration.

In the outlying provinces the four intendants of commerce worked through the intendant of each *généralité* and also its appointive, salaried inspector of manufactures. On his semiannual tours of his jurisdiction, each inspector checked on the warden-clerks (*gardes jurés, préposés*) who inspected cloth for conformity to the standards set by royal regulations, conferred with manufacturers about the improvement of their methods, and devised regional strategies for the economic strengthening of his *généra-*

lité. Each inspector, if he was worth his salt, was thinking very hard about how to render his district more prosperous. He was aided by subinspectors of manufactures, who resided in each major industrial town.[12]

The four intendants and consultant deputies of commerce believed that for the royal administration to intervene beneficially in the economy it needed information, rational interpretation of causal interrelations, and careful empirical consideration of all the angles and factors in a situation. The Bureau of Commerce, they were persuaded, did indeed have the procedures to insure rational appraisal of an interrelated reality. By these procedures a petition, let us say a petition for government aid to start a new glass factory, allegedly using superior English techniques, would be referred by the Bureau's secretariat to the intendant of commerce who was supervising the *généralité* or industry of its origin. The intendant or his *premier commis* would determine whether the question could be decided on their own knowledge or whether additional information should be sought. Such information could be obtained by asking for the previous documents on the case or by referring the petition to the intendant or inspector of manufactures of the *généralité* in which the factory was to be sited: Are the facts in the petition correct? Would the factory be advantageous to the locality? Is there a market for the product? Will it interfere with other privileges already granted? Are raw materials present in sufficient quantity? Is fuel available? Is the supply of labor adequate? Will neighboring citizens be disturbed or endangered? (Evidently the problems and principles of zoning were an acknowledged issue.) As often as not, the intendant or inspector of manufactures referred the request down the line to the man on the spot, the appropriate subdelegate or subinspector. If his reply was favorable and his intendant or inspector endorsed it, and if the factory proposed to use wood for fuel, the managing intendant of commerce sent the petition to the Administration of Waters and Forests: From your standpoint should this permission be accorded? Is the wood supply ample? Will the navy's claim to high-grade timber in coastal regions be protected? Or if the intendant of the *généralité*'s answer was favorable and the petition entailed an exemption or diminution of internal dues or an increase of import tariff, it would be sent to the Farmers General for their opinion: Do you advise granting this request? How will permission affect your interests and the king's revenue? What is the tariff policy in question? At this point an opinion was often sought from the consultant deputies of commerce: How will this proposal affect the general prosperity of the kingdom and, specifically, of your region? Because this petition prospected a technological innovation borrowed from English practices, a scientist from the Royal Academy of Sciences might also be called in: Will the petitioner's claims stand up under testing? How does the proposal fit into our general industrial strategy for glass?

Meanwhile the responsible intendant of commerce would be weighing with his *premier commis* the pros and cons of various forms of pecuniary aid. Once the information for a rational decision had been assembled and all the angles had been considered, he might (if the issue was routine) decide it on his own or consider it in his regular weekly meeting with the controller general. However, if the issue was a major one, as in this hypothetical case of the glass factory, he presented the proposal with his recommendation to his fellow intendants of commerce, who met in *comité* twice a week just before the biweekly session of the full Bureau. They then prepared collegially a joint decision. If their answer to the petition was positive and if it was approved by the full Bureau of Commerce, and/or the controller general, a decree was issued and a transfer of an English technological practice was undertaken.[13]

Although application of a twentieth-century generalization to the eighteenth is risky, Herbert Simon's comment on cooperative discussion seems appropriate here. "An important advantage of the committee over step-by-step clearance as a means of reaching a joint decision is that each participant is exposed, directly and simultaneously, to the views of all the others. There is a maximum of opportunity for the free interchange of information and ideas. . . . Apart from their effectiveness in securing a free interchange of views, and hence in securing sounder decisions, committees serve important communication functions. First, they communicate a thorough understanding to the participants of the decisions reached, of the goals and objectives sought and of the strategies applied. They thus assure continuity and consistency in policies already developed and in their implementation by action. Moreover, by providing a feeling of participation in the decision-making process and a feeling of responsibility for the decisions reached, they greatly improve the motivations of the participants in later carrying out the decisions. . . . Group participation in decision-making is an important means for securing acceptance [and support] of new programs [policies], and organization[al] changes."[14]

As individual administrators and as a group meeting biweekly in *comité*, the four intendants of commerce had thus formed over the decades the continuing center of administrative thought about the relation of the French royal government to the French economy. By 1781 they had developed strategies of improvement for the manufacture of textiles (silk, wool, cotton, linen), metal products (iron, steel, lead, tin), glass, paper, chemicals, leather, and sugar.

We still haven't answered the question: Who in the royal administration made the decisions with respect to French industry? Obviously, as in any large organization, the decisions were composite ones in which many people participated. Obviously, too, any single decision could be pushed, stalled, or ultimately checked by anyone along the route: by the petitioner himself; by the officials in the field, the subdelegates of a *généralité*, the subinspectors of manufacture, the local inspector of trees in the Administration of Waters and Forests, the lowest subaltern agent of the collector of indirect taxes for the Farmers General, the intendant and inspector of manufactures in the *généralité*; in Paris by the *premier commis* of the relevant intendant of commerce, the intendant of commerce himself, the consultant scientist, the knowledgeable deputies of commerce, the *comité*, the full Bureau of Commerce, the controller general, the secretaries for foreign affairs, for war, and for the navy, and by the king.

Nevertheless, this can be said. King Louis XVI was rarely an active force in decisions relating to the French economy. Of his controllers general and ministers or directors of finance, Turgot (1774–1776), Necker (1776–1781), and Calonne (1783–1787) were actively involved in determining economic/industrial policies and implementing measures. In contrast, the two controllers general between Necker and Calonne were nearly ciphers in economic matters. Although Joly de Fleury (May 21, 1781 to March 26, 1783) attempted to undo Necker's reforms of the administration of royal finances, he neither overturned nor added to Necker's reform measures with respect to the regulation of industry. The evidence in his papers and in the archives of the Bureau of Commerce shows him to have been mainly preoccupied with the finances of the royal government, rarely with its relations to the economy. Thus he seems to have approved and signed or to have asked the king to approve and sign whatever an intendant of commerce or the *comité* of four intendants brought to him. Of this we can be sure: he did not innovate in the realm of governmental policy regarding the economy. The same may be said of his six-month successor, d'Ormesson (March 26 to November 6, 1783).

It follows that during these two and a half years we have the opportunity to observe the Bureau of Commerce as it essentially was, sustained by the dedication, zeal, habitual procedures, and thoughtful policies of its four intendants of commerce and their consultants and undisturbed by any intruding, abrasive superior.

The question then becomes: How shall we handle the Bureau and its four intendants during these nine hundred days so as to discover and reveal administrative reality? What approach or method shall we use?

In the pursuit of certified knowledge professional historians have developed or applied an arsenal of approaches and methods from which they can choose: among them, for example, the techniques of historical criticism; empathy; content analysis; comparative analysis; typology; prosopography; psychological and social psychological theories; class and group analysis; information theory; organization theory; systems analysis; semiotics and deconstructionism—to mention only a few. From options such as these the historian selects those methods which seem appropriate to the problem at hand and to the available data.

The problems we are considering in this probe are: What were the characteristics and qualities of this segment of the French royal administration? During these months (and in later probes during the revolutionary and Napoleonic years), what of the administration continued, and why, and what changed, and why? What were the interrelations of the administrators and the French people?

In the resolution of these problems we have found it advantageous first to present the data empathetically as a flow-of-activity, flow-of-consciousness narrative, and then to ask what light the data throw on the questions we have asked. In this type of narrative we are making two basic assumptions: one, that scholarly historical investigation is a reality-seeking, reality-communicating enterprise; and two, that the genesis of historical events lies in individuals. If we push the implications of these assumptions to the utmost, certain consequences follow. We imaginatively walk alongside our intendants of commerce as they enter situations with certain attitudes, ideas, and emotional complexes that affect their perception of the situation and possible courses of action; they take an action, and this affects the situation and maybe the attitudes, ideas, and complexes that affect their perception of the *new* situation and possible courses of action, and so on. When the administrators meander, we meander; when they enter a cul-de-sac and necessarily turn back, so do we; and when they are frustrated by fellow bureaucrats (the Farmers General, for instance), we feel frustrated and exasperated too. We do not know what is coming next, any more than they did. We share, for the moment, their values and prejudices and refrain from any judgments beyond the ones they themselves make.

This stance determines the events we select: since many of the administrative procedures were routine and repetitious, there will be routine and repetitious events in our account; events that loomed important to the administrators will be important to us. This stance also governs our style: their deliberate, delaying administrative prose was not simply a mode of expression, it was a way of thought; it becomes ours. If our brief paraphrase of a long administrative document sounds just like the original, that is what we intend and desire. We shall thus not reproduce the reality of the estimated 50,000 pages of manuscript we have read but rather create a symbol of that reality, a verisimilitude, in its flow of activity and consciousness. We shall then have a body of certified knowledge from which we can seek answers to the problems we have set. We shall have also shown how an Old Regime administrative unit moved (or did not move) through twenty-nine ordinary and interesting months.

The evidence for these years is both abundant and incomplete, revealing and opaque. We have a register, that is, a *list* of the incoming and outgoing letters of the four intendants of commerce. In addition, there are all the outgoing letters themselves of two of the intendants, Tolozan and Montaran the younger. From them the incoming letters to which they were responding may be inferred. We also have the dossiers of all the major *industrial* cases considered by the four intendants. These dossiers contain the original, precipitating petition, the reports (if required) of the intendant and inspector of manufactures of the concerned *généralité*, the evaluations of the Administration of Waters and Forests, the deputies of commerce, and the consultant scientists, and the recommendation of the managing intendant of commerce—in brief, all the information presented to the *comité*. There are on occasion traces of the conversation between the intendant of commerce and his *premier commis*, between the intendant and the controller general, and between the controller general and the king. We then have within the dossier the recorded decision of the full Bureau of Commerce and/or the controller general, to be amplified in a letter to the original petitioner. In our documentation we also have a complete and splendid series of opinions rendered by the deputies of commerce, chiefly on tariff issues. Since the deputies usually give a history of the tariff duty in question from the time of Louis XIV and the changing state of the industry in France with respect to its competition in Britain, Holland, Germany, Italy, and Spain, these opinions are a rich source for industrial history and the economic philosophy of our Bureau. Added to these are the semiannual reports of several inspectors of manufacture on their tours of their *généralités*. All this information seems ample, and to a degree it is, for a rather full history of decision-making during these years. What is lacking is any record of the oral interchange that occurred within the meetings of the *comité* and of the full Bureau. We shall never know what the officials said to each other. Here, as elsewhere in historical investigation, we push back the limits of darkness and bring in light, but darkness and mystery remain, hovering just beyond.

2
The Story

When should the narrative start? Fortunately, we have a convenient date: May 19, 1781, when Louis XVI dismissed Jacques Necker as director general of finances. As controller general in everything except title and a seat on the Royal Council, Necker had supervised the operations of the Bureau of Commerce. Gifted with psychological finesse, he had skillfully mediated between the die-hard Colbertist mercantilists and the extremist advocates of laissez-faire. As much as anyone, he was responsible for the reconciling tenor of the revised industrial regulations of 1779, 1780, and 1781, which tried to meet the needs and desires on the one hand of manufacturers who were demanding the protection of strict rules and on the other of those who wanted unlimited freedom to exploit the variegated opportunities of an ever-expanding market. Necker thus personally helped to ease the adaptation of French industrial policy to the new industrial world. He gave the Bureau a direction along which the intendants of commerce could proceed in the years ahead.

To succeed Necker Louis XVI appointed as minister of finances and in effect controller general Jean-François Joly de Fleury, a respected *maître de requêtes* whose most recent post had been the intendancy of Burgundy.[1] Among the many officers listed as belonging to his jurisdiction, we find our Bureau of Commerce and its four intendants of commerce who dealt with the problems of French commerce, industry, and labor. From May 1781 to November 1783 the flow of their activity and consciousness proceeded and can be separately followed along two main lines: one, the governmental *regulation* of the quality of manufactured products, especially textiles, and of the workers; and two, the direct *encouragement* of industry by a variety of means, such as subsidies, tariffs, exclusive privileges, and the like.

The Flow of Regulation with Respect to the Quality of Manufactured Products and to the Workers

In the spring and summer of 1781 the four intendants were still fine-tuning the formulation and implementation of a batch of edicts that were intended as a comprehensive overhaul of the royal system of industrial regulation.

In the preparation of the edicts and in the installation of the machinery of enforcement the four intendants had tried to consider every angle and to leave nothing to chance. As far back as 1778 they had sounded out expert and influential industrial opinion throughout the kingdom. Casting their net wide in business and administrative circles, they had asked the deputies of commerce in Paris, the inspectors of manufacture and the intendants of each *généralité*, the chambers of commerce in each leading town, and the deputies of the estates of Languedoc to respond in writing to several questions: Should different industrial undertakings (*les fabriques*) be subjected to the execution of regulations, or should they be allowed complete liberty? (Some respondents favored the first option, others the second.) Was an intermediate system satisfying both groups possible? (A large majority said yes, and approved this approach.) Should the intermediate system be introduced by patchwork legislation, or should the entire industrial code be revised, simplified, and updated? (Again, a large majority favored an entirely new code.) So, when on May 5, 1779 the basic royal edict proclaiming the general principles of the new system intermediate between mercantilistic structures and indefinite liberty was issued and its operational date set for July 1, 1780, the four intendants had every reason to believe that they were moving with the main body of French industrial opinion and there would be no problem of securing obedience.

Still, implementing decrees had to be drafted. Particular regulations for each *généralité* had to be prepared and published. In consultation with local experts this was done between August 22, 1780 (Picardy, Auvergne, and Champagne) and September 15, 1781 (Bordeaux). Work on those of Languedoc, however, was delayed, because of the independence and peculiar circumstances of the Nîmes weavers and merchants. When it became apparent that the new regulations regarding the quality of manufactured products would not be ready soon, a decree of October 25, 1781 simply ordered craftsmen to affix to each piece of cloth a small seal bearing on one side the name of the fabricant and on the other his location. In their pipelines of supply, craftsmen and merchants had cloth that had been manufactured in conformity with an older system. Since they had to be given time to sell off these articles, the ultimate date for insistence on obedience to the new rules was moved from July 1, 1780 to January 1, 1782.[2]

Moreover, the machinery of execution had to be set up. Offices of inspection (*bureaux de visite et de marque*) had to be established in towns having guilds of merchants or fabricants, in the principal centers of commerce and manufacturing, and in localities that had fairs. Each office was to be served either by two unpaid sworn guardians (*gardes jurés*), merchants or fabricants who had been elected by their fellows for a one-year term, or by a single salaried royal official (*préposé*) nominated by the appropriate intendant of commerce in consultation with the intendant of the *généralité* and commissioned by the king. According to the new regulations *all* cloth (every item) manufactured in France was to be brought to the appropriate *bureau de visite* and inspected by the local *garde juré* or *préposé*. Cloth manufactured satisfactorily according to the rules of the kingdom, of the *généralité*, and of the particular town with respect to raw material, width of cloth on loom and after finishing, number of threads in the warp, and dye, was to receive a seal (a *marque*) bearing on one side the word *réglée* and the year of manufacture and on the other side the name of the *bureau de visite*. Cloth that was intended to meet the regulation standards, but did not, was to be cut up, a portion was to be confiscated, and the offending craftsman or merchant was to be fined by the local royal judge of manufactures. Cloth deliberately manufactured by the free choice of the fabricant according to dimensions not prescribed by the regulations was still to be brought to the *bureau de visite*; it was to receive a seal carrying simply the name of the *bureau de visite* on one side and the year of manufacture on the other.

This system of inspection was supervised by a hierarchy of inspectors: inspectors of manufactures one for each *généralité*, who were to travel throughout their jurisdiction, checking on the operation of each *bureau de visite*, conferring with manufacturers about the improvement of their methods, and devising regional strategies for the economic strengthening of their *généralité*; subinspectors of manufactures for each major industrial towh, who closely supervised the *gardes jurés* or *préposés* and kept in touch with local merchants and craftsmen; and *élèves des manufactures*, who were interning for several years as subinspectors, in preparation for becoming one.[3] In accord with the necessary proprieties of channeled communication and command the intendant of commerce in Paris could give orders directly to the intendant of the *généralité*, the inspectors, subinspectors, and *élèves* of manufactures, and the *gardes jurés* and *préposés*. However, the royal judges of manufacture belonged to the judicial hierarchy. To confirm or moderate one of their appealed verdicts, the intendant of commerce had to request the controller general himself to order the intendant of the *généralité* to take appropriate action. In major cases even the controller general might have to write to the keeper of the seals.

By the close of 1781 this machinery of inspection and enforcement was in place in *most* manufacturing centers.[4] In addition the ordinance providing for the policing of workers throughout France had been proclaimed on September 12, 1781. Unlike the regulations regarding the quality of the product, the labor code was a tightening rather than an overhaul of past legislation. The tightening was apparent in nearly every article of the decree. By Article I a worker, upon arriving in a manufacturing town, must immediately register with the police. This provision brought him at once within the network of police surveillance. Articles II and III declared that agreements between master and worker were to be faithfully executed. A master was not to discharge a worker, nor reciprocally was a worker to quit a master, until the time limit of the contract had expired. Should there be no time limit, workers could not leave a master until they had completed the articles they had started, reimbursed him for advances made, and given eight days' notice. Articles IV through VI reaffirmed, with improvements, the use of the *billet de congé*. As before, a worker could not leave a master without a written *billet de congé* from the master or local police judge; other masters were forbidden to hire a worker unprovided with a *billet*. Now, however, the worker was to record in a little book (a *livret*) the successive *billets* he had received during his lifetime. A model *billet de congé* was appended to the decree itself. Again, by Article VIII, workers were forbidden to assemble in a body or to cabal among themselves for the placement of workers. A new article, number VII, directed masters to require the local police lieutenant to record the theft by any worker of looms, tools, or materials and to have the robbers pursued. The entire ordinance was to be enforced on "merchants, artisans, apprentices, journeymen, shopkeepers, and workers residing in all the towns and places of the kingdom, and especially where there were or will be . . . guilds."[5]

The regulations were in place, the effective operational date of January 1, 1782 was near, and so was the moment of truth for the four intendants. On November 27, 1781 and for months thereafter they entered and endured a *blizzard* of inquiries and protests from craftsmen, merchants, and enforcing officers. The blizzard was probably unanticipated. The four intendants had spent months, even years, sounding out the sentiment of business circles and trying to devise regulations that were simple, clear, precise, and unambiguous. Yet here were these requests for clarification. The four intendants had tried to devise an intermediate system that would flexibly meet the needs and desires of every French manufacturer. Yet there were protests. The four intendants rose to the occasion. Patiently, firmly, flexibly, diplomatically, and always reasonably, they answered each inquiry and met every protest, surefootedly adapting each reply to the material and psychological circumstances of the inquirer and his local situation. The four intendants did this together. Whether the incoming inquiry was addressed to the controller general or to a particular intendant of commerce, almost every outgoing reply contained the phrase: "I have communicated your letter to Messieurs les Intendants du Commerce and they are of the opinion . . . ." For the four intendants this was their reform; they had spent months, even years in its preparation, and together they were going to make it work. Their effort was collegial administration at its cooperative best.

Even before November, 1781 the four intendants had received a few premonitory inquiries and protests. On June 19, by a letter from Joly de Fleury to Louis Thiroux de Crosne, the intendant of the *généralité* of Upper Normandy (Rouen), they had replied to a memoir of the "syndics and their assistants of the guild of merchant *passementiers* who manufactured all kinds of fabrics in the town of Rouen." The syndics had requested that only they and their assistants be called upon to serve as *gardes jurés* and that the duty of one sou not be levied each time a seal was affixed to a piece of cloth. Joly de Fleury firmly explicated the regulations and insisted they be adhered to: the syndics and their assistants were eligible to be *gardes jurés*, but so was every merchant and fabricant even if he did not have a *lettre de maîtrise*; consequently, even nonguild artisans could vote in the election of *gardes jurés*; the duty of one sou per piece was intentionally set so low as not to be burdensome.[6]

In early July the "Sindics du Corps des Fabricants faisant Fabrique les étoffes de soye, de Nismes" were heard from. Nîmes championed freedom to meet the varied wishes of consumers in an ever-widening market. The Nîmes *fabricants*, in their letters and in an accompanying memoir, were protesting the application of Necker's compromise system of regulations to their products.[7]

The letters patent of May 5, 1779 and January 1, 1780 and the Royal Council's enforcing decree of March 19, 1781 had ordered the Nîmes manufacturers to bring each and every bit of their silk cloth to the inspection bureau; if the item met the standards of quality set out in the regulations, it would be stamped with the capital letter R; if it did not, the mere fact of registration would be certified. In theory the fabricant was free to meet the standards or not, as he chose. In fact, the Nîmes fabricants protested in their memoir, he was not. Buyers, they said, will consder silk cloth without the R to be defective in quality, and they will not purchase it. Fabricants will be forced to conform to the Procrustean regulatory code. But, the memoir continues, "good cloth" is that which suits the consumer's taste. Tastes are changing, they vary, and they do not always harmonize with the standard heavy, ornate cloth prescribed by the regulations. In 1682, the year of Colbert's code, a grandmother bequeathed to her granddaughter a wardrobe of durable dresses that had four times the material that vestments have today, and prices were in proportion. Now, women change their frocks with the season, and they own several; they wish them of lighter material and at a cheaper price. Manufacturers must have freedom to follow changes in taste and to meet foreign competition. Since 1750, the memoir explained, the Nîmes manufacturers have had this freedom and flourished. In 1750 there were in Nîmes 500 looms producing five or six types of silk articles; now there are 3,000 turning out 120 varieties. Concluding that the "liberty" provided by the new regulatory code was illusory, the Nîmes fabricants had therefore asked the intendant of Languedoc to suspend its application to them for six months. When this request was denied, they had appealed in their letter and memoir to the new controller general, in effect to the Bureau of Commerce, and, specifically, to intendant of commerce Colonia. They now requested not simply suspension of the new code but its repeal.

Efficient execution of the regulations depended on the number and distribution of the *bureaux de visite* within each *généralité*. To decide that required a detailed knowledge of local and regional circumstance. How many *bureaux* should there be, for example, within the *généralité* of Orléans? The controller general hoped to save expense by keeping the number down to four: Orléans, Chartres, Romorantin, and St. Agnan. Craftsmen and merchants could choose among the four, and the cloth could be inspected at the moment either of fabrication or of shipment (*expédition*). However, in a dispatch of September 25 he expressed a willingness to defer to the judgment of the man on the spot, the intendant of the *généralité*, Jean François Claude Perrin de Cipierre, if he thought eight were needed for the convenience of the local artificers.[8] Or how many *bureaux* were necessary at Rouen? Hitherto there had been two, operated by two separate corporate groups: one where the "communauté des fabricants drapiers" inspected and marked the woolen cloth woven within the city limits, and the second where the "merciers drapiers" inspected that made outside the city. The latter now petitioned that the two *bureaux* be merged into one. The proposal at first appealed to the controller general on the ground of economy. But enlightened by the knowledgeable Tolozan, intendant of commerce for the region, he concurred on October 10 with Thiroux de Crosne, the local intendant, that a merger would greatly disadvantage the "fabricants drapiers" and that the two *bureaux* should be continued.[9]

And so after November 27 the dispatches went out from the Bureau of Commerce in Paris, week after week, sometimes day after day, patiently, firmly, reasonably explicating the new rules with only occasionally a sharp word of reproof. Here are a few examples paraphrased from the detailed letters of reply.

November 27, to Brunet, inspector of manufactures of Middle Normandy (Alençon). No, the fabricants of your district are mistaken; cloth selling at 40 sous per ell or less does not automatically fall under the rubric *libre*; it too is to be classed as *réglée* or *libre* as it conforms or does not conform to the regulations for quality. Do not establish a subinspector of manufactures or a *préposé* at Vire until we are certain the traffic justifies it.[10]

November 28, to Thiroux de Crosne. Rural carders and spinners who work at home must return their materials and tools to one master before changing to another, but the master fabricants of Elbeuf are wrong in insisting that they secure a *billet de congé*; the *lettres patentes* of February 13, 1766 freed them of that requirement, and the new regulation of September 12, 1781 on the police of workers left that freedom intact.[11]

November 29 (and in supplement, December 30), to Brown, inspector of manufactures for Lower Normandy (Caen). The fabricants of woolen cloth at the town of Vire wish to maintain the former number of threads in the warp, which yielded a coarser cloth that could be extensively sold at a reasonable price, but the four intendants insist that the required increase in the number of threads in the warp be maintained, since it was determined after consultation with the "marchands fabriquants" of the district; if this increase necessitates use of a finer quality of thread, so much the better; if the fabricants do not wish to meet the requirement, they can always sell their cloth under the category of *libre*. The red thread required in the border of every piece must be uniform throughout the kingdom; a suggested blue substitute for Vire would only cause confusion. It is astonishing that the police did not take action in the recent rebellion of the fullers [cause not given]; their excesses shall be overlooked this time by royal pardon freely and mercifully given, but warn the *procureur* to prosecute the offenders on the next occasion and to caution the ringleader, a Jean Levergeois, to be more circumspect or he will be punished. Weavers, fullers, and shearers of cloth, if they be fabricants, may all vote in the assembly electing *gardes jurés*. "Finally, Monsieur," the letter of November 29 concludes, "I must observe that in general you cannot be too circumspect and prudent in your dealings with the fabricants. You should make them understand that in all that it does the Council has nothing in view except the good of the manufacture. To be sure, it is appropriate to give them a hearing when they offer remonstrances that merit some consideration; but you should not listen to anything whose only aim is their personal self-interest; and especially you should guard against yielding too easily to impressions that they urge upon you in order to win you to their opinion."[12]

November 30, to Lepage, subinspector of manufactures at Aumale in Upper Normandy. With respect to the traditional rights of the duc de Penthièvre over the *bureau de visite* of Aumale, try to reconcile his inherited interests with the well-being of commerce. Let the bureau in Aumale with its customary boundaries be maintained and allow the duke to have, as before, one-third of its fines. Encourage neighboring merchants and craftsmen to use the bureau perhaps by naming several of them *gardes jurés*, but leave them free to patronize other bureaus if they find sale outlets there; to compel them to come only to the bureau in Aumale would be contrary to the letter and spirit of the new regulations.[13]

December 6 and 7, a cluster of letters to Boisroger, *inspecteur honoraire*, for transmission to Claude Lazowsky, subinspector of manufactures in Upper Normandy for Elbeuf and Louviers, about the derelictions of their craftsmen and *gardes jurés*. The few fabricants of woolen cloth who still try to conform to the regulations complain that those who manufacture under the category *libre* deceitfully try to make the borders of their cloth indistinguishable from that denominated *réglée*: let the *gardes jurés* intervene to check that abuse. The merchants of Toulouse report that the cloth from Elbeuf and Louviers is not being marked correctly as the new regulations prescribe: let the *gardes jurés* be more careful, for in the future no excuses will be accepted.[14]

Then, on December 19, a tactful note from the controller general directly to Messieurs les Gardes Jurés de la Fabrique d'Elbeuf, with thanks for their recent letter and a reminder of their power to promote the success of the manufactures of Elbeuf. The Royal Council, in issuing new regulations, has no other object in view than the greatest possible advantage of the manufacturers. As they know, unlimited liberty has already injured the reputation of Elbeuf cloth within France and abroad. In that situation, the fabricant cannot compete on equal terms with dishonest ones. To eradicate the evil at its source, the *gardes jurés* must be vigilant that not a single piece of cloth leaves the Fabrique of Elbeuf without having been inspected and marked in conformity with the new regulations. They may rest assured that the controller general will always zealously try to be useful to the industry in general and to each of the fabricants in particular.[15] In brief, I have your interests at heart, and let us work together on these problems.

On January 1, 1782, Elbeuf and Louviers having been dealt with, the four intendants turned to Nîmes, another great textile center. The bishop of Uzès had forwarded a memoir from the fabricants of stockings in the towns of Uzès and Nîmes, who requested a six-month delay in the application to them of the new regulations requiring the apposition of a mark on goods in the *libre* category. The request revealed that the fabricants had no intention of manufacturing stockings meriting the stamp of *reglée*. More than that, they wished even the *libre* goods to escape inspection and designation. The response of the four intendants was adroit, diplomatic but firm. It showed an awareness of the situation in Nîmes and of just how far the royal administration might press the fabricants, how much obedience it might obtain. Through a letter of Joly de Fleury to the bishop, the four intendants professed not to understand what the fabricants meant (again I paraphrase the details): The new regulations for knitted goods, including stockings, are still in preparation; the old regulations are still in force. To be sure, at Nîmes the latter have not been observed with exactitude, and the Bureau of Commerce does not intend to enforce them with any more rigor in the future than in the past. Nevertheless, there is one essential the fabricants must observe if they do not wish their cloth to be seized: they must place on each piece of knitted goods a small seal designating the place of fabrication and the name of the fabricant. This procedure, already outlined in the old regulations, is necessary to prevent confusion of French "national" merchandise with foreign.[16]

And so through the winter and into the spring, in a steady stream of letters to intendants of *généralités*, inspectors of manufactures, and *gardes jurés*, the four intendants of commerce were elucidating, modifying, supplementing, and maintaining the new regulations and fine-tuning their enforcement.[17] During the same months, meanwhile, they were receiving feedback as to what was actually happening to the new regulations out in the country, outside Paris. Sometime in 1781, probably during the summer, the Bureau had issued a circular to all of its inspectors of manufactures in the provinces. Always avid for information that might illuminate the darkness in which they worked, the intendants instructed the inspectors to discover what was going on, and to report. They were also encouraged to make their customary observations on the condition of manufacturing and commerce in their districts and submit suggestions for improvement. Apparently, in January, 1782 these reports began to come in.

A model report was that of Vaugelade, inspector of manufactures at Poitiers.[18] Dated January 14, 1782 and directed to Montaran, the intendant of commerce in charge of the *généralité* of Poitou, it left nothing to be desired in thoroughness. Vaugelade had made his tour in the autumn. Poitou was one of the poorest of regions, and as Vaugelade traveled from village to village and from town to town he was always on the lookout. What could be done to render the economy more productive? How could the government help to create regular employment for more people? At Fontenay-le-Comte and the parishes nearby, some hemp of good quality was being raised. If the administration could arrange to provision the naval vessels of Brest and La Rochefort with hempen rope from Poitou, the cultivation of hemp could be extended. Already there were merchants who, with slight encouragement from the administration, would undertake such a speculation. Other localities had similar potentialities for development.

Vaugelade also commented, as he had been instructed to do, on the enforcement of the new regulations. There were seventeen inspection bureaus (*bureaux de visite*) in his jurisdiction, and he called on each one. As he watched the bureau clerks (the *gardes jurés*) register, classify, and mark cloth submitted by the neighboring manufacturers, he suggested how the bureau personnel might bring up their performance to the expected standard of operation. He was hopeful that although the enforcement of the new regulations had not yet reached the standard of order desired, the measures he had taken at each bureau would move the personnel imperceptibly and gradually in the direction of exactitude and regularity. Over the years steady pressure from the central government in Paris and from its inspectors in the provinces would thus teach the subordinate clerks the role behavior expected of an effective bureaucracy. But it would take time, Vaugelade thought. Besides, he wrote, the problem of enforcement lay not merely with the administrative personnel, who were slack, but also with the manufacturers, who were frequently disobedient. At Partenay de Niort and other places as well, the fabricants of linen cloth simply refused to affix their personal trademark to their product, as the law required. What should be done? Could the *gardes jurés* enter the shops of disobedient producers and seize all the cloth lacking this mark? Only this drastic measure, Vaugelade believed, would ensure observance of this particular rule.

In general, the reports of the other inspectors of manufactures confirmed that of Vaugelade. They brought bad news to the four intendants of commerce in Paris: the new regulations were not working out. Some manufacturers openly disobeyed them; others, while technically obedient, responded in a manner not expected by the Bureau (in Normandy, for example, manufacturers whose cloth clearly met the quality standards for the regulatory code did not claim the mark *R* for fear that not every article would pass muster).[19] The lower administrative personnel (*gardes jurés*, *préposés*) was not always efficient. The attitudes of the inspectors of manufactures themselves were diverse. Several inspectors (among them Charles-François Quentin Crommelin, subinspector at Valenciennes in Hainaut) wished to return to the more stringent, inflexible rules of an earlier decade; others, such as Vaugelade, accepted the compromise of 1779–1780 and wished to see it enforced honestly and effectively; a few, such as Jean-Marie Roland de la Platière, inspector of manufactures in Picardy (Amiens) desired complete freedom from regulation and truculently refused to cooperate in enforcement.

For the moment the intendants followed a policy of diplomatically overlooking direct defiance of the new regulations while steadily, and quietly, elaborating the machinery for their enforcement. Montaran's comment on Vaugelade's journal beautifully expressed the spirit of the intendants' approach toward the enforcement of regulations. Montaran recommended to Vaugelade "celerity without precipitation, gentleness and forbearance without weakness, with a sustained attention to keep me informed of local obstacles." He also endorsed Vaugelade's proposals to extend industry within his jurisdiction by multiplying commercial relationships with the interior of the kingdom and with foreign lands.[20]

The Bureau's handling of two opposite extremes, Crommelin and Roland de la Platière, is no less revealing of its diplomacy. Born in 1732, member of a family that had been long identified with the production of linen cloth in Valenciennes, Crommelin had entered the administrative hierarchy of the Bureau of Commerce in 1750 as an *élève de manufactures*.[21] Appointed subinspector of manufactures of Valenciennes in 1751, he dedicated his hard-working life to maintaining through enforcement of regulations the superior quality of the linens and lace for which Valenciennes was internationally celebrated. In his dedication to his job, to his locality, and to its chief industry he was a model civil servant. He was also at one in spirit and belief with most of the craftsmen, fabricants, and merchants of his town.

When Necker's new code was being considered and introduced, Crommelin protested its formulation and installation. From 1780 he inundated the younger Montaran, intendant of commerce for linens, with proposed detailed refinements of the new local regulations of the linens produced in his jurisdiction. Montaran, finally fatigued by the subinspector's loquacity, protested to Sénac de Meilhan, intendant of the *généralité* of Hainaut. Of Crommelin's latest project for detailed implementation of existing regulations, this time on the bleaching of linen thread, Montaran wrote the intendant: "Nearly all the articles of his proposal contain details and discussion that are not usually inserted in a general regulation." He concluded, in exasperation, "This proposal is worthless in both its separate parts and its totality."[22] But to Crommelin himself, who after all was a loyal, hardworking, and vigilant inspector, Montaran was more restrained. When the subinspector pointed out a discrepancy between two of the Bureau's local regulations with respect to linens, Montaran simply reminded him of the general purpose of the Necker codes: namely, to accommodate the needs and wishes of every variety of manufacturing enterprise in France.[23]

At the other, laissez-faire extreme, the prickly Roland de la Platière made life equally difficult for the Paris intendants of commerce. Born at Thizy near Lyons in 1734, he tried business for two years before entering the royal administration at age twenty. He served at the textile center of Rouen for ten years as *élève de manufactures* (1754–1764) before becoming subinspector of manufactures at Clermont-de-Lodève in Languedoc (1764–1766) and finally full inspector of the *généralité* of Picardy (1766–1784), whose capital, Amiens, was the center of the third most industrialized area in France. At every location Roland, industrious, intelligent, and ambitious, always worked closely with craftsmen and large-scale manufacturers to improve their methods of production. He traveled widely through England, Germany, and Italy to learn of better industrial procedures. An indefatigable writer, he prepared a series of "in-house" memoirs on the bleaching and dyeing of cotton goods that won him the esteem and praise of his early superiors, Daniel-Charles Trudaine (1703–1769), and his son, Jean-Charles Philibert Trudaine (1733–1777), who protected his career. After the untimely death of the younger Trudaine, Roland began to publish technical treatises. In 1780 he signed a contract with the publisher Panckoucke to prepare a monumental *dictionnaire* of the industrial arts and trades, whose three quarto volumes duly appeared in 1784, 1785, and 1790. From 1781 to 1783, aided by his wife Manon, Roland was simply swamped by research and writing for this huge enterprise, as he prepared articles on "the methods of tanning leather, dyeing wool, weaving cloth, preparing soaps and oils, processing peat for fuel," and the like.[24] His publications won him international recognition, and he was elected to foreign and French academies.

Always fiercely independent, outspoken, and tactless (even his friend the elder Trudaine had gently to reprove him for his irascible tone), Roland became increasingly haughty and even insubordinate to his new superiors, the four intendants of commerce. The chief bone of contention was enforcement of the new regulations in Roland's inspectorate of Picardy. By 1778 Roland had become an impassioned advocate of total abolition of the regulation of methods of manufacture. In June of that year Necker had asked him for "a memoir preparatory to reaching a simplification of the regulations." Roland responded with a learned diatribe against "the inept tyranny of regulations and of agents who still carried their enforcement to excess."[25] "In the course of a single morning," he declared, "I have seen them cut to bits eighty, ninety, one hundred pieces of fabric . . . I have seen them descending with a band of satellites upon fabricants, overturning their workshops, spreading terror in their family, cutting the warp on the loom, carrying them off, seizing them, serving writs against them, postponing the process, subjecting them to interrogations, confiscations, fines, and sentences publicly posted and all that follows, anguish, disgrace, shame, expense, discredit, and why? For having woven pannes of wool, which are manufactured in England and which the English sell everywhere, even in France, but which are not mentioned in French regulations that speak only of pannes of hair."[26]

Despite his outspokenness the intendants of commerce needed and valued Roland's knowledge. They had brought him to Paris for the entire year of 1780 to confer about the content of the new regulations, especially those respecting the manufacture of stockings and other knitted goods, a major industry in Picardy. Their new compromise regulation of 1781 went far to meet his viewpoint by granting French artisans the freedom *not* to manufacture according to the rules. Yet the new code was not completely laissez-faire: there was still a machinery of inspection and registration. Now the time had come for Roland to report on the code's enforcement in Picardy: what would be the response of the irascible, laissez-faire extremist inspector?

Roland's answer was silence. As inspector of manufacture of Picardy he toured his *généralité* from July 22 to August 7 1781. In his report on the tour he wrote about everything except the subject in which the four intendants were most interested: the *bureaux de visite* for the inspection of cloth—had they been established? were the *gardes jurés* efficient? what were the attitudes and actions of the manufacturers? Instead he inveighed against the royal officials, who he said were arbitrary; he accused the *gardes* of Abbeville of dishonesty; he described the state of manufactures in vivid detail; but of the *bureaux* nothing or next to nothing did he write.[27] When on March 3, 1782 Montaran remonstrated and ordered him to report circumstantially on the inspection bureaus in his district,[28] Roland simply denounced an administration "whose principles vary according to the necessity of circumstances and the differing viewpoints of superiors who succeed each other," proclaimed his own virtue, and ignored the command.

His second report, on a later tour in the summer of 1782, offered no additional information on the bureaus. Bruyard, formerly chief clerk of the two Trudaines, recommended that he be called sharply to account. But someone wrote on the margin of Bruyard's comment, "Rien à Faire." [29] And indeed, there was little else the four intendants could do with an angular, independent, self-righteous fanatic inspector except to fire him, and they were not ready for that. For the larger problem of law enforcement during a period of transition perhaps "Rien à Faire" was the most prudent policy for an administration to follow in instances of overt disobedience. It avoided confrontation while the Bureau quietly developed its local agencies and smoothed out minor difficulties; it gave French manufacturers time and freedom to learn how to live with the new arrangements.

Upon reflection it would seem that the reform in regulations, designed to allay all controversy by meeting everyone's desires, had in fact reawakened it. The reform that promised to diminish the four intendants' expenditure of time and energy on the regulatory aspect of their activity had for the moment increased it.

By April and May, 1782 the vexatious problems of interpretation of the new regulations seemed to be moderating. A supplementary royal decree of April 18, originating no doubt in the Bureau of Commerce, ordered the establishment of *bureaux de visite* in all the provinces of the kingdom that had not yet received particular regulations; their *gardes jurés* were to affix the national mark on all stuffs fabricated within their province, as provided by the basic general regulation.[30] On May 13 Montaran dispatched a general circular to all inspectors of manufactures under his jurisdiction: that is, the inspectors of Roussillon, Languedoc, Provence, Dauphiny, Montauban, Auvergne, Auch, and the *généralité* of Paris (outside the town itself), as well as all inspectors of linen throughout the kingdom. He announced that the new regulatory regime was "now sufficiently established" that its functioning could be counted on and accurate reporting could begin. He instructed his inspectors to investigate and then report, on a six-column form, the number of *bureaux de visite* in their district and the number of pieces of cloth marked.[31]

Yet just as Montaran was dispatching his bland instructions, Colonia was receiving on May 18 a blockbuster petition from the syndics and *gardes jurés* of Lyons.[32] They opened respectfully enough: "The Syndics-Jurés, Gardes, royal inspectors of manufactures of fabrics of silk, gold, and silver of the town of Lyons are obliged by the conservation of the factories whose police and interests are confided to them, to bring to the foot of the throne of Your Majesty their very humble and very respectful representations on the dispositions of [articles 7 and 11] of the *lettres patentes* of 5 May 1779." These articles provided, it may be recalled, that throughout France all cloth was to be brought to an office of inspection (*bureau de visite*): cloth manufactured satisfactorily according to the rules would receive a seal bearing on one side the word *réglée* and the year of the manufacture and on the other side the name of the *bureau de visite*; cloth manufactured according to the free choice of the fabricant would receive a seal carrying simply the name of the *bureau de visite* on one side and the year of manufacture on the other.

The syndics and *gardes* of Lyons now quite bluntly asked for the total exemption of all silk goods manufactured in Lyons from the inspection provided in those articles. The national system provided by the *lettres patentes*, they explained, was already written into the local system at Lyons. The "Fabrique de Lyon," acting under prior royal regulations, had its own *gardes jurés* who daily visited the shops while pieces of cloth were being developed on a loom. No deviation could escape their vigilance. Besides, the honor of each craftsman and the reputation of each merchant in the marketplace required perfection of the product. Indeed, the reputation of Lyons's good quality stood so high that at international fairs, as at Leipzig, the dealers traded packets of Lyons silk cloth without ever opening the parcels. If a craftsman wished to deviate from the regulation to fulfill a particular commission or simply to realize an idea of his own, he could do so on the simple permission of the consulate. He was then subjected, of course, to even closer surveillance. The needless second inspection required by articles 7 and 11 of the *lettres patentes*, furthermore, would only cause endless trouble. Each Saturday the Lyons craftsmen brought their cloth, six thousand pieces in all, to the warehouse-store. They were immediately paid off, so that they might enjoy themselves on Sunday after a week of excruciating toil. To order them to reopen their packets, to submit to another ruffling inspection, and to add the weight of another seal to one already affixed would occasion immeasureable delay and destroy slim profits. If articles 7 and 11 were enforced, the petition concluded, the commerce of Lyons would be ruined in no time whatever.

So read Colonia, the other members of the Comité, and Joly de Fleury, the controller general. On June 1 the latter suspended the application of the articles in question to the silk goods of Lyons until he could find the opportunity to study the question. Concurrently, the vigorous protests of the fabricants of Nîmes had forced the administration, once again, to defer even drafting the regional regulations for the *généralité* of Languedoc.

Meanwhile the deputies of commerce were considering two cases that turned on the interpretation of the labor ordinance of September 12, 1781, originally drafted by Tolozan and governing the interrelations of employers, employees, and the government. From the western textile region came a petition from the fabricants of Elbeuf. They requested the Royal Council to decree that for the next ten years only the sons of master craftsmen could become apprentices. In an astoundingly strong dispatch to the intendant, Thiroux de Crosne, on April 16, Joly de Fleury, counseled by Tolozan, came down hard on the fabricants. "I would not think of adopting such a resolution. It is contrary to the natural right (*droit naturel*) of every citizen (*citoyen*) to acquire the knowledge he needs to take up an occupation that is agreeable to him."[33] An unusual example of the language of natural right, freedom, and careers open to talent from the pen of a staid, well-balanced, middle-of-the-road bureaucrat—Tolozan!

The scene for the second labor case was also laid in the west, in the Norman town of Laigle. The plaintiff, Sieur Pottier *fils*, was one of its leading manufacturers of pins. On May 23, 1781 one of his workers, Jullien *dit* Campis, had suddenly left without giving notice and without securing a *billet de congé*. Pottier tracked him down and six days later found him occupied in "tirer du fil" in the shop of a Sieur Boucher. When Pottier failed to persuade Jullien to return and Boucher to release him, he brought suit before the judge of the marquisate of Laigle. On June 1, 1781 the judge decided against Pottier on the ground that Jullien was now doing a different type of work at Boucher's than what he had been doing at Pottier's. On Pottier's appeal the Parlement of Rouen, on December 7, 1781, confirmed the local judge's decision; Pottier now requested the cassation of the high court's ruling.

The deputies of commerce, in rendering their opinion, went directly to the point. A worker is always a worker, no matter what type of work he is doing. As a worker he cannot, under the law of September 12, 1781 and of previous legislation, quit an employer without fulfilling his contract. Nor can he leave without securing a *billet de congé* from his employer or from the local judge. Nor can a new employer hire him without asking for that *billet*. It is of unmost importance for manufacturing, the deputies concluded, that these rules be adhered to. "These rules are enunciated from the wisdom of the Sovereign, and neither the Sovereign Courts nor any other judges have the right, for any cause whatever, to evade them or even to modify their dispositions. If the judgment of the Parlement of Rouen were confirmed, all workers would claim to be free and would leave their masters whenever it pleased them. There would ensue an insubordination and an anarchy that would lead manufacturers to their ruin. . . . That is why the Deputies of Commerce are of the opinion that there is good ground to quash the judgment of the Parlement of Rouen."[34]

In the measured and persistent action of the Bureau, the second semi-annual reports for 1782 from its outlying inspectors of manufactures began to come in during September, October, and November. From the inspectors' reports we learn of the situation with respect to the enforcement of the new industrial regulations of the quality of product. By September the regulations had been registered locally; except in the two major *généralités* of Lyons and Languedoc, the *bureaux de visite* were in place, two *gardes jurés* or a single *préposé* for each bureau had been designated, in each *généralité* the supervising inspector, subinspectors, and *élèves* of manufactures were at work, and the backup royal judges of manufacturing were ready. The number of letters that had to be written to interpret the new stipulations was diminishing.[35]

But once the uniform machinery of enforcement was spread across the kingdom, nothing could surpass the variety of regional response to the new regulations. In the town of Orléans the fabricants of blankets (*couvertures*) and linens (*toiles peintes*) as well as the knitters of stockings and caps simply refused to bring in their products for inspection and marking, and the *bureaux de visite* stood empty, totally without activity.[36] Across the *généralité* of Poitou the merchants and manufacturers continued openly to disobey. Those of Lyons, as we have seen, demanded to be exempted and to be permitted to continue older local regulations that were as strict and yet as flexible as the new. The merchants and craftsmen of Nîmes in the *généralité* of Languedoc, independent as always, simply went their own way. In Normandy the abler weavers of linens and cottons who manufactured very good cloth and might have been expected to ask for an *R* (*Réglée*) still chose the system of freedom (*libre*) for fear that a single deficient item in a packet, a single involuntary lapse, might subject their goods to confiscation.[37] The less able weavers chose freedom and varied the width of their cloth irregularly. The manufacturers of *blancards*, destined for Spain and the French sugar islands, followed a uniform, compulsory regulation that was still in force. The merchants of Normandy complained of the variety and sighed for a return to the simpler days when a compulsory rule guaranteed a uniform quality, but to no avail.[38] In contrast, the manufacturers of Sedan chose *R* and welcomed the opportunity to proclaim thus the well-earned, well-known excellence of their woolen cloth.

And nothing could surpass the persevering pressure of our four intendants of commerce for order and their flexible adaptability to the varied regional responses that emerged out of persistent local material conditions and mentalities. However, as the months passed, the Bureau's policy was an *evolving* adaptability as elements of the situation changed. Now that the machinery of inspection was in being, the intendants and the controller general no longer wrote across cases of open defiance: "Rien à faire." Through the intendant of a *généralité* and the local inspector of manufactures they warned the disobedient merchants and fabricants of Orléans and Poitou that their cloth would be confiscated; they themselves would be subject to the full penalties of the law, without mercy (*sans aucune grâce*). (An exception, the seemingly inevitable exception of any situation in the Bourbon monarchy, was to be made for the knitters of stockings and caps; since the new regulations for knitted goods were not yet ready, these craftsmen need only attach to their products the small seal giving the name of the fabricant and his place of manufacture.)[39] For Lyons the intendants asked for time to reflect. To the inspector at Nîmes they conveyed instructions to insist on the simple seal required by goods of the *libre* category, but otherwise let the manufacturers alone pending the preparation of a special local version of the new regulations for the *généralité* of Languedoc. Although the behavior of the weavers of Normandy was unexpected, it was within the letter of the law and even in accord with its spirit of freedom; so, no comment. The upright stance of the fabrique of Sedan was welcomed.

Here again, the journal of Vaugelade, inspector of manufactures for Poitou, of "his tour among the *bureaux de visite* established for the inspection of linens, begun September 2," is revealing both of a local situation and of the Bureau's evolving policy.[40] He was responding in the journal to the request of the four intendants in Paris for "enlightenment concerning the fabrication of linens in this province as well as the difficulties that thwart at several points the execution of the new regulations." We pick up Vaugelade in the midst of his tour. He has just been in Niort; he is now in Saint-Maixant, and he is writing in his journal what he has seen there. "This bureau is in the same condition as that of Niort, that is to say, all the regulations are registered and two linen-drapers [*marchands toiliers*] are *gardes jurés*. But the weavers still refuse to bring in their cloth to receive its particular stamp." In the face of massive disobedience what does Vaugelade do? "I made," he continues, "the same representations and the same recommendations" as before. Why doesn't he do more, as the law empowers him? The answer disclosed the initial policy of the four intendants in Paris. "However, I am reluctant to command the seizure of the cloth because I have not been positively authorized to do so, and because in taking measures to establish order I have been enjoined to proceed always with gentleness and circumspection." By now, though, Vaugelade is fed up. He personally has had enough of "gentleness and circumspection": "Two years of patience and exhortations are enough." Only force, confiscation of the cloth, will bring obedience. "As long as the merchants stubbornly persist in buying unmarked cloth, this obstinacy will sustain negligence, which only confiscation will correct." The four intendants of commerce now concurred with this new rigor in confronting widespread disobedience in Poitou.

Yet at the same time an "unofficial" letter from Tolozan (a rare survivor in the documentary evidence; if only we had others like it!) illuminates their flexible adaptability. The letter arose in correspondence about Bureau personnel, old and new. Tolozan and his colleagues each had in their *premier commis* in Paris good steady hands, intelligent civil servants who directed the flow of business: Bruyard the *premier commis* of the two Trudaines, father and son, now retired, but on occasion still sought out for counsel; Fourcade, the *premier commis* of the Montarans; and Valioud, placed by the elder Trudaine in his bureau in 1752, promoted to *sous-chef* in 1765 and ten years later to *chef*, and shortly thereafter named Tolozan's *premier commis*. Tolozan saw to it that on November 25, 1782 Valioud's remuneration was raised from 2,100 livres to 2,400, the same as Fourcade's.[41] While retaining the faithful chief clerks, the four intendants recruited for the inspectorate of manufactures active-minded young men, preferably but not necessarily those with some background in physics and chemistry.[42] Two of these were Claude Lazowski, appointed subinspector of manufactures in 1781 and advanced to the rank of inspector the following year, and J. Antoine Lansel, named subinspector on July 2, 1782.[43] It says something about the atmosphere within the Bureau of Commerce that the intendants could both hold on to its steady civil servants and also attract, retain, and utilize educated, progressive-minded young men. Although the staff of the Bureau might not always be happy with each other or with every decision, they felt probably that something important was going forward and that they had a share in what was happening. They knew that they were free to make suggestions and that their suggestions carried weight.[44]

It was about Lansel, one of the younger men, that Tolozan was writing on October 22 to the intendant of Languedoc, Guignard de Saint-Priest.[45] Tolozan opens: "I beg you to allow me to claim your good graces for M. Lansel, who goes to Nîmes as subinspector of manufactures. He is a young man of good family who first thought of practicing law, but whose taste for the crafts and manufactures decided him to follow another career." Tolozan is pushing Lansel ahead. "As much as possible we have abridged in his favor the usual tests, and I am persuaded that with his desire to succeed and with his cast of mind, he will be very useful to the manufactures of Nîmes, even though this district is not easy [for an administrator], especially with respect to regulations." That was the local situation, as Tolozan well knew. And what counsel does he offer Lansel? "I warned him of this, and I told him that the most prudent course to follow was to appear to enter the region more for self-instruction than for rigorous enforcement of the laws." Again, "gentleness" and "circumspection" and flexible adaptability! And Tolozan closes with a courteous flourish of his pen: "If your son and you, Monsieur, would honor him with your counsel and your protection, I shall not be uneasy about his success."

We may speculate: why this complex, evolving policy of the four intendants with respect to the implementation of the new regulation, moving from "Rien à faire" to rigor, yet in moving always flexibly adapting the Bureau's policy to the local situation? Were the intendants thinking that over the years flexible, persevering pressure would ultimately bring uniform order? And meanwhile, to secure obedience, did they have any other option than flexible adaptabiility? Massive constabulary and military forces for repression were not available to them. The old regulations had been laxly enforced for more than fifteen years, and the habit of routine obedience had lapsed; in the minds of many merchants and manufacturers obedience to any regulation was an annoying, nonuseful act. The French economy was indeed varied; local economic situations and attitudes were diverse; the new two-channel regulations had added needed flexibility, but perhaps even more local flexibility was now advisable.

During the winter and spring of 1783 the four intendants closed in on three disobedient regions that remained in the kingdom. Lyons was still one trouble spot. Through the controller general, Joly de Fleury, Montaran was still trying to persuade the *prévôt des marchands* of that city to permit the installation there of a *bureau de visite* for linen. The *prévôt* was unyielding.[46] Languedoc was another. Particular regulations acceptable to Languedoc and hence to the craftsmen of Nîmes had yet to be drafted. Auvergne was a third, and here an answer was found that could be applied to Lyons as well.

Cloth from Languedoc, uninspected as to quality, was flooding adjacent provinces, including Auvergne. The weavers of Auvergne, in turn, simply refused to bring their cloth to the local *bureaux de visite* and sold it unmarked. In early December the inspector of manufactures of the *généralité* of Auvergne, Jubié, assisted by the local *juge des manufactures* at the town of Mariaguer, tried to enforce the law; the local weavers rioted. Jubié and the judge now wished to bring the two instigators of the riot to trial, but Montaran invited the intendant of Auvergne, Charles Antoine Claude de Chazerat, to propose other measures.[47]

One can appreciate Montaran's dilemma. In the face of massive disobedience of the weavers of a province what could he do? The machinery of routine enforcement—*gardes jurés*, *préposés*, *élèves*, subinspectors, inspectors of manufactures, and *juges de manufactures*—had broken down. The rural constabulary in the field was too weak (three thousand men to preserve order in a kingdom of 24 million people was almost laughable); and how could the royal army be brought in to enforce a commercial regulation? Yet if the instigators were not punished, and the province was not controlled, riot and massive disobedience would be affirmed and might even spread.

Montaran was in a corner, with his back to the wall. But desperation, if it does not paralyze thought, sometimes stimulates it. Someone, perhaps Montaran himself, perhaps the intendant of Auvergne, or some obscure clerk, had an idea: Enforce the law, but avoid direct confrontation of the royal administration, the rural constabulary, and the army with an angry mob. Instead order into action the Farmers General, which collected indirect taxes. It had more than fourteen hundred customs houses at strategic points throughout the kingdom to collect general import and export duties as well as internal tariffs between regions.[48] These posts were manned by a private "army" of thirty thousand inspectors, clerks, and guards. Every merchant and every craftsman traveling down the roads was forced to declare his merchandise at a customs house and submit to its examination by customs inspectors. Let these inspectors (this is the idea!) seize all unmarked cloth, and the new regulations will be enforced on that product moving out of the village and down the roads.

So, on January 8, 1783, Montaran through Joly de Fleury ordered the intendant of Auvergne to stand firm and enforce the regulations by the seizure of the illegal merchandise.[49] The next day he instructed Vilevault, the fifth intendant of commerce, who was in charge of foreign trade and also the liaison with the Farmers General, to instruct that organization specifically to enforce the law on merchants and merchandise traveling through Auvergne.[50] Then, on January 15 and 16, to remove a basic cause of the difficulties in Auvergne, Montaran through Fleury informed Saint-Priest, the intendant of Languedoc, that he was setting to work on a set of particular regulations for Languedoc adapted to the special needs and desires of such textile centers as Nîmes.[51]

The solution invented to handle the disobedient weavers of Auvergne was then applied to another major holdout, the craftsmen of Lyons. On May 28 Joly de Fleury's successor, d'Ormesson, simply ordered Flesselles, the intendant of Lyons, to establish in Lyons a *bureau de visite* for the inspection of cloth, to enforce the law, and to accept no nonsense from protestors.[52] When in consequence there was in Lyons on August 1 an "effervescence" of protesting workers, the intendants of commerce avoided a direct confrontation and yet enforced the law by ordering the Farmers General to seize at their customs house unmarked cloth from Lyons.[53]

A crisis of enforcement during the summer of 1783, at the textile center of Laval in the *généralité* of Tours, enabled the intendants of commerce to clarify further their cooperation with the Farmers General. The artisans of Laval produced linen cloth that in its category was on a par with the excellent woolens of Sedan and Abbeville. In a long process "the flax of the locality was spun into thread in the farmhouses, woven into cloth by professional weavers (dispersed throughout the countryside) for the account of merchant/fabricants who sold it on the market of Laval to wholesale merchants, who in turn gave the cloth its final finish before exporting it," either through Lyons or "directly toward the French West Indies and the Iberian peninsula and its colonies."[54] For two years, unbeknownst to the inspector of manufactures of Tours, Huet de Vaudour, and to Montaran, Libour, the subinspector of manufactures at Laval, had allowed the local merchants and craftsmen to ignore the new regulations with impunity. The merchants, for example, were simply shipping their goods abroad unmarked or were eliminating the mark and substituting their own names. Because the law concerning inspection, registration, and marking of cloth was not being enforced, there had been no protests, and Huet de Vaudour and Montaran had assumed all was well. But when in April, 1783 Libour, spurred perhaps by the attentiveness of d'Ormesson and Montaran, abruptly began to enforce the regulations brutally, and when Huet de Vaudour seized at Tours three bales of unmarked Laval cloth, merchants and fabricants in Laval defied the royal administration during the last week of August and refused to bring their cloth to the local market and the *bureau de visite*.

Montaran was at first inclined to blame the protestors until his persistent investigation revealed both the initial negligence and the abrupt, arbitrary brutality of Libour, both so contrary to the principles of a sound and consistent administration that operated in accordance with the law, principles that Montaran cherished.[55] He replaced Libour as subinspector with a M. Chaix, a young and zealous *préposé* who had been active in the Lyonnais.[56] Avoiding a direct confrontation with the Laval protestors, Montaran ordered Vilevault to have the agents of the Farmers General seize unmarked cloth from Laval. But why hadn't the agents been doing this before? Montaran discovered that they had not been confiscating unmarked cloth, as ordered. Rather they had assumed it was produced for export from France and under the new system did not have to be marked, or they had assumed it was "foreign" cloth coming from another tariff area and exacted an import duty. In a strong letter to Vilevault on September 16, Montaran corrected both misconceptions. All cloth manufactured in France, whether produced for export or for domestic consumption, was to be marked; all unmarked cloth was to be seized, not taxed, and the malefactor fined.[57] With the application of these various measures the "fermentation des esprits" in Laval subsided, calm was restored by mid-October, and the law was being enforced.

More significant, with the letter to Vilevault it seemed that the machinery for enforcement was finally in place and operating throughout the kingdom outside the *généralité* of Languedoc. After days, months, years of queries, clarifications, disobedience, evasions, and even a mass mutiny, the firm yet gentle perseverance of the four intendants was finally paying off in the enforcement of regulations concerning quality of cloth. Aside from the unresolved situation in Languedoc, they were in the summer and autumn of 1783 handling individual cases and petitions by administrative routine in decisions that seemed to the administrators discriminating, fair, just, and adapted to the long-term interests of the royal administration, the French economy, and the governed.

Thus, the "merciers quincailliers" of Lisieux asked to be excused from performing the functions of *gardes jurés* for the inspection of woolen goods. After consulting on June 25 with the intendant of the *généralité* of Alençon, Antoine Jean-Baptiste Alexandre Jullien, and receiving his reply on July 6, the Bureau wrote to him on July 15 that the requested exemption could not be accorded. When the guild of "merciers quincailliers" persisted in their request via a letter of August 26, the controller general wrote Jullien on October 7 that the answer was still "Néant," or nothing doing.[58] The same answer to an identical request was given through the same intendant on the same date to the "marchands détamines" of Nogent-le-Rotrou.[59]

When the Bureau learned that the *juges des manufactures* of Bolbec, Havre, Aumale, Evreux, and Monancourt were charging higher fees than the law prescribed for their presence at the election of *gardes jurés* and the reception of their oath of office, it had the controller general write on May 7 to the keeper of the seals, Hue de Miromesnil, asking him to discipline his subalterns in the judicial hierarchy.[60]

Whenever an individual craftsman from anywhere in France was accused by a *garde juré* or *préposé* of violating a regulation—perhaps by submitting cloth that was too short or too long or dyed in a manner contradictory to its label—and fined (usually 300 livres) by the local *juge des manufactures*, if that craftsman appealed the judgment, the responsible intendant of commerce carefully studied the *procès-verbal* of the individual's case, however humble. If the accused was by reputation a "bon sujet" and a first offender, it was assumed the violation proceeded from ignorance of the new regulations, and the fine was reduced to 10 livres.[61] The reduced penalty in effect said, "this is a violation and do not do it again," but did not ruin the craftsman. In the administration of the four intendants there was almost always an element of "give" and even of humane and prudent consideration for the necessities and feelings of the governed. A negligent artisan or a second offender, whose ignorance might be difficult to prove, was fined 50 livres.[62] But if the violation seemed the result of deliberate fraud, the full penalty was sustained.[63] Since an intendant of commerce could not give orders to a judge concerning any case, he would have the controller general inform the intendant of the *généralité* of the decision, to be passed on to the judge. Thus were the necessary proprieties of channeled communication and command observed.

In several instances where uniform application of the regulations would diminish the sale of French products, the Bureau flexibly considered each case on its merits and reached a nuanced decision. To insist, for example, that cloth destined for the African slave trade receive the French seal of inspection would betray its French origin and thus destroy the belief of the African recipients that it came from India. Trudaine had permitted this exceptional absence of the seal; the deputies of commerce now recommended continuance of Trudaine's policy, and presumably the Bureau went along.⁶⁴ When the *passementiers* of Rouen observed that by long usage and by the regulation of August 11, 1748, they had been permitted to market their mixed cloth of silk and cotton without indicating its dye was "petit teint," the Bureau allowed the practice to continue. To add a description of *teinture* now would imply to the consumer that the cloth's quality had deteriorated, give English competitors an advantage, and curtail French sales.⁶⁵ On the other hand, in a slight variation of the same situation, this argument of immediate competitive survival did not move the Bureau. Two merchants of Rouen, Sieurs Morin and Bigot, were marketing under the description of "bon teint" a new type of cloth of mingled colors whose base (*fond*) was of a "petit teint." The Bureau commanded the release of the two merchants without penalty but ordered that in the future the cloth be labeled "bon teint mêlé de petit teint." Here protection of the consumer, the long-term reputation of French cloth, and hence long-term sales were the decisive considerations.⁶⁶

Other details of law enforcement were also clarified. By a decree of August 28, two seals were to be affixed to each piece of cloth, one at the top and one at the bottom.⁶⁷ For small articles such as stockings and other knitted goods it was decided on October 30 that a single seal on each packet of six pairs of stockings or of a dozen of other items would do. To require a seal for each pair or item would augment the weight of the package and increase transportation costs.⁶⁸

The same delicate fine-tuning appeared during these months in the intendants' dealings with French workers. Throughout the eighteenth century the general socioeconomic structures of French society had been operating against the urban worker. Employed journeymen were receiving lower real wages at the close of the 1780s than fifty years before. The main lines of the Bureau's policy—the support of guild organizations, the requirement of the written *billet de congé* and the *livret* (the registration of migrant workers with the local police), and the prohibition of workers' combinations—also placed the worker in a network of surveillance and control.

Yet in the administration of policy during the mid-months of 1783, the Bureau was often understanding of the workers' viewpoint and did not automatically identify with that of the employer. For example, when the master fabricants of Elbeuf again petitioned that only the sons of masters might be admitted to mastership, thus turning the guild into an inheritable private preserve of a few families, the Bureau rejected their plea. Though the fee for a certificate of mastership might remain high, no insurmountable barrier of hereditary privilege should block the rise of the industrious journeyman.⁶⁹

With the same calm impartiality the intendants dealt with complaints of disorder among workers and of illegal combinations of journeymen in *compagnonnages*, which had reached not only the controller general but the keeper of the seals and the minister of foreign affairs as well. Such complaints had long been a subject of discussion in the Bureau of Commerce.[70] Yet when the keeper of the seals wrote the *procureurs générals* of the parlements, they replied either that such infractions of the law did not exist in their jurisdictions or that the law on the books prohibiting worker combinations was adequate. Only the *procureur* of the parlement of Toulouse insisted on a new law that would specifically forbid workers from having in each town a center of assembly "at the home of a woman they call their *Mother*. In addition, this magistrate proposes to forbid more than three workers to meet together in a tavern, to carry staffs, canes, or any other weapons whatever, under the penalty of being prosecuted as disturbers of the peace." The Bureau declined to act along these lines. In the Bureau's view, the keeper of the seals should explain to the *procureur* of Toulouse that the institution of "Mothers" had its usefulness. Allowing workers to have "Mothers, in the several towns," was one way to contain them "in the path of duty, since she in a sense is answerable for them and can give them useful advice on their conduct" as well as "little handouts" without which they might run wild into "dangerous delinquencies." So let the police simply keep an eye on "the Mothers and the workers, and have them punished in case of abuse and disturbances." To do this the police and the judges would need no other laws than those already existing.[71]

The Bureau displayed the same tact in dealing with the emigration of skilled craftsmen to foreign countries. Discussion of the problem in the Bureau was precipitated by a letter from Saint-Priest, the intendant of Languedoc, who proposed a new series of severe penalties for workers who migrated as well as for those who enticed them to leave. Confiscation of property and corporal punishment were among the penalties he recommended. At the Bureau's request, Tolozan, its labor specialist, reported to the Bureau on July 24 on laws that forbade subjects of the king to leave his states without his permission. No law, it came out, really covered the case of migrating workers. Yet when the Bureau tried to formulate one that did, it was baffled by the complexity of the problem. It was extremely hard to establish that the worker intended to expatriate himself permanently. To forbid him to leave might be in some cases inhumane, if he needed work and hence subsistence. At other times the exit was habitual and authorized, as in the seasonal migration of harvest workers to Spain. It might seem easier to focus on those who sought to seduce workers into departing, but here too formulation of a law both just and efficient would be difficult. "These reflections and others of the same kind, drawn from the principles of justice and humanity, lead us to think that it would not be without danger to enact a new law on this matter." Saint-Priest would be well advised, the Bureau concluded, to alert the "commandant of the province" of the evil. He in turn might order his officers to arrest workers without passports;

interrogating these and threatening them with punishment if again caught might be intimidating and hold them at home. Meanwhile, the Bureau would inform Ségur, minister of war, of the problem.[72]

On the other hand the Bureau was much more exercised by the smuggling of French looms abroad, another subject raised by Saint-Priest. Yet even on this issue it displayed restraint. When Saint-Priest had alerted the Bureau to the problem in June, the four intendants had simply asked the Farmers General to excite their frontier agents to the utmost vigilance.[73] Saint-Priest, however, was not to be put off. In September, with his usual vigor, he recommended an aggressive attack on the problem. In his proposal (1) carters (*voituriers*) engaged in the transport of looms were to be required to show the municipal authorities of the town of their departure the certificate already prescribed by law; (2) the seller of a loom was to file with the consul of his town a written certificate giving the name of the buyer, who whenever challenged by the authorities was to give the loom's destination; (3) the sale of looms to unknown persons was to be forbidden. Upon reflection the Bureau decided that recommendations (2) and (3) could not be enacted without impeding the free flow of commerce; however, recommendation (1) might be implemented without disadvantages.[74] So on October 7 the controller general dispatched a circular to all intendants of the provinces, instructing them to order all carters transporting looms to show the municipal authorities the certificates that had been given them.[75]

Meanwhile, throughout these months of 1783, Tolozan, acting for the Bureau, was gathering from the intendants of the *généralités* information about workers' chronic theft of scraps of wool waste thrown off during the process of weaving woolen cloth. By early November he was nearly ready with his report on the problem, and the Bureau seemed on the verge of an informed discussion of the issue.[76] However, just as the four intendants were turning their attention in that direction, they learned, on November 2, 1783, that d'Ormesson had been dismissed as controller general and, on the following day, that Charles Alexandre de Calonne, intendant of the *généralité* of Flanders and Artois, had been designated his successor.

The procedures of our four intendants of commerce formed a system of ascertaining and improving reality by rational and legal means. Initially the attempt to introduce an intermediate program of regulation into the industrial/administrative life of French craftsmen had gone wrong. The four intendants had taken every precaution, so they thought, to ascertain French industrial opinion, to formulate an intermediate program that apparently met everyone's needs and desires, and to assure advance approval and eventual obedience. Yet as the program of enforcement went into operation, it provoked a blizzard of queries and protests, and even mass mutinies.

What had gone wrong? The four intendants, it may be suggested, had asked the wrong people the wrong questions. They had asked questions of members of the administrative/industrial elite—deputies of commerce, intendants of *généralités*, inspectors of manufactures, and chambers of commerce—who were already tied in with the royal administrative complex. They had not asked everyday, hardworking craftsmen who brooded, sometimes in fury, over their looms. And they had asked the elite either/or questions that led to approval of the conclusion that the four intendants already had in mind.

Yet after two years of troubles the four intendants had stood fast and except in Languedoc had apparently prevailed in installing their intermediate program and securing obedience to it. Why had they succeeded? A few obvious answers might be advanced here, pending more extensive reflections later. For one thing the four intendants were seasoned, unflappable civil servants, used to governing by bureaucratic procedures in accordance with the law. They believed in the soundness and ethical rightness of their procedures, in their mission to improve the French economy, and in the contemporary utility of the intermediate program: namely, in an economy where rapidly changing tastes and better roads were diversifying and widening the market, some flexibility in regulation was advisable; let each entrepreneur decide how much flexibility he needed and when. Furthermore, once the four intendants were in difficulty, they did listen to what their inspectors of manufactures and the petitioning craftsmen were telling them, and surefootedly adapted their response to local situations. As a last resort, they could still count on the coercive force of the royal judiciary and the Farmers General. Sharing common administrative practice, knowledge, and values, the four intendants on this issue worked well together.

The Flow of Direct Encouragement to Industry

In the area of regulation the four intendants of commerce were innovating new policies. In the area of direct encouragement of industry they were applying standard operating procedures and industrial strategies inherited from the past.

By 1781 the four intendants had inherited from their predecessors an immense array of types of encouragement that could be accorded an inventor or a business firm. These formed a rich variety of government supports that the intendants could selectively mobilize in special strategies for each industry and region, and each petitioning firm. They constituted an arsenal of devices from which the intendants could draw when they were formulating that combination of inducements which would best aid a region, an industry, or a particular business concern. Simply listing the devices is one way to convey their multiplicity. They included money, as either an outright gift or loan; exemptions from the major royal levies, such as the *taille*, the salt tax, the *corvée*, and militia duty; a *privilège exclusif* or monopoly of the market in France, a region, or a district; and special permission to undertake certain manufactories that used fire (blast furnaces, forges, foundries, glassworks) or to exploit a vein of coal.[77]

By 1781 the four intendants had also inherited strategies for developing five major manufacturing areas: glass; textiles (wool, silk, linen, cotton, and an adjunct endeavor, dyeing, common to all); chemicals, including soda; metals (iron and steel, tin, lead, and latterly copper); and paper. In telling the story of the Bureau's activity we might proceed by industries: what, chronologically during these nine hundred days, did the four intendants do with respect to glass? to textiles? to chemicals? to metals? and to paper? But such an organization of the material would be untrue to the reality of the four intendants moving together through the complexities and surprises of the Old Regime economy, society, and government, turning their attention, with incoming petitions, now to glass, then to textiles, back to glass, on to chemicals, again to glass and textiles, then to iron and steel, and eventually to paper.

To represent that reality and to communicate a vision of the Bureau moving in time, I offer an *interbraided* narrative, each strand being sequential action with respect to a major industry. We open, as did the intendants, with a petition concerning a glasswork, turn with the intendants to the manufacture of silk—a textile—back to glass, then to soda—a chemical—on to iron and steel, and eventually to paper. I conclude with a summary of how effective the Bureau had been in each industry.

This flowing narrative, corresponding symbolically to the flow of administrative activity, imposes the strain of sustained attentiveness upon the reader, who must keep in mind (as the four intendants kept in mind) the strategic policies with respect to five manufacturing areas. However, the interbraided narrative has the great advantage not only of conforming to reality but also of offering data for the resolution of the three problems with which this study opened: What were the characteristics and qualities of this segment of the French royal administration? During these months, what of the administration continued, and why, and what changed, and why? What were the interrelations of the administrators and the French people?[78]

We begin our narrative once again in May 1781, when Joly de Fleury succeeded Necker as controller general. In that month Antoine-Louis Blondel, the intendant of commerce responsible for the *généralité* of Picardy (Amiens), was following the procedures of the Bureau with respect to a petition from the comte d'Artois requesting permission to build a glass manufactory within the appanage his brother had granted him for his lifetime.[79] In the closing decades of the eighteenth century contemporaries estimated there were more than three hundred glass manufactories in France. Far and away the largest was the Royal Plate Glass Company, which enjoyed the extraordinary exclusive privilege to manufacture plate glass in France. It had grown to be the second largest French business concern, exceeded in size only by the coal mines of d'Anzin. Since its privilege had been renewed for thirty years in 1757, its affairs do not enter our narrative. Other glass firms were smaller, using local clays as raw material and wood from neighboring forests as fuel, and employing customary methods of production. They graded down in magnitude from dark-bottle factories annually producing 600 to 900 tons of glass containers to medium-sized concerns fabricating 150 to 250 tons of whiteware (tumblers, goblets, and the like) to the local factory, tucked away in some mountain covert, turning out 25 to 50 tons of common ware for the local market. These lesser concerns using wood and a traditional technology were happy to have simply the permission to exist and, if possible, the exclusive privilege to produce glass of a certain type for an area only ten leagues around. The comte d'Artois's project belonged to this category. Then, a few innovative glass manufactories were seeking to use coal as fuel and/or to manufacture a sparkling crystalware rivaling in brilliance that of England.

Whatever its size, methods, and purpose, a new glass firm used fire in its manufacturing processes and hence had to seek royal permission to start up. In the interests of protecting French forests and controlling their exploitation the Royal Council had decreed on August 9, 1723 that no glasswork should be established without specific *lettres patentes* from the Royal Council of State prepared (in effect) by the Bureau of Commerce.[80] Even the king's brother was subject to this law.

His proposed factory was to be erected within the "Forêt l'abbaye," near the towns of Abbeville and Amiens on the river Somme. Blondel was assembling information on which to base the Bureau's recommendation to the controller general. He received the opinion of Sainte-Foy, the intendant of Picardy. Sainte-Foy noted, what everyone realized, that approval would be "très agréable" to Monseigneur the king's brother. Erection of the factory, moreover, would enhance the value of property that upon Monseigneur's death would revert to the royal domain. Blondel also read the advice of Des Forges, director in charge of waters and forests, who on July 18, 1781 counseled approval: roads in this forest were so bad that it was very difficult to get the wood to market; besides, in the forests of this region there was a superfluity of supply, far beyond the immediate needs of the inhabitants: "In this case there should be no apprehension that a glass factory would cause a dearth of wood."

Against this opinion Blondel, and later the four intendants of commerce, had to weigh the objections of the municipality of Abbeville: the forest, only three leagues from Abbeville, was connected with it by two highways: it was little distant from the Somme River, which carried wood to Amiens as well as to Abbeville. Abbeville was always short of wood in winter; the price of wood had been steadily rising; the erection of the glass factory, a great consumer of wood, would cause prices to rise higher; the costs of soap manufacturers, brewers, brickmakers, and building contractors would thus increase, and they would become less able to compete with other French and foreign manufacturers. At the close of 1781 the decision of Blondel was still in suspense.

The petitions of other would-be glass manufacturers were before the Bureau during the late spring and early summer of 1781. One brought into consideration the state of the glass industry in the Lyonnais. There were two older substantial glassworks in the province: that of Joseph Esnard at Pierrebénite, one league from Lyons, and that of Michel Robichon at Givors, three leagues from the city and employing as many as 250 workers.[81] They fabricated chiefly bottles and windowpanes. They more than supplied the needs of the province for these articles, their warehouses were clogged with unsold merchandise, and they were desperately seeking an export market down the Rhone River. Their problems were complicated by the recent entrance of two upstarts.[82] In September 1774 a Sieur Sonnerat and in April 1778 a Demoiselle Eléonore Bouvier had each secured the Royal Council's permission to erect glass factories near Lyons, but on the express condition that they produce only white glass and various assortments noncompetitive with the articles manufactured by Esnard and Robichon. However, the upstarts, like the camel nudging into the tent, were not content with what they had obtained. Sonnerat, quite illegally, began to produce bottles. Bouvier, as early as November, 1778, pressed the Bureau to accord her permission to manufacture all types of glass. At first the Bureau refused, but she was not to be denied. Contrary to their principle of orderly, balanced industrial development, the four intendants of commerce yielded to her importunity. On June 19, 1781 a decree accorded her permission to produce glass of all kinds including bottles and windowpanes.[83] A seasoned administrator could anticipate that Esnard and Robichon would soon be heard from.

Two other glass-factory petitions were in process. In one petition a father and son named Fréjard were asking permission to reestablish a glass factory in the village of Longchamp in the *généralité* of Dijon. The petition was duly referred to Colonia, who sent it on June 22 to Des Forges in waters and forests, for his opinion.[84] Des Forges's investigations always took time, and we must wait, along with Colonia and the petitioners, for his reply. In another petition, that of Sieurs Guiraud and Montmarillon, Colonia had already received the opinion of Nicolas Dupré de Saint-Maur, intendant of Bordeaux, dated July 9, and was now seeking that of Des

Forges. The proposed glass factory would be in the Landes, south of Bordeaux, a very poor region where the wood was normally ruined by the sea, which crept among the trees and rotted them.[85] Again, the reply of Des Forges must be awaited.

We must pass without transition, as did the four intendants, from one item to another as these came in, from one industry to yet another, from glass on to textiles. From the viewpoint of the four intendants the textile industries were the most rewarding of manufacturing processes, if the raw material was raised within France or its colonies. The production of raw wool, cotton, silk, and flax kept many rural inhabitants occupied and gave them a cash crop to sell. The fabrication of woolen, cotton, silk, and linen cloth as well as hempen products taught habits of industry to another set of producers and added value to native raw materials. If the finished product was marketed among the peasants, they could purchase it with the money received for the raw material they produced, thus completing the circuit of trade. On the other hand, if the product was sold abroad, the cash obtained was thought to be pure gain, since nothing imported had been used in the product's manufacture. At every step, from the purchase of the raw material through the organization of the handicraft producers to the sale of the final article, merchants could usefully make a profit.

As a consequence of the number of producers involved and of the value to be gained, textiles had been a focus of the four intendants' attention throughout the eighteenth century. The reform regulation of 1781 had been concerned largely with the regulation of textiles. The interest in new machinery for the spinning of silk and cotton thread was a concern with maintaining French superiority in silk and catching up with the recent daunting British advances in cotton spinning. The sustained attentiveness of the Bureau of Commerce to the discovery and scientific testing of new dyes as well as the dissemination of the best dyeing procedures among ignorant French craftsmen was a textile concern, since unless the cloth was left white, woolen, cotton, and linen products were dyed. At the same time, these problems in machinery and dyeing offered opportunities to innovative French entrepreneurs and amateur chemists, who applied to the Bureau for direct encouragement and implementation of their dreams.

Thus, out in Evreux, in the *généralité* of Upper Normandy (Rouen), a member of the Society of Agriculture of Rouen named Morize had invented what he considered an improved reeling machine for the winding of silk thread.[86] On May 23 he presented it to the local Academy of Sciences at Rouen. Encouraged by the approbation of the examining commissioners the academy had appointed, Morize on June 27 forwarded the machine with two memoirs to Jean-François de Tolozan, the intendant of commerce in charge of Normandy, who in turn referred it to Colonia, the intendant in charge of the silk industry. Colonia, an intelligent administrator but no expert on machines, was in no position to appraise the invention. Perhaps it was a breakthrough; perhaps not. Who knew? The approbation of the local experts of the Academy of Sciences of Rouen was encouraging but scarcely decisive. Local experts had been wrong before. Colonia needed help. So two years later (the delay is inexplicable) he sent the machine and the memoirs to Vandermonde, a mathematician of world renown and a scientific consultant to the Bureau: what was his opinion?[87]

As the summer wore on, the Bureau, operating under a new, noninnovating controller general, seemed to be driven more by the momentum of its procedures than by its own will. On the Bureau's recommendation the Royal Council on July 17 granted a Sieur Sturgeon 2,000 livres per year for five years to support the establishment of an earthenware factory at Rouen.[88] On August 26 the Council, probably on the Bureau's recommendation, prohibited the export of ashes, salts, and potashes.[89] These were badly needed as raw materials in the chemical industry and were in short supply in France, and the prohibition followed customary mercantilistic policy. On August 19 Le Noir, lieutenant general of the Police of Paris, asked the four intendants whether Sieur Stoucard, a Paris manufacturer of copper and tin sheets, should be permitted to apply them to any articles he wished. On September 8, Jacques-Marie-Jérôme-Michau de Montaran, in the name of all four intendants, returned a negative answer: such a practice, he wrote, would facilitate fraud. This decision too accorded with a mercantilistic practice, that of governmental protection of the consumer.[90] On August 30, the day after Le Noir's note was received, Vergennes, the minister of foreign affairs, forwarded to Joly de Fleury, the controller general, a letter from Philippe de la Salle, the ingenious inventor of silk-weaving machinery in Lyons. La Salle recommended that the French government attract from Bologna an artisan well-versed in the Italian secrets of bleaching and finishing gauzes and crepes. He further suggested that the offer of an annual pension of 4,000 livres, devolving upon his death to the artisan's widow, would be a sufficient inducement. "Since this subject concerns trade and consequently your administration," Vergennes wrote, "I thought I should inform you. I shall wait to hear what you think about it." Vergennes's inquiry and La Salle's memoir were referred to Colonia, the intendant in charge of the silk industry.[91]

Soon after, a Sieur Jean Joseph Gaspard d'Audouard was asking the controller general for permission to operate in the neighborhood of Marseilles a factory to produce all kinds of glass in furnaces heated only by coal; he requested that he be given for twelve years the exclusive privilege to use the process of coal-fired glass furnaces within the jurisdiction of the Parlement of Provence. The petition was referred to Montaran, the intendant of commerce in charge of that region. In accord with the Bureau's procedure, he wrote on October 12 to Charles Jean-Baptiste Des Galois de La Tour de Glené, the intendant of Provence (Aix), for information and counsel. Montaran's letter is interesting: it reflects the changing attitude of the Bureau toward grants of exclusive privilege. After summarizing d'Audouard's petition, Montaran said that if his allegations were true, the administration should recompense him for the expenses of his researches. But, the intendant warned, the compensation should not take the form of an exclusive privilege. "The Council is becoming miserly in granting these types of favors, which tend, as you know, only to restrain trade by concentrating it in the hands of a single person, to curb industry, and to deprive the consumer of the advantage which would necessarily result from competition between several establishments of the same kind." So, he concluded to La Tour, "I should be infinitely obliged if I could obtain from you the necessary clarifications and information with respect to the potential usefulness of Sieur d'Audouard's establishment, as well as your ideas about the type of exclusive privilege which he solicits. It will be in conformity with your opinion that I shall propose to the Minister a decision in this matter."[92]

Early in January 1782 Montaran had in hand a letter from La Tour, the intendant of Provence since 1744, giving him the information needed for a rational decision concerning the petition of d'Audouard.[93] Montaran's original inquiry to the intendant, dated October 12, 1781, was already three months old. La Tour tactfully reminded him of the facts of the case: d'Audouard "requests the exclusive permit for a period of twelve years to establish in the area of Marseilles, a factory for all types of glass, on condition that he use only coal. . . . He certifies that he has been the first manufacturer of black glass bottles made with hard coal." But, La Tour observed, that claim simply was not true: there was already a similar manufactory at Marseilles; d'Audouard's factory would not be unique, even in Provence. Besides, La Tour continued, the grant of an exclusive privilege would hamper the development of industry, just "at the moment when the spirit of research is agitating manufacturers," especially those who were engaged in chemical operations; La Tour recommended a simple turn-down of d'Audouard's request. His opinion was in accord with his own hostility to recommending within his intendancy the grant of an exclusive privilege to manufacturers who were not pioneering an industrial innovation.[94] Montaran had promised to follow La Tour's lead, and he did. On January 15, presumably on Montaran's recommendation, the controller general wrote "Néant" in the margin of d'Audouard's petition.

In January 1782 the steady search for better and cheaper dyes again surfaced in the flow of the administrators' consciousness and correspondence. Since Colbert, French administrators, scientists, and manufacturers had perseveringly sought a scarlet dye equal in quality to the imported variety. A native French supply of the root of the herb madder, which yielded the dye, would free French manufacturers from uneasy dependence on foreign sources, check a drain of specie abroad, perhaps reduce the costs of French textile firms, thus giving them a differential advantage over foreign competitors, and conceivably furnish an article of export. Apparently madder grew in several provinces in the kingdom. Time and again, throughout the eighteenth century, inspectors of manufacture, societies of agriculture, intendants of a *généralité*, and private entrepreneurs sent samples of the root to the Bureau of Commerce in Paris, there to be appraised by its permanent salaried consultant chemists in the art of dyeing, Jean Hellot (1685–1766) and Pierre Joseph Macquer (1718–1784).[95] As recently as August, 1779 Macquer, a master of the comparable testing of raw and manufactured products, had thoroughly examined a sample of uncultivated madder growing near Issoudun, in the *généralité* of Berry. It had been sent in by the intendant of Bourges at the request of a painter named Geoffrey, who proposed to cultivate experimentally two or three *arpents* of it in October. Macquer, after a series of comparative tests, reported the sample yielded dye of excellent quality, substantially equal to that imported at considerable expense from the Levant. He recommended that Geoffrey be encouraged.[96] This report had been prepared at the request of Tolozan, the intendant of commerce in charge of Berry. Similarly, in January 1782, at the insistence of Montaran, Macquer had tested madder root from Pontoise. It too, he reported on January 17, was among "the best roots of this species."[97]

Several days later the perennial question of local monopoly versus competition in the glass industry was again brought before the Bureau, this time by petitions from the comte de Melfort. The count's glassworks had existed at the town of Ivoy in the *généralité* of Berry since 1725 and manufactured bottles. But in 1778 the Royal Council, upon the recommendation of the Bureau of Commerce, had granted a Sieur Piéton the right to establish a glass manufactory near Ivoy, at Boucard. Since the new factory was three leagues closer to the Loire River and to the market than that of Ivoy, the count feared he might be ruined. In successive petitions he requested the demolition of the rival factory. Tolozan, the administering intendant of commerce for the *généralité*, referred the petition to its intendant, Jean-Baptiste Claude Dufour de Villeneuve.

Dufour's reply, dated January 20, was interesting.[98] In the broad flow of administrative correspondence, it was only an item. But it symptomatically illustrated the transitional spirit of administrators who, perhaps without realizing it, were moving ever so gradually from the known, staid forms and formulas of mercantilism toward a freer, more competitive economy. Dufour granted that simply by seniority the older factory of Ivoy merited preferential protection, if it could not subsist beside that of Boucard. But it was apparent from the investigations of the preceding intendant and from Necker's decision that such was not the case. The older concern did not saturate the potential market: there was room for both factories. Besides, the new firm would stimulate commerce. It would utilize wood now going to waste, give employment to poor people of a poor province, and increase its wealth. Thus far Dufour's mind was traveling down the traditional grooves of mercantilistic reasoning. But he concluded with an idea that belonged to another universe of thought: even if competition diminished the profits of Ivoy, that was all to the good—consumers would benefit, presumably from lower prices. Following Dufour's recommendation, Tolozan, the Bureau, and the controller general turned down the count's request. A slight move toward freedom had been made.

As we have seen in our first probe, the two great branches of the chemical industry in the eighteenth century were the manufacture of acids and the manufacture of alkalis. Concentrated sulfuric acid was used widely, in making hats, in the manufacture of paper, in tanning hides, in the production of tin and copper, and, above all, in dyeing and bleaching. As late as 1760 nearly all the 70,000 livres of sulfuric acid consumed in France had been "made in England." However, in the next two decades Trudaine and the Norman industrialist John Holker established near Rouen a large sulfuric acid factory that used British procedures of manufacture to capture the French market and then moved to challenge British manufacturers in the export area of France's continental neighbors Holland, Germany, Switzerland, Italy, Spain, and Portugal.

This stunning success encouraged our four intendants to press French scientists and inventors to achieve a technological breakthrough in the chemical production of alkalis. Soda and potash, the two major alkalis, were essential in bleaching and in the making of soap, glass, and alum. Soda especially was in tremendous demand in France. But the native supply of soda was relatively meager, and foreign imports were becoming increasingly expensive. Throughout most of the eighteenth century soda was derived almost entirely from natural products. The ashes of trees was one source, but a diminishing one as the forests became depleted. "Natural soda," or *trona* (natron), occurred as a mineral deposit in Egypt. Imported by French soap boilers, it was used to saponify olive oil. It was the best source, but it was also the dearest, and its purchase drained France of specie. Barilla, or the ash from several species of the glasswort plant (*Salsala soda*) found on the Mediterranean littoral of Spain and southern France, was an important source, as was the ash of kelp, a seaweed gathered along the coasts of Brittany and Normandy. But most barilla came from Spain, and its price too was rising.[99]

The variable quality of the vegetable alkalis as well as their rising price spurred the search to make soda chemically. In time the search drew in the Bureau of Commerce. In February, 1780 the Bureau had granted an exclusive privilege to Father Malherbe, a Benedictine *abbé* at Saint-Germain-des-Près in Paris, along with Sieur Athénas (who was perhaps his assistant in the abbey's apothecary shop), and an Angevin capitalist to produce soda economically from common salt by a process Malherbe had invented. In 1781 the finance minister, probably Necker, had persuaded the Academy of Science to offer a prize of 2,400 livres to those "who had found a practicable method to derive soda from common salt in quantities large enough to supply all our industries" (Macquer's paraphrase).

Meanwhile, Louis Bernard Guyton de Morveau (1737–1816), an amateur scientist, and a brilliant one at that, had been applying himself for years to finding a commercially profitable method of extracting soda from marine salt.[100] He himself was the product of the interplay between the vigorous intellectual life of a provincial capital (Dijon in Burgundy) and the more sophisticated culture of Paris. Born in Dijon and educated there at the Godran (Jesuit) College and Faculty of Law, Guyton had practiced law in his home town from 1756 to 1762. He then entered the Parlement of Dijon as *avocat-général du roi*—one of the public prosecutors. His performance in that post and his occasional literary writings brought him in 1764 election to the local Académie des Sciences, Arts, et Belles-Lettres of Dijon, where chemistry was often discussed. "In 1768 he installed a laboratory in his new home. He was entirely self-taught, studying initially the books of A. Baumé and P. J. Macquer."[101] His published experiments on the calcination of metals brought him to the attention of Lavoisier and in 1772 election as correspondent of the Paris Academy of Science.

From general gossip Guyton knew that the purchase of "natural" soda from the Levant and Spain was draining France of specie. From personal experience, as owner of a *nitrière* producing saltpeter, he had become acutely aware of how the shortage of soda was hampering the glass manufacturers. Unable to obtain soda, they had turned to using potash and sharply driven up its price. But Guyton required reasonably priced potash or, better yet, soda in his *nitrière*. Animated probably by a complex of motives—business necessity, desire to serve France, ambition to win the Academy's prize, and simply the craving to know—he devoted his spare time to experiments in the synthetic production of soda that seemed to be leading to a favorable conclusion. On hearing of the privilege granted Father Malherbe, he had abandoned his search, thinking the problem of producing commercially profitable artificial soda had been resolved.

But when Malherbe and his associates did not erect a successful factory, Guyton resumed his experiments. By February 16, 1782 he was writing the controller general from Dijon that he had discovered a practicable way to extract soda from marine salt in large quantities. Its price, he assured, would be competitive with that of the natural product. What did the royal administration wish to do? Did it wish to operate its own soda factory using Guyton's process under his supervision? Or did it wish him to set up his own factory under the protection of an exclusive privilege that would guarantee him a recovery of his expense? And where should the factory be located? His principal ambition, he assured the controller general, was simply "to do something useful for the State" (again, the concept of utility). He hoped that in light of this consideration the administration would grant his memoir favorable attention.[102]

The memoir reached the Bureau of Commerce on February 20 and was referred to Colonia for study and report.[103] He immediately noted a key question: before the administration could go any further, it needed to ascertain whether Guyton's "secret" was not the same as Malherbe's. In accord with the Bureau's standard operating procedure of involving an expert scientist, on March 9 Colonia invited Guyton to submit his procedures to Macquer, the Bureau's consultant chemist, for appraisal.[104]

While Guyton and Macquer were corresponding with each other, the Bureau considered the problem of how to instruct industrial entrepreneurs and ignorant, illiterate artisans in the use of new tools and machines. Vaucanson, the inventor of the silkthrowing machinery through deliberate application of scientific theory, had recently died. The Bureau had invested him with the title of *Mécanicien* to the government. Independently, in part with government subsidies and in part at his own expense, Vaucanson had formed in his own residence a collection of the silk mills, towers, and reeling machines of his own invention as well as models of other mechanical contrivances. George Villard, the empirical inventor of silkthrowing machinery and Vaucanson's great rival, now asked that the title of *Mécanicien* be given to him, along with Vaucanson's depot of technological devices. Villard promised to make the devices available to innovative manufacturers.

For more than a century the idea of an industrial museum had been in the air. In the vision of Descartes it would house the most modern machines, and professors of mathematics and physics, one to each industry, would explain to artisans their operation and the nature of new discoveries. Moved to action, perhaps by Villard's petition and certainly by the problem of disposing of Vaucanson's depot, the Bureau gave to the idea of a technological museum a habitation and a name.

The intendants ordered that the depot be housed in the Hôtel de Mortagne, with the distinguished mathematician Alexandre-Théophile Vandermonde (1735–1796) of the Royal Academy of Sciences as curator. Aside from his four major mathematical papers (1771–1772), which made him a genial precursor of such nineteenth-century giants as Gauss and Cauchy, Vandermonde had for years frequently served with Vaucanson, Lavoisier, and other scientists on commissions to appraise allegedly new machines and craft procedures. As curator of the depot he was instructed to enlarge Vaucanson's collection. He was to "assemble all that was technologically interesting in French and foreign factories; construct those machines of recent invention that the government wishes to diffuse; gather rare and expensive tools that the Paris workshops lack and loan them on occasion."[105] To assuage Villard's disappointment at not gaining the post of custodian, the Bureau accorded him on February 26 an outright gift of 5,000 livres and an annual *pension viagère* devolving on his widow of 3,000 more.[106]

The four intendants were now ready to consider in Comité the petition of Sieurs Guiraud and Montmarillon for permission to establish a glass factory in the Landes, south of Bordeaux. Colonia, in whose jurisdiction the Bordeaux *généralité* lay, had already secured the favorable opinion of its reforming, progressive intendant, Dupré de Saint-Maur, who wrote on July 9, 1781 that the factory would bring vivifying new industry and commerce to a poor region and give its inhabitants work. Eight months later Colonia had received the opinion, dated March 4, 1782, of Des Forges, director in charge of waters and forests. (Of course Des Forges, while the petitioners and the Bureau waited, had had to pass the petition down the line of the appropriate *grand maître*, *maître particulier*, and *lieutenant de maîtrise*, until it finally reached some subordinate forest official on the spot who could secure the information and pass it up the administrative ladder.) Ultimately Des Forges' opinion was favorable: the factory would be a market for trees that the sea water was otherwise rotting. On Colonia's recommendation, based on the information thus obtained, the Comité accorded on April 9, 1782 the requested permission to Guiraud and Montmarillon, who had been waiting for over a year.[107]

The next day, April 10, Joly de Fleury took favorable notice of the research of Dambourney, a chemist at Rouen, on dyeing. The chemist had recently given the Chamber of Commerce of Normandy a collection of 576 samples of woolen cloth, each dyed a different nuance of color. He had expressed the wish that the results of his investigation be communicated to the dyers of Normandy. In a letter drafted probably by Tolozan and addressed to the syndics of that Chamber of Commerce, Joly de Fleury thanked them for informing him of Dambourney's gift, highly praised his dedication to the improvement of dyes used in textiles, and blandly suggested that depositing the samples in the archives of the Chamber of Commerce was the best way to make them available to local weavers.[108]

Simply as another example of the steady flow of routine petitions and decisions passing across our intendants' desks, we might cite the case of Madame D'Auxon of Abbeville. The word "routine," however, should bring us up short. To us the petitioner is only a name, and her petition and what became of it only an illustration of an administrative process. But the petitioner who bore the name was once alive, tense, anxious, looking to Paris for the fulfillment of her hopes, calculating, above all calculating, how to use the bureaucratic system to her profit. She proposed to set up a soap factory under the auspices and within the appanage of the king's brother, Monseigneur the comte d'Artois. She chose first to send a sample of the soap her company could make, not directly to the intendants of commerce, but to the Royal Academy of Sciences, for an appraisal and praise. She declared that her soap was better than all others for bleaching and for the scouring of wool.

Macquer and Baumé, the two distinguished chemists deputed by the Academy to examine her product, let her down but let her down gently. Perhaps the name of the comte d'Artois had its effect. Or maybe they were merely being courteous and kind. Her soap, they agreed, had all the properties that one could desire in a product so important in domestic life and in many crafts; indeed, in quality it closely approached the good white soap of Marseilles. But, they added, as there was nothing novel in the procedures used to prepare it, the Academy could not give it the approbation that it accorded only to new discoveries and inventions. The opinion concluded, "Fait au Louvre le six mars. Macquer et Beaumé."

Not deterred by this first repulse, Madame D'Auxon secured from the Academy a copy of the opinion, dated March 18 and certified by Condorcet, the Academy's secretary, and presented it to the Bureau of Commerce with a request for financial support and protection. By its own processes the Bureau could move rapidly on this one: it had the opinion of scientific consultants; it was the Bureau's standard policy to support only persons using innovative procedures. The decision of the Comité, dated June 7, was brief and pointed: "Néant." [109] The Comité's decision, like Madame d'Auxon's petition, was only a bubble, a soap bubble if you please, in the flow of administrative activity and thought.

In contrast, during the summer of 1782 the four intendants were considering three significant cases in iron and steel, glass, and chemicals. The first was that of a persistent petitioner, Jean-Baptiste Delaplace. An obscure artisan, "manufacturer of rouge, he lived and kept a shop in Saint-Germain-des-Prés, at the corner of the rue des Petits Augustins [now the rue Bonaparte] and the rue des Marais [now the rue des Beaux-Arts]." He called himself a chemist, and "the coloring matter that he fabricated had won approbation from the Academy of Science." [110] Living with his wife and children in very pinched circumstances, he hugged a secret that he dreamed would make him rich. From 1778 he repeatedly announced that "he had discovered the secret for making iron more pure, more ductile, more malleable, very much easier to forge, and far more suitable for conversion into steel of excellent quality." [111] His iron and steel, made from native French iron ore, would equal, he promised, the best Sweden or England produced.

To understand the importance of his petitions and the Bureau's patience with him over the years we need to recall how iron and steel were then manufactured in France. At that time the manufacture of an iron product might pass through several stages. In the first stage, a mixture of wood charcoal, iron ore, and limestone was packed into a blast furnace and set afire. After the iron was melted, it might either run directly into molds to form, after cooling, *cast iron* kettles, grates, and so forth, or be directed into a bed of sand called in England the "sow" and down connecting furrows in rivulets to form "pigs" that, when cooled, were called *pig iron*. Pig iron could be taken to a forge, reheated in one or two hearths with a charcoal fire animated by a water-powered draught, and then hammered under water-powered hammers to form *wrought iron*, or, if slit into bars, *bar iron*. It was malleable, and a blacksmith could fashion it into wrought iron articles.[112]

There were also three kinds of steel, each having properties that fitted it for certain usages. *Acier naturel*, produced chiefly in Dauphiny, was usually made by reheating pig iron that contained manganese to lower its carbon content below the threshold of 1.2 to 1.5 percent, the level of iron. *Acier naturel* was used in the manufacture of "three varieties of merchandise: the finest grade for the production of weapons (swords, bayonets, for example) and cutlery; a coarser steel, for edge-tools; and an iron-like steel, for [certain] agricultural implements" such as plowshares.[113] *Acier cémenté*, or cementation steel, was partially recarbonized wrought iron. Alternate layers of bar iron and powdered charcoal (the cement) were packed in closed chests of refractory brick or sandstone in a furnace; the chests were heated for several days; the resultant cementation steel was more even in grain than *acier naturel* and more brittle, and it required more care in working, but it was excellent for such articles as files, sickles, scythes, and hardware.[114] In *acier fondu*, or crucible steel, cementation steel was fused in a crucible heated to a very high temperature by a coke fire. *Acier fondu* was free from the ashes that marred even cementation steel and took a higher polish. The most precious and refined of the three types of steel, it was used in fine cutlery, surgical instruments, watch springs, and steel jewelry.[115] Here and there in France in the early 1780s, *acier naturel* and cementation steel were being manufactured, but not in great quantity nor of first-rate quality; French iron was still an unsatisfactory base for cementation steel. The production of *acier fondu*, the most precious type of all, the one in which the English excelled, was not even being attempted.

With this situation in their minds the four intendants of commerce naturally regarded with interest anyone who promised to improve the manufacture of iron and that of steel, and Delaplace promised to do both. He had a secret additive that he stirred into the molten pig iron as it was being reheated to form wrought iron. In the cementation process he placed a small metal cube of undisclosed ingredients amid the bars of wrought iron that were being reheated to become cementation steel. For three weeks in 1779, in a test arranged by Tolozan for the Bureau, Delaplace had demonstrated his two processes at the forges of the comte de Buffon and under the watchful eyes of two appraising ironmasters. The results were ambiguous. The experts differed in what they perceived. The two eyewitness ironmasters reported that Delaplace's iron and steel products were superior to the customary ones; the Bureau's respected and influential metallurgical consultant, the chevalier Grignon, who had not been present at the trials but had performed a cost analysis, objected that Delaplace's procedures were more expensive in time, material, and fuel without a significant gain in quality.[116] On the basis of Grignon's report, Necker had first written "Néant." Then, softened perhaps by Delaplace's earnest perseverance, he granted him a lump sum of 800 livres but no substantial encouragement for the erection of a foundry.

Not deterred by this first defeat, the irrepressible Delaplace somehow got directly to the controller general, Joly de Fleury, in the summer of 1782, and asked him for the *procès-verbal* of the 1779 demonstration and the signed opinion of the eyewitness ironmasters. Since their opinion had been quite favorable, Delaplace's request placed the Bureau and specifically Tolozan, its supervising official of the case, in a most embarrassing situation. Tolozan took refuge in the principle of confidentiality. He transmitted Delaplace's dossier to the controller general with the observation that it was part of the Bureau's protocol generally to maintain the confidentiality of minutes of a demonstration and of the opinions of the appraising experts; otherwise they would not dare to be forthright in the future. Joly de Fleury conformed to the Bureau's policy and transmitted the dossier, not to Delaplace, but for some reason to the intendant of the Department of Mines, De la Boullaye.[117]

The second significant case of the summer of 1782 was the petition of two ambitious glass manufacturers, Lambert and Boyer, sponsored by the duc de Guines. The English had pioneered in the production of crystalware of great brilliance and clarity, known technically as flint glass. By 1755 the English manufacturers had discovered that the replacement of some lime in the original mixture of sand and soda or potash with lead oxide yielded a sparkling white ware that was suitable for cutting other glass and that bid fair to capture the French market. For years the Bureau of Commerce had welcomed any entrepreneur who promised to transfer the process to France. In the early 1780s "Lambert, Boyer and Company [had] tried to set up works at St. Cloud. After costly experiments they embarked on expensive buildings. The first two furnaces built were 'so badly made as to be no use at all.' . . . Large-scale trials produced flint glass, but it could not be shaped. Then the furnaces were found to be too big for the working hall, so that the men could not work the glass. Down came furnaces and hall and a larger set-up was planned. Hereabouts the two partners came to terms with their own ignorance. They saw that they lacked [both] 'the information necessary to have made furnaces on the scale of the English ones so as to burn coal without damaging the crystal *and* . . . the methods of making pots necessary for this type of furnace.' " Nor did French workers know the subtle, sleight-of-hand maneuvers that went with the process. "So the two partners smuggled themselves into England" in the middle of the American War of Independence. They secretly conveyed to France not only English glassworkers but "their families and tools" as well.[118] It was probably at this point, in early July 1782, that the partners petitioned the French government for aid and submitted samples of their product. The Bureau passed on the samples to its consultant, the able chemist Macquer, for appraisal. Acting very rapidly (was it the influence of the duke?), Macquer tested the glass and reported within a week that while the glass was interesting it had defects. Before approval of their project could be granted, Montaran wrote to the duke, defects would have to be removed.[119] The influence of a duke might speed the Bureau's process of appraisal but could not impair its integrity.

The third significant case of the summer was that of Guyton de Morveau, who had asked for support of a manufactory that extracted soda from salt and whose petition had also been referred to Macquer. By July 31 Macquer had his report ready. He was enthusiastic. Guyton, "ce savant chimiste," had arrived at not one method of manufacturing soda synthetically but two, elaborated through more than four hundred experiments. Both procedures were totally different from the one of Malherbe, and they were "more simple, much more sure, much easier, and consequently far more practical and inexpensive." However, Macquer observed, their success on a large scale predicated access to large quantities of marine salt, priced at no more than one livre ten sous per quintal. Guyton had proposed two ways of bringing his method into large-scale production: let the king establish a factory on his own account; or let the government authorize Guyton to do so. Passing from the realm of scientific appraisal to the domain of public policy, as the Bureau's consultant scientists were increasingly doing, Macquer recommended the second route. The first, of royal ownership, did not seem to enter into the current plans of the administration. But the second did, and in adopting it, "M. de Morveau should be favored by exemptions and privileges, by ease of procuring quality of marine salt exempt from dues, and even by cash advances if he needs them." In a word, the administration should support Guyton's enterprise by all means within its power, "because it is one of the most useful, one of the most important, and one of the best understood projects that has been proposed in a long time." [120]

Such enthusiasm was as refreshing as it was rare among our administrators, who were more skilled, perhaps, at defusing excitement than awakening it. One can imagine what Daniel Trudaine would have done with a recommendation to go all-out for a strategically important large factory, manufacturing a product crucial to several industries. However, Colonia was not a Trudaine in ability; nor did he control all elements of the situation as Trudaine did. Macquer, with his eye on the jugular issue, had already focused attention on the next key question: granting that Guyton's method was novel and superior, was reasonably priced salt available? So, after a delay of several weeks, on August 20 Colonia inquired of the Farmers General, who sold salt at monopoly rates, what would be their attitude to making salt available to Guyton at a reasonable price?

Through August or early September Macquer was verifying for Montaran the pretensions of another inventor, Sieur Dino Stéphanopoli, a native of Corsica who claimed to have discovered a substitute black dye for that derived from gallnuts. Macquer betook himself to the dyeing shop of Guénault on the rue to Huchette. There in his presence, in accord with the usual dyeing procedures, the workmen plunged 125 hats into a boiler of water containing nothing but a mordant "of logwood, verdigris, and green vitriol" and Stéphanopoli's secret chemical, which was fawn-colored and astringent to taste. After two days the hats were withdrawn, washed, dried, and examined. Macquer thought their blackness to be "very beautiful, very soft" and equal in every respect to articles dyed with gallnuts. Guénault, the craftsman, who seemed to know his business, was of the same opinion. However, since Stéphanopoli refused to divulge the nature of the chemical, no test could be made of his claim that it was considerably cheaper than the one in use. This question, as Macquer observed, was now the essential one. Not having the answer, Montaran could only direct his clerk to file Macquer's report in Stéphanopoli's dossier and await his appearance.[121]

While the Guyton de Morveau and Stéphanopoli cases were in process, the Bureau was also considering a third petition involving chemicals, and also a state monopoly. Guyton's petition had originated in Dijon, Burgundy. This time the setting was Nîmes, the textile center of southern France. There a Sieur Lapenne had erected a chemical factory, manufacturing nitric and sulfuric acids and mineral salts used in arts and crafts, and especially in dyeing. In his chemical operations he employed a raw material, *eaux-mères de salpêtre*. Currently he manufactured the *eaux-mères* himself by boiling and decomposing saltpeter, but the process was costly, and he wished permission to import them from the neighboring foreign city of Avignon. He also desired the title of *Manufacture royale*. Seeking information, the Bureau sent this petition to the intendant of Languedoc, Jean Emmanuel Guignard de Saint-Priest, and he in turn passed it on to his subdelegate at Nîmes.

After an inspection trip through the factory, accompanied we may imagine by Lapenne himself (phrases in the report seem to echo the entrepreneur's promotional élan), the subdelegate was glowing. The establishment was extensive; large buildings enclosed several galleries and furnaces skillfully arranged for the distillation of nitric acids; there was one room for the distillation of sulfuric acid, and another one a-building capable of rendering France independent of foreign imports of this product. Because heat-resistant stoneware retorts were used, only coal was employed as a fuel; import of the indispensable *eaux-mères*, instead of manufacturing them, would indeed reduce the cost of operations. Lapenne's factory, the subdelegate concluded, "presented great advantages and promises to endow the state with a most interesting branch of commerce."

In transmitting his subdelegate's report to the Bureau of Commerce on August 26, Saint-Priest appended his own comments. For all the value of Lapenne's factory, it probably should not be granted the title of *Manufacture royale* until it had in fact rendered France independent of foreign supplies of sulfuric acid. As for permission to import *eaux-mères*, would that not have to be taken up with the Compagnie des Poudres? The Compagnie was a *Régie*, that is, the administration of a monopoly under state supervision. Since July 1, 1775 it had enjoyed the monopoly of fabricating, importing, and selling gunpowder and its major ingredient, saltpeter. The Compagnie was an efficient *Régie*. Under the direction of Antoine-Laurent Lavoisier, a French chemist who was also a *régisseur* (administrator) of the organization, the Compagnie was establishing French self-sufficiency in munitions of war with a gunpowder "reputed to be the best in Europe."[122] Obviously Saint-Priest was correct: Lapenne's request needed to be cleared with the Compagnie. Probably in early September, the Bureau of Commerce inquired of the Compagnie's *régisseurs*, what is your attitude to Lapenne's proposal?[123] While a reply was awaited, another affair and, for that matter, another entrepreneur were in suspense.

Also in September, 1782 the semiannual reports of the regional inspectors of manufactures upon their semiannual tours of inspection began to come in. By now the accent in the reports was less on the enforcement of regulations than on positive measures of encouragement, either recommended or in process. In his journal inspector Vaugelade observed that industrially his responsibility, Poitou, was one of the poorest and most indolent provinces in the kingdom.[124] In Poitiers itself thirteen master fabricants supervised the knitting of woolen stockings and caps; but the loss of Canada to the British in 1763 had reduced their market. Seven others fabricated woolen cloth, but they were little occupied. However, private and public initiatives were forming new establishments that could become very useful. One fabricant was manufacturing woolen blankets, for sale in Poitou and elsewhere, thus using Poitevin wool. The charity hospital was at any one time training fifty to sixty children, mostly girls, in the use of the spinning wheel; they would spread this skill throughout the province, thus preparing the way for cotton weaving. And a Sieur Reignier had set up eight looms for weaving cotton cloth, with enough spinners of cotton yarn to keep the weavers supplied—he had requested government aid. It was essential, Vaugelade wrote, for the government to favor these enterprises in some way. Otherwise Poitou would never emerge from its depressed situation.

At the other end of the scale from Poitou, in the *généralité* of Upper Normandy (Rouen), everything, apparently, had been accomplished. There private initiatives and the long-term strategies of Holker and the Trudaines in support of the textile and chemical industries had borne fruit. With unconcealed satisfaction the inspector of manufactures, Goy, wrote November 12, 1782: "The Rouen linen industry is immense, extending throughout a large portion of the *généralité*. The industry has grown quite far there; there is no one who is not employed, despite wartime fluctuations. . . . Its commerce extends not only throughout *le Royaume*, but abroad as well. The soil there is generally good and well cultivated; the majority of the handicraftsmen throughout the countryside cultivate farms that they either own or rent. Manufacturing and Agriculture lend each other mutual support."[125] Statistics lend support to Goy's glowing description. Whereas during the first six months of 1782, the weavers of all Poitou produced only 8,624 pieces of cloth (a gain of only 8 pieces over the corresponding months of 1781),[126] those of Rouen and its environs manufactured 183,714 pieces, 64,046 in Rouen itself and 120,668 in the surrounding countryside.[127] "The large number of persons of all ages and both sexes occupied by the manufactures [of linen and cotton cloth] render these 'très intéressantes' for the State."[128]

Indeed to Goy the *généralité* of Rouen seemed the showpiece and the justification of the administrative policy of developing the French economy in a sound, balanced, interrelated way. Farmers supplied raw materials (food, wool, flax) and a market that craftsmen needed; the craftsmen in turn furnished clothing the farmers desired; merchants linked artisans and farmers in trade; the royal government, taxing the commercial processes at various points of production and exchange, gained revenue; and all grew prosperous together. No wonder Goy contentedly concluded his report that there seemed no need to form new manufacturing establishments (in Normandy), but merely to protect and encourage those already in operation.[129]

It was in line with this overall strategy of balanced development that the Bureau resumed consideration of Guyton de Morveau's offer to establish a soda factory, an offer glowingly endorsed by the chemist Macquer. To Colonia's inquiry of August 20, the Farmers General replied: in no way could they grant Guyton a special rate on the price of salt; the concession to one person, however honorable, would simply open the door to fraudulent evasion of the salt tax by others. When Guyton protested, the Farmers General stood firm: the proposed soda factory could not be sited in the "Pays de gabelles"; the salt pans of Brittany were the only possible location. The Bureau of Commerce perforce deferred to the adamant decision of the Farmers General, and through Joly de Fleury communicated it to Guyton on November 6: the factory could be formed only in Brittany, "in proximity to the salt pans." The controller general added: "I am quite aware that the journeys and sojourns you would have to make, in this distant province, in order to acquire the necessary site to lay out the workshops, and to take other indispensable measures, would inevitably involve you in a very considerable expense, which it seems you could not undertake unless the Government came to your aid; and since existing circumstances [a reference probably to wartime fiscal stringency] do not allow this, I come to the conclusion that it is necessary to postpone to a more fortunate time the execution of your project."[130] Though the controller general tried to soften the blow by adding, "I shall then gladly do whatever is in my power to promote its success," he was in effect saying "Rien à faire à présent." By reason of the intransigent opposition of a powerful monopoly, perhaps the most promising industrial initiative of the year was indefinitely postponed.

Meanwhile, throughout the autumn another industrial chemist, Jean Antoine Chaptal (1756–1832), was beginning to chat with the Bureau about the many interesting experiments he was conducting at Montpellier. Like Guyton de Morveau, he was the product of the interplay between the sophisticated scientific culture of Paris and the vigorous intellectual life of a provincial town. For centuries the Faculty of Medicine at the University of Montpellier had been internationally famous, and the local Royal Society of Sciences, chartered in 1706, was on a legal equality with the Royal Academy of Sciences at Paris. Educated at the local *collèges* of Mende and Rodez, Chaptal enrolled in the Faculty of Medicine and in 1776 was received as a doctor of medicine. He persuaded a rich uncle, who was a wealthy physician, to finance a broadening educational experience in Paris, where he was captivated by the public lectures of distinguished chemists. "His enthusiasm for chemistry led to his appointment in 1780 to a special created chair" on the subject at Montpellier.[131] In his popular public lectures he emphasized the multiple uses of chemistry in manufacturing, in "the belief that the application of science to industry would yield *useful* fruit [again the concept of utility] and would contribute to material progress," especially to the progress of the local economy.[132] With the dowry of 70,000 livres from his wife, the daughter of a cotton merchant, and the wedding gift of 120,000 livres from his rich uncle, he erected in 1782 a factory to manufacture sulfuric acid and related chemical products. The enterprising young Chaptal was off and running.

In a breezy, engaging style he wrote to the controller general on November 22 about his wonderful lava bottles, which were half the weight of ordinary glass bottles and much stronger. When a brewer had filled with a very heady beer 230 ordinary bottles and 25 of Chaptal's, corked them firmly with blows of a mallet, and buried them in sand, 61 of the regular bottles had burst, but none of Chaptal's. They could be used also to bottle wine, a major local product of the Languedoc. Chaptal announced that 120 of these bottles had been consigned to the controller general; they had left Montpellier on November 12 and should reach Paris by December 8. The professor of chemistry of the province of Languedoc, as he signed himself, also ran on about the marvelous tin he was making: "very hard; whiter in color, less leaden; and with a very clear sound approaching that of silver." "Metal thus purified," he assured the controller general, "makes an excellent tinplate, proof against all the agents that are most used in the kitchen." He then alluded to his experiments on the perfection of dyeing and promised to communicate the results when they were finished. He finally reminded Joly de Fleury of his proposal to improve that species of the glasswort plant, *Salsola soda* or barilla, found on the Mediterranean beaches of France, from which soda was derived. The soda extracted from maritime plants found on French beaches sold for only 3 to 4 livres per hundredweight, but that extracted from Spanish barilla brought 20 to 25 livres. Chaptal proposed with an associate to naturalize Spanish barilla by sowing the plant on a strip of French coastline. Bottles, tin, dyeing, and soda, he cheerfully and repeatedly pointed out, were all projects of immediate practical utility to industry.[133]

The controller general and the Bureau were charmed with a scientist who was working so fruitfully for the public good. "M. Chaptal merits every consideration, by reason both of the useful discoveries he has made already and of the trouble he takes to perfect some very interesting branches of industry."[134] Yet they were not so enchanted as to forget to bring Chaptal's discoveries within the Bureau's appraisal procedures. Joly de Fleury (or his chief clerk) singled out his letter as one to be acknowledged at once, before reference to the Bureau of Commerce for routine consideration— an unusual mark of distinction. On December 1, he thanked the scientist in advance for the shipment of the 120 bottles "made of lava" and promised to comment on their quality upon their arrival. He also asked for a sample of his tin, presumably for testing. Chaptal's letter was then referred to Montaran, the intendant in whose jurisdiction Montpellier and the *généralité* of Languedoc lay, and he brought it before the Comité of intendants of commerce on December 10.

The Comité instructed Montaran, in turn, to investigate Chaptal's request for permission to use a stretch of French Mediterranean beach for experiments in naturalizing Spanish barilla. Montaran's investigation in Paris soon revealed that in September of October Chaptal had already requested, through a M. De Joubert, the same permission from Joly de

Fleury, and that unbeknownst to the four intendants and perhaps Joly de Fleury, the controller general's own bureau had taken the request unto itself. In correspondence with Saint-Priest, the intendant of Languedoc, it had already arranged the details of the concession and granted it.

In according the grant the reasoning of the controller general's bureau reveals much of the *Ancien Régime* in miniature. The issue, it said, was relatively simple, since the coastal stretches belonged to the king. What he owned, he could give. However, in the thicket of grants inherited from centuries past, a few neighboring villages (*communautés*) might have acquired rights over the beaches, including the right to impose the *taille*, and they might object. But Chaptal was petitioning, not for ownership, but for permission to cultivate uncultivated land. As for his associated request for exemption from a local *taille*, it was best to say nothing for fear mention might awaken discussion; if a village attempted to levy on Chaptal, the administration could proceed by mediation (*conciliation*). Operating within a crazy-quilt of legal privileges so complex that no single person in France knew what they all were, even the king had to tread warily. Chaptal would discover them only as he tripped against them. So, in conclusion, on November 14 the controller general had authorized Saint-Priest to issue an ordinance according Chaptal permission to use for one year two leagues of coastal beach between "le Gran de Frontignan et celui de Perals" in his experiment to naturalize barilla. Saint-Priest was to inform the controller general of the results of the attempt. Joly de Fleury's letter of permission addressed to Saint-Priest had crossed Chaptal's inquiry of November 22.[135]

Throughout 1782 the deputies of commerce associated with the Bureau were meanwhile rendering a series of "Avis" on individual tariff rates, their interpretation, their revision, and their impact on French industry and on the French economy in general. In the maze of multifarious customs duties and amid the pressures of interested groups, the deputies kept their heads and consistently followed the nuanced protectionist tariff policies and philosophy described in probe 1 of this study.[136] As they fine-tuned the application of the policies during this year, their recommendations for specific products included the following: Paper: prohibit the export of raw material used in its manufacture. Chemicals (soda, potash, alum, sulfuric acid): prohibit export of potashes and saline ashes useful in the manufacturing of saltpeter. Sugar: match British bounty with a countervailing import duty. Lead: a low import levy for "pig" lead, high for finished product. Tapestry: continue prohibitive duty of 25 percent, English tapestries to be admitted at only a single customs bureau. Brass: a moderate duty of 3 livres per hundredweight, since it is needed for further manufacture. Copper articles: 6 livres per hundredweight to protect copper mines and foundries. Oak bark suitable for tanning hides: renew and enforce 1720 prohibition of its export. Gold jewelry: reduction of export duties on this finished product. Worked coral objects: import tariff of 10 percent, protective but not prohibitive, to encourage a new industry. Glass: prohibit export of raw materials used in its manufacture. Silks: import duty on all silk cloth from China and India; but since manufacturers of gauzes need 90 million livres worth of Nanking silk, continue to accept it. In an interesting exception to protectionist policy, but justifiable in terms of the overall welfare of France, scientific instruments were to be admitted free.[137]

An "Avis" of October 8 illustrates their participation in the process of the decision.[138] The Merchants Merciers of Lyons had petitioned the controller general for an increase in the import duty on colored ribbons. The deputies recognized that the merchants were moved by private interest. Yet they thought their request conformed to the principles of the administration. Here was an industry, indefinitely expansible, that could occupy a large number of craftsmen in town and country. Hitherto the import tariff, 10 livres per hundredweight, had been too low to be protective, and many shops had closed. The deputies recommended doubling the tariff to 20 livres: the labor force of "le Royaume" would thus increase, and so would its wages. Their opinion was listened to, and on October 22 a royal decree doubled the import duty to 20 livres.[139]

Throughout the year the deputies were conducting a running fight against the Farmers General, who were nervously insecure, and hence firmly adamant, about the modification of any duty, internal or external, that reduced their revenue or enhanced the chances of smuggling and fraud.[140] The deputies, in contrast, took the broader view of enlightened self-interest: certainly the king's revenue must be protected, but so must the interests of commerce and industry from which royal revenue is, in part, derived. How did the proposed modification affect these broader and more ultimate concerns? After a series of confrontations with the Farmers General, the deputies finally could contain themselves no longer. In measured prose that rose to the dignity of a peroration, they described the antagonism between the Farmers General and the operations of commerce.

The occasion of the deputies' eloquence was a request from the Farmers General for *lettres patentes* regulating the customs declarations of importers. The debate turned on a crucial issue. If an importer declared a quantity that upon verification turned out to exceed the actual amount, should the duty be levied on the declared or the actual contents? The Farmers General, anxious for money, said, on the larger quantity—the declared amount. But suppose the declared quantity was inferior to the actual. Obviously this was a case of fraud, unintentional or intentional, and again the duty must be applied to the larger amount—in this case the actual. Heads I win, tails you lose. Whatever the situation, the Farmers General would come out ahead. They had already surprised the unwary controller general into approval: the *lettres patentes* embodying their viewpoint were only awaiting registration before becoming a law.

To the deputies all this seemed outrageous. In their "Mémoire" of

December 7 they tried to keep their temper.[141] Almost impersonally they stated their thesis in the first sentence. "If smuggling is detrimental to the royal treasury, if it is harmful to commerce itself, the excess of precautions taken to prevent it is even more dangerous, because in frightening commerce it unquestionably diminishes the revenues of the Public Treasury [*Trésor Public*]." They then bluntly placed the Farmers General and the operation of commerce in polar opposition. "The Farmers General always distrust the operations of commerce, commerce always complains of the shackles with which the Farmers General overwhelm it." From this polar antagonism two harmful consequences must follow. "The royal government, alarmed by the representations of its Farmers, fears to lose a branch of its revenues; it accumulates decisions upon decisions, it denatures, so to speak, the original laws, it imposes new constraints, and it strangles commerce, which requires liberty if it is to expand; commerce, in turn, fatigued by hindrances, disheartened by formalities, often seeks to simplify and speed up its operations, and sometimes is tempted to withdraw from obedience to laws that are too overwhelming; persuaded that its interest is sacrificed to that of the Farmer, it believes it is being unjustly treated; and, then, it is to be feared that a merchant who in society and in civil acts is honest and scrupulous may allow himself to be drawn into breaches of regulations. . . . [The minister, better instructed,] retraces his steps, but the harm has been done; commerce has suffered reverses and the merchant may have become habituated to fraud and breaches of the law that he had first considered only as measures that he had been forced to take in order to repulse the losses and injustices that were being inflicted on him."

The deputies conceded that the Farmers General did not intend the oppression of commerce; nevertheless, their ignorance has the same effect as malice. "We are far from wishing to suggest that the Farmers General *intend* to oppress commerce, we render them that justice, but we cannot dissimulate our belief that continually occupied with making the most of the proceeds of their *Régie*, they do not sufficiently take into account the relations with all the other interests. Strangers to commerce, how could they do this? They know neither its mechanisms, nor its competitive rivalries, nor its needs; often they deal it the most deadly blows, while believing that they are achieving the double good of serving commerce and augmenting the revenues of the King. How many times has this error been fatal!" It was up to informed officials—that is, the intendants and deputies of commerce—"charged with the ensemble of the administration to maintain the balance between the tax collector and the taxpayer, and to reject measures proposed to them, when those measures that are presented to assure the collection of the tax are fit only to dry up its source."

In conclusion, the deputies were not optimistic about the ultimate success of their protests. The Farmers General were always there, and they would persevere. "We cannot resist observing that the tranquility of the subjects of the King depends essentially on the stability of the decisions he gives to shelter them from the attacks to which they are continually exposed, and that it is very important to be on guard against the attempts of powerful corps [*corps puissans*] to take unfair advantage of them because these corps steadily subjugate private individuals by their spirit of continuity and their ability to revive, under different forms, pretensions on which they had been rebuffed. A condemnation that is absolute [in its effects] for a private person, for a corps is only a momentary reverse, and a single success avenges it for all the checks it has suffered."

From objection to a particular initiative of the Farmers General concerning customs declarations the deputies had risen to reflection on the general polar opposition between the Farmers General and the interest of commerce and of merchants: from that intermediate reflection they achieved the broader perspective of the exposed position of all the king's subjects to the powerful, continuing bureaucratic "corps puissans." With pardonable pride they had viewed themselves as on a height, above the warfare of individual and corporate interests, and as attempting to manage the conflict so as to protect the individual subject and to secure the welfare of the king and his kingdom.

Meantime, during December and into the winter months of 1783 the routine of business in the Bureau of Commerce continued under the benign presidency of its noninnovating controller general, Joly de Fleury. Petitions were coming in; petitions were being referred to later months; and cases (that is, petitions) were being wound up and their documents filed.

On December 9, a Sieur Moyroud, "Maître de Forge" at Perouzét in Dauphiny, presented a memoir announcing a new process to manufacture natural steel (*acier naturel*) with a one-fourth saving in coal and labor-time and no diminution in quality. The process seemed to merit attention, and the Bureau asked the intendant of Dauphiny (Grenoble), Christophe Pajot de Marcheval, to investigate and report.[142]

Year after year in Lyons a Sieur Rivey had invented improvement after improvement in intricate knitting looms. Year after year he had received awards from the Caisse des étoffes étrangères in Lyons: 1,000 livres in 1774; 120 in 1775; 5,000 in 1777, and so on. On December 18, 1782 Joly de Fleury accorded him an annual pension of 300 livres.[143]

In mid-December a second petition from the chemists Lambert and Boyer was passing through. This petition was an example of where under Bureau guidance a process had been matured until it met Bureau standards. The first petition had been turned down six months before on the advice of the expert chemist Macquer. In the second time around the petitioners asserted that they had discovered and now had improved a process to manufacture crystalware equal to that of England. They proposed to erect their factory in Paris, and they asked for an exclusive privilege to sell throughout the kingdom "des Cristaux, Emaux, et Cendre bleu" of their manufacture. Their request was now backed by both the duc de Guines and the duc d'Orléans, and perhaps for this reason was labeled urgent ("comme MM. Lambert et Boyer étaient pressés"). The petition was referred to Macquer, who on December 17 quickly endorsed their process and product.[144] Acting very promptly, the Bureau through Joly de Fleury denied the request for an exclusive privilege but accorded Lambert and Boyer on January 14, 1783 a subsidy of 50,000 livres to be paid in ten annual installments. The money was to be used to discharge the interest on the debt Lambert and Boyer had incurred to erect the factory.[145] The Bureau could act with dispatch because favorable conditions now coincided—the dream and drive of innovative, persistent petitioners, the support of influential patrons, the endorsement of a scientific expert, and the long-standing Bureau policy to encourage any firm whose product promised to match sparkling English white ware.

On December 30, the next-to-last day of the year, the controller general could finally inform the intendant of Languedoc of the fate of the petition of Lapenne, the genial, enterprising chemical manufacturer of Nîmes.[146] The *régisseurs* of the Compagnie des Poudres would not permit him either to manufacture *eaux-mères* or to import them from Avignon, since to do so would infringe the *Régie*'s monopoly, diminish its revenue, and hence reduce the king's profit. However, the Compagnie would give orders that Lapenne might purchase saltpeter at its warehouse in Montpellier or buy *eaux-mères* from its refineries. The price, of course, would be that set by the monopoly. Nor could the Bureau of Commerce accord his factory the appellation of *Manufacture Royal* since it was not unique of its kind. Such was the New Year's message for Lapenne, his promotional plan for the moment stunted by a royal monopoly.[147]

After a lapse of nearly a year and a half the Bureau reached a decision on the petition of the comte d'Artois requesting permission to build a glass manufactory within the appanage his brother had granted him for his lifetime.[148] The four intendants had before them two diametrically opposite opinions: that of Des Forges, the director in charge of waters and forests, recommending approval because there was a superfluity of wood, and that of the municipality of Abbeville protesting approval because there was a shortage. The protest of the municipality seems well substantiated. Yet the Royal Council, presumably on the recommendation of the four intendants, listened to Des Forges and on January 7, 1783 accorded the requested permission.[149] This decision was probably an instance where the personal interests of the monarch (the glass factory would enrich the royal domain when the appanage reverted to the king upon the count's death) overrode the Bureau's policy (to protect the forests of France and the welfare of local communities). It was another example of where the intention of forest legislation, to conserve fuel, was being undermined, in this case by administrative action, in others by administrative inaction.[150]

As February slipped into March and March into April, one controller general gave place to another: after twenty-two months in office Joly de Fleury withdrew on March 26, 1783 to be succeeded three days later by Henri François-de-Paule Lefèvre d'Ormesson (1751–1808). From a family that for more than two hundred years had served the monarchy with distinction in the magistrature and the administration, d'Ormesson was only thirty-one years old when elevated to the post of controller general. He had begun his career as councilor of state and intendant of finances in charge of the department of taxes, the "free" gift of the Catholic clergy, the *régie* of powder and saltpeter, and the works of charity.[151] His responsibility for the administration of the house of Saint-Cyr had obliged him to work with Louis XVI, who had taken a liking to him and appointed him controller general. When d'Ormesson protested his youth and inexperience, the king reportedly replied: "I am younger than you, and I occupy a position greater than the one I am giving you."[152] Yet d'Ormesson's self-distrust was justified by the event. Although a hard worker of unimpeachable probity who performed well in subaltern administrative posts, he had no knowledge of the complex business and intrigues of the controller general's office. He became buried in detail and committed blunders of fiscal policy that endangered the credit of the state.[153] After seven months he was dismissed and retired to the subaltern duties of councilor of state, where he continued to work with zealous efficiency in matters that he understood.

It is difficult to discern from the documents what effect, if any, d'Ormesson had on the ongoing operations of the Bureau of Commerce and our four intendants. In the area of positive encouragement of industry, the processes of the collegial administration of the Bureau seemed to go on as before.

On June 2, 1772 the Bureau had granted a Sieur Priqueleur permission to install a tilt-hammer to fashion squares of iron used in watchmaking. His ironworks at Plancher-les-Mines in the *généralité* of Franche-Comté had prospered, and now in February 1783 he requested permission to add a forge. His petition entered the standard operating procedures of the Bureau. It was referred to Colonia, the intendant of commerce in whose jurisdiction Franche-Comté lay. He passed it on to Charles André de la Coré, the intendant of the *généralité*, with the inquiry: what do you think? La Coré responded favorably on February 24. The utility and success of Priqueleur's first establishment, he wrote, had earned him the government's protection for its expansion. The firm already employed workers in an agriculturally barren district that otherwise would be without occupation, and the forge would enhance their well-being. Its fuel requirements would triple or quadruple the price of wood, much of it from the king's own forests, and thus contribute to the wealth of the state and the region. With the intendant's opinion in hand Colonia promptly applied on March 15 to the director of waters and forests: what is the opinion of your corps? And under d'Ormesson's controller generalcy he awaited a reply.[154]

Early in 1783 Sieurs Glaesner and Prudhomme of Lyons had proposed to establish there a watch factory for their own profit and to capture for France an industry that was drawing specie to Switzerland, the home of fine watchmakers. The two promoters planned to lure one thousand discontented Genevese craftsmen to work in their factory, and they asked the support of the French government. Not at all modest in their demands, they requested an outright subsidy of 200,000 livres, the title of *Manufacture Royale*, and exemption from all import and export duties. Under Joly de Fleury the petition had been referred to Colonia, intendant of commerce in charge of the Lyonnais, and he addressed a specific question to Jacques de Flesselles, intendant of Lyons: what arrangements do the Protestant Swiss craftsmen expect with regard to their worship services and their acts of baptism, marriage, and burial, which are outlawed in Catholic France? (Here was another instance of privilege, in this case a privileged church, potentially cramping free industrial innovation; at least the Bureau was obliged to handle the obstacle.) Flesselles replied on March 24, during the last week of Joly de Fleury's ministry: there is no problem; the Swiss intend to submit to the laws of the kingdom (*Royaume*) without soliciting any exemption whatever.[155] Under d'Ormesson the Bureau continued to consider the petition, only in the end to turn it down. On May 1 Colonia wrote to Glaesner explaining why: the discontent of the Genevese might be transitory, and besides the French government did not wish to seduce workers away from a friendly country; in any case the title of *Manufacture Royale* could be granted only to an enterprise that in some way was novel.[156]

In early April the chemist Guyton de Morveau took advantage of the appointment of a new controller general to renew his application for government protection of his project to extract soda from salt by two methods of his invention. In a letter of April 5 written from Dijon, he accepted the limitations imposed by the Farmers General: his manufactory would be erected near the salt pans of Brittany. He likewise accepted the restriction imposed by the prior privilege of Sieur Athénas: the factory would not be sited within ten leagues of Nantes. Guyton also assured the government that he needed no royal subsidy: he had wealthy financial backers anxious to make a fortune from a "good thing." He asked only for an exclusive privilege to manufacture soda by his two methods and to market it throughout France. Within the Bureau of Commerce his letter was referred to Tolozan, now in charge of the affair.[157]

Scarcely had Tolozan read Guyton's letter than he found himself perusing a memoir from a Sieur Hollenweger announcing *his* discovery of an economical method for extracting soda from salt on a large scale. "He was a former pupil of the Saint-Gobain glass company, France's premier glass concern, and his scheme followed trials he had made at Saint-Gobain and at the same firm's Tourlaville works near Cherbourg. This firm must have been one of the largest alkali consumers in the country, employing more than a thousand tons of soda a year in 1770. It had refused to support its pupil in large-scale manufacture, however, lacking faith in his method; his complaints having led to his dismissal, Hollenweger was now embarking on a soda venture of his own."[158] He wrote the controller general that the example of Athénas had encouraged him to request an exclusive privilege to establish a factory for the large-scale implementation of his process. He desired, as well, exclusive rights to market its product throughout France.[159]

Tolozan now had before him two petitions of almost identical import. He had several options, whether he was aware of them or not. He might have plumped for one enterprise, perhaps Guyton's, which was already thoroughly tested, and thrown the resources of the French government behind it. This would have accorded with Trudaine's practice of going big with something big; this would have been strategic policy. Or he might have brought together the two entrepreneurs, Guyton and Hollenweger, in a joint effort. This would have been the policy of tactical thoughtfulness. But in the spring and summer of 1783 he selected neither of these options. Instead, apparently governed by the Bureau's administrative routine, he considered each petition separately and sent each one through the Bureau's standard operating procedures for the consideration of a petition. The procedures incorporated the Bureau's principle that each inventor had a right to his invention and to its profitable exploitation.

By April, 1783 Guyton's petition was farther along. Its process had been tested and praised by Macquer, its proposals trimmed by the Farmers General. In brief, it was ready to go. By June 3 Tolozan had secured from his fellow intendants in the Bureau of Commerce, from controller general d'Ormesson, and finally from the Council of Finances consent to a royal decree granting Guyton what he essentially desired: for fifteen years the exclusive privilege to manufacture soda by the two methods he had described and to sell it throughout the kingdom. The grant was subject to three conditions: Guyton was not to erect his factory within ten leagues of Nantes; he would give the royal administration a detailed description of the two methods; and he would not oppose the manufacture of soda by methods different from his own.[160] Greatly rejoicing in the grant, Guyton headed for the salt pans of Brittany. There at Croisic, two hundred leagues from his home in Dijon, at considerable expense, he began energetically and rapidly to put his plans into execution.[161]

Meanwhile, unbeknownst to Guyton, Tolozan was processing Hollenweger's petition. As was customary, he referred it to Macquer for expert appraisal. On July 22 the chemist reported that Hollenweger's procedure for extracting soda from salt was economically feasible. More than that, it was totally different from Guyton's.[162] On that assurance, Tolozan, the Bureau, and the controller general recommended and on September 23 the Royal Council decreed that Hollenweger be accorded the exclusive privilege to produce soda chemically by *his* method for fifteen years.[163]

Guyton was stunned by news of this decree. On October 18 he protested to d'Ormesson that the Royal Council had set up between Hollenweger and himself a knock-down, knockout competition that could only be ruinous to both contestants. His financial backers, he said, were already dropping out, and he did not know whether he could continue.[164] Guyton's initiative was too important to lose. After checking with Macquer, Tolozan (through d'Ormesson) officially informed Guyton that legally he had no case: his own grant of June "bound him not to oppose any enterprise manufacturing soda by a method different from his own." [165] Unofficially, Macquer (at the instance of Tolozan) assured Guyton that Hollenweger's method, while feasible, was so inferior that he need not fear his competition.[166] Upon that assurance Guyton began to produce soda at his Croisic plant.[167]

However, the last word in the incident lay not with Athénas, Guyton, and Hollenweger, nor with Tolozan, d'Ormesson, and the Royal Council of Finances, but with the Farmers General. As Guyton had anticipated, Athénas's process was so impractical that it was never put into operation; it was said that Athénas used his privilege simply "to deceive those who would loan him money." Hollenweger never even built a factory.[168] As for Guyton, when he tried to ship "trois tonneaux" of his own soda from his manufactory in Brittany to his glassworks near Dijon, the agent of the Farmers General at Nantes impounded the consignment, perfectly legally, until the customs tariff had been paid, as if it were being imported from a foreign country! Appeals from Guyton to the controller general and from him to the Farmers General for the release of the cargo were unavailing, and it lay in the Nantes customs house for three years, until 1787. Naturally, Guyton suspended operations.[169] One of the most promising administrative-industrial initiatives of 1783 had been daunted by the implacable opposition of the Farmers General. The problems Guyton and the Bureau were attempting to solve—the exploitation of French manufacturers by foreign soda producers, the annual drain of 2 million livres of specie abroad, the shortage of both soda and potash in many lines of French industry—remained unresolved, their solution held up, actually and symbolically, by the impounded cargo of "trois tonneaux" of soda in the Nantes customs house.

As the four intendants of commerce moved from spring through summer into early autumn under the new controller general, they participated in yet other administrative-industrial initiatives. Several lay in the realm of textiles. As we have seen, Dambourney, secretary of the Academy of Rouen and a member of other academies, "had been seeking since September 1779 among plants native to France those that could be substituted for foreign ones that are used in dyeing." In the language of Tolozan's report, "he had not only found them but he had added several new nuances of colors." The journal of his experiments, approved by the chemists Macquer and Claude Louis Berthollet and entitled *Receuil des procédés et d'expériences sur les teinture solides que nos végétaux indigènes communiquent aux laines et lainages*, was to be published at the government's expense. In Tolozan's view, its publication would "certainly mark an epoch in the art of dyeing." By a decision of June 3, Dambourney himself was accorded an annual pension of 1,000 livres.[170]

In another textile project, Colonia, after two years, revived the petition of Morize, the member of the Society of Agriculture of Rouen who had invented what he considered an improved reeling machine for the winding of silk thread. Encouraged by the approbation of the examining commissioners of the Academy of Rouen, Morize on June 27, 1781 had forwarded the machine to Tolozan, who turned it over to Colonia, the intendant in charge of the silk industry. Only now, on July 7, 1783, more than two years later, did Colonia refer the machine to Vandermonde for examination and report: "Could we have your opinion of the use that could be made of this machine?"[171] On July 10 Vandermonde, curator of the depot of machines at the Hôtel de Mortagne, acknowledged receipt of the memoirs relative to the instrument and promised to give his opinion "after I have read and examined these documents with the necessary care."[172] With that acknowledgment the Morize petition again dropped out of sight.

Wishing to secure from England several special looms for the knitting of stockings and other articles, the Bureau dispatched to London an expert mechanic named Le Turc to spy them out. His trip of espionage was eminently successful. He soon sent back to France "(1) a loom *à chaîne* to knit stockinet [an elastic fabric used for stockings and undergarments] that is still superior to the looms of Sieurs Sarrazin and Germain; (2) a loom fit to imitate lambskin and brocaded fabrics; (3) a mechanism to make velvet that can fit another loom; (4) a mechanism to make stockings that operates so that they stretch at will and then return to their original, natural state; (5) a mechanism to manufacture ribbed fabrics." By a decision of October 4 the Bureau granted Le Turc the lump sum of 10,000 livres for his expenses and to compensate him for all his trouble.[173]

In cotton spinning the Bureau had been working closely with the Holkers, father and son, to domesticate in France the most recent English inventions—the Hargreaves spinning jenny and that complex of machinery known as the Arkwright water frame. In 1771 the younger Trudaine had sent Holker's son to Britain "to surprise the latest [industrial] secrets." He had returned with a Hargreaves spinning jenny, "concealed, disassembled, in kit form."[174] Installed first at the Holker manufactory at Sens, its use had soon spread; by 1789 there would be nine hundred in France.[175] The jenny produced a thread soft and smooth, especially suitable for the woof of the cloth.

The use of mechanical spinners put pressure on the carders to produce enough carded cotton. In 1779 the Holkers had made contact with a Jacques Milne, an English artisan who had brought from England an improved set of cards. The following year, 1780, Milne introduced the Holkers to an Arkwright water frame, which required little skill of the operatives, could be moved by water, wind, or steam power, and produced a thread smoother, stronger, and more uniform than that of the jenny. The yarn of the water frame was especially suitable for the warp. In 1782 the Bureau of Commerce had authorized Milne to construct a factory that would use his carding process and Arkwright's spinner.[176]

However, Milne's version of the water frame had "bugs" in it. It tore the cotton and thus weakened the strength of the thread.[177] The Holkers and the staff of the Bureau of Commerce, inspectors of manufactures as well as intendants of commerce, searched for a more perfect Arkwright process—and so did individual entrepreneurs, who knew that anyone who installed a perfect water frame in France would make a fortune. At first the elder Holker seemed to have the inside track. In a letter of May 27 addressed to the controller general and referred to Tolozan, he recommended two English artisans who had worked for years in a cotton-spinning factory near Manchester. They offered to build a model water frame that, unlike the Milne version, would preserve without tearing the silkiness of the cotton fiber throughout its length.[178] But even as Tolozan was considering Holker's letter, Jacques Martin, a protégé of Roland de la Platière, the inspector of manufactures for the *généralité* of Picardy (Amiens), was breaking through to success. Born about 1758, Martin had given himself as a youth to the study of science, the industrial arts, commerce, and political economy. Directed in his studies by Roland, he had accompanied the inspector of manufactures on his tour of the industrial enterprises of Germany and had shared in the preparation of his articles and books. At considerable risk he stole into the cotton-spinning factories of England and returned with a perfect version of the Arkwright water frame. Now, upon the recommendation of Roland and Vandermonde, the Bureau of Commerce accorded him the astounding subsidy of 70,000 livres. His factory, erected at Lepine near Arpajon in Picardy, prospered from the start.[179] And no wonder! It produced a thread that was not only cheaper than the product of hand-spinners but better—smoother, more uniform, and stronger.

Other decisions of the intendants concerned the production of metals—copper, iron and steel, and lead. The manufacture of copper products, hitherto neglected by the intendants of commerce,[180] entered their flow of activity via the route of private petition. Before 1780 Great Britain had supplied French merchant and naval ships with rolled copper sheets to sheath the underside of their hulls. But in 1780, during the American War of Independence, the British government forbade the export of sheet copper to France. In December of that year a talented French industrialist, Michel-Louis Le Camus de Lamare, who had already established in France one of the first mechanical spinners, proposed to the French Department of the Navy to erect a copper foundry at Romilly near Rouen to supply the navy with all the copper articles it needed, including copper sheets to sheath its ships. By 1782 he had six reverberatory furnaces, fueled by coal, and the necessary rollers, animated by water power, reworking smelted copper (drawn mostly from Sweden) and turning out copper sheets for the French navy. At some point he found it necessary to import a colony of skilled British copper foundrymen and their families to transfer the technology involved.[181] During the war the French Royal Navy took all the firm's product. However, with the coming of peace in 1783 and the reduction of navy orders, the firm needed to enter the market of the private sector. Supported by secretary of the navy Castries,[182] Le Camus de Lamare now petitioned the controller general for (1) the prestigious title of "Royal Foundry," to be inscribed over the factory's door (a Swiss guard in royal livery would also be posted there); (2) the lucrative exemption of the factory's products from all circulation and export dues; and (3) the mediation of the intendant of the *généralité* of Upper Normandy (Rouen), Thiroux de Crosne, in the acquisition from neighboring proprietors of parcels of land necessary to changing the course of a navigable stream and constructing a highway, so that the copper articles might get to market. The response of the intendants was prompt. In their meeting of July 27, they quickly approved the title of "Royal Foundry," referred the request for exemption from dues to the Farmers General, and asked Thiroux de Crosne to report on the negotiations with respect to the parcels of land. The reaction of the Farmers General was likewise quick—but entirely negative. In their meeting of July 21 they observed that as a well-established firm Romilly was not entitled to any special fiscal favors; an exemption granted it would in all fairness have to be extended to every competitor.[183] Only the intendant Thiroux de Crosne was dilatory. Days, weeks, and months passed, and still the intendants at Paris received no word from him.[184]

The testing of allegedly new or advanced procedures in the manufacture of iron and steel meanwhile continued. An old acquaintance, the indomitable artisan-chemist manufacturer of rouge, Jean-Baptiste Delaplace, who hugged secrets for improving French iron and steel, petitioned once again for another hearing. In 1783 the four intendants of commerce relented and gave him another chance. This time Liouville, inspector general and administrator of the forges of the royal iron works of La Chaussade in Lorraine,[185] supervised the procedures of Delaplace and compared them, step by step and product by product, with those of La Chaussade. Liouville submitted a balanced report. There was something to be said for the operations of "M. de la Place." There was "a small economy of time and coal." On the other hand, there was a slight increase in labor and in difficulty of skimming off the slag and extinguishing it.[186] Not being sure of what to recommend, Liouville suggested further testing of Delaplace's products by Vandermonde at the Hôtel de Mortagne in Paris. The Bureau complied and dispatched the samples to Vandermonde. Knowing the never-say-die perseverance of Delaplace, we can expect to see him again in the Bureau's offices, pressing his case.

Another persistent petitioner was Sanche, the master of the large and celebrated foundry of Amboise.[187] Something of a braggart and always a promoter and propagandist for his products, Sanche delivered to the Bureau in the spring of 1783 a consignment of three bars of steel, which he alleged to be *acier fondu*. The intendant of commerce in charge, Colonia, sent it to the chemist Macquer for examination. Macquer's investigation and report were models of disciplined, scrupulous inquiry and a justification of the Bureau's careful procedure. He gave the steel to a Sieur Perret, a "maître coutelier" of the rue de la Tissanderie, who was a specialist in steel and author of a book on the craft of the cutler that had been approved by the Academy of Sciences. Perret submitted Sanche's steel to all the known tests—reheated the bars, made of them scissors, knives, and razors; and subjected these to the operations of the forge, the file, and the polishing wheel. It was while polishing the razors that Perret discovered that Sanche had lied: the bars were not *acier fondu* but *acier cémenté*. It was very good *acier cémenté*, Perret reported, equal to any made in France and useful in the manufacture of files and other tools not requiring an absolutely homogeneous metal. Nevertheless, Macquer observed, Sanche had not resolved the problem that had hitherto baffled French ironmasters: how to make *acier fondu*. He should direct his attention to the resolution of that frustration.[188]

A third ironmaster whose petition was passing through the Bureau during the mid-months of 1783 was Moyroud, "maître de forge" in Dauphiny. In a memoir of December 9, 1782, it may be recalled, he had announced a new process to manufacture *acier naturel* with a one-fourth saving in coal and labor time and no diminution in quality. The Bureau had asked Pajot de Marcheval, the intendant of Dauphiny (Grenoble) to investigate. He in turn had sent an engineer of mines, M. Binelly, to set up comparative tests of the customary methods and Moyroud's. In these tests Moyroud's procedures performed as predicted. But the Bureau still wasn't convinced. So on June 14, 1783 it commissioned Jars, the inspector general of mines, to verify the results. His experiments, as reported on October 31, confirmed Moyroud's claims for his method but also revealed that its execution required two furnaces instead of only one. Not satisfied with the assurances of Moyroud, Binelly, and Jars, the Bureau passed the cumulative dossier of test results to Vandermonde, custodian of the museum of arts and crafts: what do you think? There the affair rested for days, weeks, and months, as the Bureau and not too incidentally the original petitioner, Moyroud, awaited a reply.[189]

Two petitions, one minor and the other major but both illustrating the Bureau of Commerce at work, concerned the iron and steel complex at St. Etienne. In the minor one, Clément Palle, ironmaster of the parish of Chambon-en-forêt near St. Etienne, asked for his enterprise the prestigious title of *Manufacture Royale*, which was granted only to firms that were distinctive in some respect. The petition was referred to Colonia on July 23. He referred it in a routine way to Flesselles, the intendant of Lyons, for investigation and report. Flesselles replied on October 18. Palle, he explained, manufactured iron for the nail-makers in the vicinity of St. Etienne; his service to the industry, to the region, and to the kingdom was thus very useful, but it was not unique since other foundries in his canton did the same. However, his procedure was novel in that instead of making steel by placing cold bars of iron under the hammer he rolled the iron while still hot under cylinders; this process saved considerable labor time but wasted a large quantity of metal and impaired the quality of the final product. Flesselles concluded that Palle should be encouraged by a few slight favors, but his improvement, if it was an improvement, should not win for his foundry the title of *Manufacture Royale*; let him return a few years later, after cutlers and other experts had had time to appraise his steel. The Bureau of Commerce concurred, and "Néant" was written across the petition.[190]

The major petition, at least in its implications, was that of a French merchant in Turin who had contracted to supply the Piedmontese government with 24,000 gun barrels. If he purchased them in France, he would be required by royal regulation to buy them of the privileged entrepreneur-armorers of St. Etienne, who had the monopoly of manufacturing muskets for the royal army. But he wished permission to buy 4,000 of them from the nonprivileged armorers of St. Etienne. On September 18 he was supported in his request by the controller general, d'Ormesson, but his petition was denied by the Maréchal de Ségur, the minister of war: to ensure the supply of the royal army, the privileged armorers must be protected and sustained; granting the monopoly of sale of arms to foreign governments was one way of doing this.[191] Though as late as January, 1782, Colonia (the responsible intendant of commerce), the Bureau, and the controller general (then Joly de Fleury) had accepted this argument, this time they did not. In a letter probably prepared by Colonia and reviewed by the Bureau, d'Ormesson on October 28 protested to Ségur that the monopoly privilege of sale to foreign governments was disastrous ("funeste") for French commerce and industry: since the privileged armorers fobbed off on foreign governments muskets the French royal inspectors had rejected for the French army, and since they charged high monopoly prices for inferior work, foreign governments were inclined to take their business elsewhere. "All these considerations," d'Ormesson went on, "have determined me strongly to insist upon the indispensable necessity of destroying or modifying the exclusive privilege enjoyed by the royal manufacture of St. Etienne and of substituting, if necessary, indemnities of another kind." On the abolition or retention of the privilege depended, he warned, "the preservation or annihilation of a line of manufacture that it is important to maintain in the kingdom."[192] Ségur was unmoved, and the privilege stood. Once again privilege had thwarted the free flow of commercial and industrial initiatives, despite the mediation of the Bureau on behalf of individual enterprise and freedom.

In the early autumn, the Bureau of Commerce participated in decisions leading to the establishment in France of two manufactories of lead. Again it was private initiatives that set the Bureau in motion; again the Bureau mediated in a maze of privileges to open a way for individual enterprise. In one case a Sieur D'Archambault petitioned for permission to build and operate in Bordeaux a rolling mill for the manufacture of lead plate useful in the construction of buildings, ships, and pipe and to do this without being obliged to have himself accepted as a member of the guild of "marchands plombiers." Upon the endorsement of the enlightened intendant of Bordeaux, Dupré de Saint Maur, dated October 8, and the recommendation of Colonia, who was managing the case, the Bureau granted D'Archambault on November 18 the permission and the freedom he requested.[193] In a variation of the same theme of release from guild requirements, Labréaux and Charpentier, two inventors of a machine for making lead pipe without curving and soldering lead sheets, petitioned on October 23 that Labréaux be admitted as master in the guild of "marchands plombiers" of Paris without being obliged to pass through the stages of apprentice and journeyman or to submit a *chef d'oeuvre*. Again on the recommendation of Colonia, the manager of the case, the Bureau in December accorded this request. It also gave Labréaux an exclusive privilege to use the machine for ten years throughout France, a privilege that was equivalent to a patent.[194]

Also in the autumn the Bureau was facilitating the founding in Normandy of a manufactory of crystal ware after the English method. A Birmingham glass manufacturer, Mayer Oppenheimer, who had already been granted two successive patents in England but had been denied a third, had decided to transfer his operations to France. Petitioning first alone and then in partnership with a Rouen merchant, a Sieur Mercier *père*, he requested an exclusive privilege to manufacture crystal ware and ordinary glass by the English method and using only coal. In considering the petition, the intendants of commerce moved along the rails, so to speak, of long-established Bureau policy and procedure. They were inclined to deny Oppenheimer's request for privileged production of ordinary glass, for that was widespread in France, but to view favorably the idea of an exclusive privilege for the production of crystal ware, which France still imported from England—the privilege, *bien entendu*, to be only for a limited arrondissement and for a specified number of years. However, in the philosophy and practice of the Bureau all angles needed to be considered. In a routine procedure the Bureau directed Tolozan to check with the intendant of Rouen, Thiroux de Crosne. "What do you think," Tolozan wrote him on November 11, of giving Oppenheimer an exclusive privilege to manufacture crystal ware in a restricted arrondissement for a specified time period? ("Je vous prie de me marquer ce que vous en penser. Je suis avec autant d'attachement que de respect . . . .")[195]

Not only the four intendants but other scientists, administrators, and entrepreneurs were operating along the rails of well-established Bureau policy. Out in the provinces the scientist-engineer Nicolas Desmarest was personally supervising the transformation of paper factories so that they might operate after the Dutch manner. At that time Dutch manufacturers of paper, using techniques developed by French Huguenot émigrés to Holland, were producing the best paper in Europe, far superior in quality to the French product. In order to teach and persuade French manufacturers to change their ways, Desmarest was setting up four model factories: at Essone (1775–1777), the enterprise of the brothers Saurade de Richard; at Annonay (1780) the factories of Montgolfier and of Johannot, the changeover being subsidized by the Estates of Languedoc; and now, starting in 1783, at Angoulême, the factory of Henry Villarmain, who received two Dutch cylinders to triturate rags, paid for from the funds of the *généralité* of Limoges and of the Caisse d'Escompte.[196] At the last three factories and perhaps the first, Desmarest set his own terms. Dutch machines and procedures, as described in his memoirs for the Royal Academy of Sciences, were to be introduced throughout; a skillful Dutch carpenter, M. L'Ecrevisse, was to preside over the construction of the machines, the instruction of the workers, and the execution of all the Dutch manipulations; and, most interesting and from Desmarest's standpoint most important, each factory, when active, was to be open "to all the manufacturers of the province who will be free to follow the sequence of operations, to copy the machines, and to have their workers instructed in those manipulations which they need."[197]

Through the spring, summer, and early autumn of 1783 the intendants of commerce seemed to be mediating, in a society of privilege and rules, openings for individual initiatives.[198] They were seeking to release human energies and to encourage their application in freedom and in knowledge. In accord with this philosophy they were disinclined to intervene in the free play of market forces that governed production and prices. For example, in late September 1783 the close of the American War of Independence left the merchants of Marseilles with six thousand unsold bales of woolen cloth, which they had ordered from the fabricants (weavers, carders, spinners) of Carcassonne and were now unable to pay for. The fabricants of Carcassonne in turn had to discharge their workmen, who were unemployed. The *gardes jurés* of Carcassonne petitioned that woolen cloth sold abroad be exempted from the "droit d'usage." Montaran, in a letter ostensibly from d'Ormesson to Saint-Priest, the intendant of Languedoc, declined to grant even this small concession. If merchants got into trouble because of market difficulties, he wrote, it was the policy of the royal administration to let them work their way out. However, he requested Saint-Priest to investigate the human distress in Carcassonne and recommend what the government might do to relieve it.[199] In another philosophical dispatch Montaran declined to intervene directly to reduce the high price of linens in Morlaix (*généralité* of Brittany). Such prices, the result of the play of market forces, were not the concern of the government. He did suggest that the intendant, Gaspard Louis de Caze de la Bôve, should encourage the cultivation of flax.[200]

Pending more extensive reflections on the operations of the Bureau of Commerce as a whole, it might be useful briefly to summarize the effectiveness of the Bureau's direct encouragement in the five major industrial areas that have formed the themes of this section. What is most impressive is the Bureau's loyalty to its procedures of sensitive response to petitioners, of rational inquiry, and of thoughtful implementation of administrative/ industrial strategies already in place.

In the manufacture of glass the decree requiring new firms to have royal permission to start up was used by the Bureau to direct and, to a degree, to control the industry's expansion. It generally used its power to protect French forests, to protect French consumers by allowing more competition between local firms producing for a local market, and to facilitate the establishment of two innovative firms that promised to produce brilliant crystal ware rivaling that of Great Britain. In textiles the Bureau continued its disciplined search for new and better dyes. By industrial espionage it purloined two great British inventions—the Hargreaves spinning jenny and the Arkwright water frame—along with lesser techniques brought back by the spy Le Turc. In chemicals it backed promoters who promised to produce soda by chemical means. Here the Bureau probably made a mistake by not bringing together Guyton de Morveau and Hollenweger, and going all out (à la Daniel Trudaine) to found a major factory in this field. Instead they allowed Guyton de Morveau to fend for himself, and he was stymied by the implacable antagonism of the Farmers General. The net result was frustration for him and for the Bureau. Frustration, too, was the Bureau's experience in iron and steel. Despite several leads that seemed promising, the Bureau could not domesticate in France British methods of using coke to produce iron of quality equal to the British product; though gains were being made in the French production of "natural" and cementation steel, the Bureau could find no one to produce crucible steel. On the other hand, in its efforts to sustain the copper-producing firm at Romilly, staffed by a colony of British workmen, the Bureau was bringing another metal within the orbit of its action. But at the close of the period the fate of the Romilly enterprise was still in doubt. In the realm of paper a Bureau agent, Nicolas Desmarest, was successfully founding four model paper mills that used the best Dutch processes. It was hoped that backward French producers would learn from them.

We now have the data and the vicarious experience for comprehensive reflections on the Bureau's administrative operations with respect to French industry.

3
The Yield in Conclusions and Reflections

We opened this second probe into the operations of the Bureau of Commerce in regard to French industry from May 1781 to November 1783 with three questions: What were the characteristics and qualities of this segment of the French royal administration? During these twenty-nine months what of the administration continued, and why, and what changed, and why? What were the interrelations of the administrators and the French people? Now that the data have been presented, we can begin to explore possible answers.

Suppose we consider the first two questions together, and approach them from three angles, each approach yielding a gain in understanding. We might initially compare our first probe with the second. The first probe of this history presented a cross-section of the Bureau as it appeared in 1781. Time, movement, and flow were arrested, as we described the Bureau's structure, its personnel, its purpose and goals, procedures and policies; the latter for France, for each major industry, and for the *généralités*. The impression emerged of a rational, disciplined, densely complicated administrative operation, dedicated to the well-balanced economic development of France through an arsenal of means. The operation seemed to be trending toward freedom, toward the liberation of French industry from the trammels of regulation. In this second probe we have now followed this densely complicated administrative operation through twenty-nine months, by means of a narrative that symbolized the ongoing, interbraided flow of the Bureau's multiple activities. When we compare the cross-section of probe 1 with the flowing operation of probe 2, what do we see? Is there anything in the cross-section to correct? to modify? to disallow?

The answer to the question is a no and a yes. No, there are in the cross-section no major inaccuracies of fact to be corrected. The physical facilities, organizational structure, personnel, purposes, procedures, and policies of the Bureau were as described; the trend of its operation was toward freedom. Yet yes, there is something to be modified in the description. Although the facts were accurate, they yielded the misleading impression of a smooth-running, orderly operation. Why? Because in probe 1 the four intendants spoke for themselves. We allowed them to present the ideal Bureau as they conceived it, as they would have liked to have it. We presented, that is, a model of the Bureau's operations, using the word "model" in two senses—of mathematical abstraction and of moral, efficient rightness. This had one great advantage: it presented the Bureau as it *essentially* was.

But now we have placed the essential core Bureau—the four intendants of commerce and their information network of clerks, deputies of commerce, collaborating scientists, inspectors of manufactures, and intendants of *généralités*—in the midst of moving actuality and watched it operate over months and years. Here we have placed the four intendants in the midst of 28.5 million Frenchmen whose automatic obedience to royal decrees could not be depended on, in the midst of other entrenched, powerful administrative and judicial organisms (ministries of war, of the navy, of foreign affairs, of the keeper of the seals, the Farmers General, the Division of Waters and Forests, the Division of Bridges and Highways, the parlements) whose chiefs might be capable but whose diverse concerns and actions were uncoordinated by a chief minister or a zealous administrative monarch, and in the midst of a maze of multitudinous favors and privileges so numerous and varied that no one knew what they were in their total complexity. The four intendants had continually to negotiate openings for the free play of the initiatives of French industrial entrepreneurs.

Here too we have watched the working of the Bureau itself. Its own procedures of careful, rational appraisal of a project by scientists, directors of waters and forests, the Farmers General, intendants of *généralités*, deputies of commerce, and finally intendants of commerce, took weeks, months, and, if a single individual in the chain procrastinated, sometimes years. The Bureau's own regulations of quality and of workers inhibited the free exercise of entrepreneurial initiatives. The intendants and deputies of commerce might complain of the Farmers General and the internal tolls and tariffs they collected and of the maze of favors and privileges: all of these were tying down the energies of French business and preventing France from being as productive industrially as England. Yet from the narrative one gains the impression that the four intendants themselves may have been part of the problem of why French industry did not move ahead rapidly. For all their dedication and their rational encouragement of French business, their own procedures of careful appraisal and inspection were delaying.

A second overall approach might be to compare the Bureau of Commerce on May 21, 1781, with the Bureau on November 2, 1783. Resemblances would indicate continuity; differences would call our attention to movement and change.

What continued during these twenty-nine months? The answer is astonishingly simple: the Bureau continued. The same collegial structure continued: four intendants of domestic commerce, each with a batch of *généralités* and a single major industry to supervise, and a small office staff to aid him; a fifth intendant to handle foreign commerce and the liaison with the Farmers General; an advisory group of deputies of commerce; an outlying network of inspectors and subinspectors of manufactures; and the intendants in each *généralité*, who along with their many other duties served as delegates of the Bureau in the locality.

The personnel of the Bureau massively continued, with one exception. On August 5, 1782, the dean of the four intendants of domestic commerce, both in age and length of service, Jacques-Marie-Jerôme Michau de Montaran, died at the age of eighty-one. He was succeeded by his son, who had been long associated with him in the performance of his duties. Paradoxically, the change strengthened the continuity of current Bureau policy. Montaran *père* had entered the Bureau in 1744, when rigid mercantilistic regulations, more Colbertian than Colbert, were being enforced. He was a firm believer in regulations and on most issues was a standpatter until his death. Montaran *fils*, though remaining true to basic mercantilistic theorems, was willing to consider the adaptation of old measures to new conditions. His entry upon his succession meant that all four domestic intendants (Blondel, Colonia, Montaran *fils*, Tolozan) were now like-minded in their dedication to the Bureau's current policy of moderate, adaptive reform.[1]

The Bureau continued also in its long-term purpose ("to develop French agriculture, commerce, and manufactures in a sound, balanced, interrelated economy"), in its procedures for reaching informed, rational decisions with respect to proposals for government action, and in its rich repertory of measures, policies, and programs that in varying combinations could be used in particular cases. In the realm of values the intendants of commerce were dedicated to the morality of a disciplined, orderly, and "sound" administration that governed according to the laws of France, the regulations the Royal Council had decreed, and the protocols and procedures of measured administrative action. This was an administration that governed by law and rational policy and that was rarely diverted by favoritism or intrigue. Yet in applying a uniform policy (of regulation, for example) to the economic diversities of the French *généralités* and localities, the Bureau flexibly adapted local execution to local variations. It thus perpetuated the centuries-old tradition of the Capetian monarchy: through accommodation to local customs, assure central control.[2] Moreover, in dealing with individual laborers and artisans in difficulty the Bureau often showed understanding, consideration, restraint, and flexibility. In those instances there was often more "give" in the application of administrative rules than historians of the "absolutist" Bourbon monarchy usually notice. This patience with the governed was good policy; it may also have been compassion. In any case, all this represented continuity.

And yet within continuity there was movement. The continuous rational activity of the essential Bureau, day by day, week by week, yielded accomplishments, and these constituted change. Descartes's dream of a technological-industrial museum received a local habitation and a name: a depôt of machines at the Hôtel de Mortagne; its curator, the eminent mathematician-engineer Vandermonde. Industrial espionage yielded fruit. Le Turc, a government spy, sent back from England several advanced looms, chiefly in knitting technology. Jacques Martin, a private entrepreneur, returned from Britain with designs for an effective water frame. With a government subsidy he set up a factory that finally domesticated in France the Arkwright spinning complex. The manufacture of copper articles for the first time was brought within the orbit of the Bureau's activity, when the Romilly factory was accorded support. In the realm of the regulation of textiles, the four intendants at great cost of time, energy, and self-control insinuated Necker's intermediate system into French habitual practice. By that system all woolen, cotton, and linen cloth was to be inspected, and weavers who wished certification that their cloth did indeed meet quality standards could receive it; those who for one reason or another did not desire certification were freed of the necessity of conforming to requirements. They were now free to match the multiple, varied wishes of consumers in an expanded market. This flexibility was an important change, but it was also continuity. It continued the trend in the Bureau toward greater liberty.

These were all significant accomplishments in which the intendants of commerce might legitimately take pride. And yet there were certain things that did not happen, that were not achieved. The decline of the leather industry, occasioned by an oppressive system of taxation, was not arrested. The Bureau failed to break through in the synthetic manufacture of soda; its most promising lead, that of Guyton de Morveau, was blocked by the implacable antagonism of the Farmers General. Although the operation of the Bureau, day after day, week after week, was generally regular and incessant and it tried to settle matters as they came along, inefficient and maverick officials still disturbed the smooth running of the bureaucratic machine: dossiers were unaccountably lost for months, even years, in the office of the intendant Colonia; requests for scientific appraisal of inventions lay neglected on the desk of the curator of the Hôtel de Mortagne, Vandermonde; the inspector of manufactures Roland de la Platière ignored direct commands that crossed his inflexible laissez-faire principles; in his hauteur the intendant of Languedoc, Saint-Priest, considered it beneath the dignity of his office to correspond with the intendants of commerce and dealt directly with the controller general; Thiroux de Crosne, the intendant of the *généralité* of Rouen, had to be prodded to answer requests for information. The Bureau's lack of a system for following up its requests and seeing if they were acted upon aggravated the delays caused by these personal lapses.

Finally, the gap between English and French industry, a problem to which the Bureau devoted so much thought, was widening in these twenty-nine months of collegial administration, rather than lessening. The story here is complex, and the degree to which the Bureau should be held responsible for this failure to overtake England is debatable. Nevertheless, overtaking England was a goal of the four intendants, and if only for that reason we should note what was happening. In certain issues of enterprise, as in silks and plate glass, the French were ahead of England and everyone else; in other lines, as in paper, chemicals, the spinning of cotton thread (the spinning jenny and water frame), and the manufacture of iron and steel (use of coke, better iron, *acier cémenté* as well as *acier naturel*) the French were working to catch up. Yet the rate of innovation in cotton textiles, in iron and steel, and in the intertwined uses of steam power was slower in France than in England.

A few dates are revealing. In England Hargreaves's spinning jenny was in operation about 1764; Arkwright installed his water frame in the Cromford factory in 1771; Crompton invented his "mule," which combined the strength of Arkwright's thread with the fineness of Hargreaves's, in 1779. (Crompton's machine often carried 150 spindles and from one pound of cotton could draw a single fine thread seventy-one miles in length.) The corresponding dates in France were for the jenny 1771 and for the water frame 1783 (four years after an even better device was already available in England); the installation of a "mule" was in 1783 still in the future. The more the French cotton industry advanced, the farther it fell behind.

The intricate story of developments in iron and steel and in steam power is equally devastating. As early as 1709 an English ironmaster, Abraham Darby, had successfully replaced charcoal with coke in the blast furnace to manufacture pig iron. By the middle of the century his example was being increasingly followed in England. French ironmasters lagged far behind. Only in 1769, in one of the blast furnaces of the Wendel ironworks in Hayange, did Gabriel Jars make the first batch of iron to be produced with coke in France. After his death that very same year, the publication of his memoirs further disseminated his knowledge of the process, but in 1783 it was used only at the iron and steel complex of Le Creusot, and there the product was inferior. Meanwhile, in England the superior cast iron from coke-fired blast furnaces and the improved cylinders from John Wilkinson's cylinder boring machine made it possible for James Watt to construct in 1776 his first marketable steam engine, which could drive an even stronger blast of air through the blast furnaces. This basic Watts engine was known to the French intendants of commerce as early as 1778, and they were at once interested, but during the ensuing decade only a few were installed in France. And nothing prepared our four intendants for the inventions that were occurring in England in 1781 and 1782. Watt was adding significant improvements to his basic engine: in 1781, a sun-and-planet device for converting to-and-fro action into rotary movement, thus making possible the application of steam power to the new textile machinery; in 1782, a set of valves that permitted steam to be injected at both ends of the stroke. Coincidentally, in 1782 Henry Cort invented his puddling and rolling process to purify pig iron in a coal-fired reverberatory furnace and to roll it after limited hammering into wrought-iron bars. Mercifully, as the four intendants worked head-down, day by day, week by week, along the flow of their rational procedures, they were unaware of what the future held for them in the sudden improvement of Britain's competitive position in cotton textiles, iron and steel, and steam power.

The question arises, why was there continuity of the Bureau's basic operation? Also, why was there change, when change did occur? To answer these questions, suppose we informally introduce a third approach, that of systems analysis, and see what, if anything, it will yield. "A system," to adopt the general definition offered by James Grier Miller, "is a set of interacting units with relationships among them."[3] Living systems, again to follow Miller, can be arranged in a hierarchy of levels.

> *Cells* (a single cell in our body, or in any animal or plant on Earth) are at the simplest level, composed of atoms, molecules, and multimolecular organelles. At the next level is the *organ* (our heart, liver, brain), made up of cells aggregated into tissues. Then there is the level of *organism* (ourselves, our dog, a fruit fly, a tree), with organs, tissues, and organelles. At the fourth level there are *groups* (herds, flocks, forests, families, teams, committees, tribes) of organisms. Next is the *organization* (cities, hospitals, corporations, universities), comprised of groups and individual organisms. Then there is the *society* or nation, made up of organizations, groups, and individuals; and finally *supranational systems* (United Nations, European Economic Community, NATO), composed of societies and organizations.[4]

Each living system has mechanisms or subsystems for processing inputs of matter-energy and of information and then extruding outputs.

The level at which the historian dives into this hierarchy of living systems depends on the availability of the data. For the Bureau of Commerce we usually have few data on the individual organisms (Trudaine, Necker, Blondel, Colonia, Montaran *père* and *fils*, Tolozan, and their colleagues). They appear almost as impersonal units in a bureaucratic process; we cannot watch the processes within each one. We have more information on the face-to-face groups: each intendant of commerce and his staff of chief clerk, *rédacteur*, *expéditionnaire*, file clerk, and office boy; the Comité of four or five intendants; and the nonexecutive full "Bureau pour les affaires du Commerce," whose members included five *conseillers d'état* and the five intendants of commerce. We can at least watch a petition or report (input) coming in, its being given a file number, the preparation (sometimes) of an administrative summary, the intendant's directed search for additional information, the reference of the petition to several knowledgeable persons, the reception of the results of the research, and the recommendation of a course of action to the Comité (an output for the intendant and his staff, an input for the Comité), some of the discussion there, and the Comité's decision (output) and/or recommendation to the full Bureau or controller general. However, since for each group (the intendant and his staff, the Comité, and the full Bureau) we rarely have records of the face-to-face discussion but only, usually, the input (petition or report) and output (decision and some of the reasons for it), we can rarely observe the internal processes by which the decision was reached. When we rise to the level of the organization, to the total Bureau of Commerce, we have more data. The total Bureau then comprises the nonexecutive "Bureau pour les affaires du Commerce," each intendant of commerce and his staff, the Comité, the advisory deputies of commerce, the outlying network of inspectors and subinspectors of manufactures, and the intendants of the *généralités*; here we have much of the correspondence among these units.

Whether we consider a group (the four intendants in Comité) or the organization (the total Bureau), the first impression, as we have suggested, is one of massive systemic continuity during these twenty-nine months, continuity of physical facilities, organizational structure, personnel, presuppositions, principles, purposes, and cherished values, roles, role expectations, role norms and values, procedures, documents, and policies. The question arises, why continuity? Why massive continuity? The answer that first slips easily into mind is habit, both individual and group. If left undisturbed, people are apt to do the same thing in the same way, especially if they are well-paid administrators who have made it within the bureaucratic system. The key phrase here is, *if left undisturbed*. From what quarters had disturbing inputs come in the past? From innovating intendants of commerce (Gournay), directors of commerce (Trudaine), directors of finance (Necker), and controllers general (Turgot). Both from within the system (Gournay, Trudaine), or without (Necker, Turgot), these had offered inputs that provoked change. But during the twenty-nine months of collegial administration (1781–1783), there were no creatively innovating intendants of commerce or controllers general. Only occasionally during these months did a vigorous intendant of a *généralité* (Saint-Priest) or a recalcitrant inspector of manufactures (Roland de la Platière) stir the Bureau into action, and then only on a matter of detail. Disturbances (inputs) had also come in the past from outside: incoming petitions from manufacturers who had an idea for a factory, incoming news of massive disobedience of regulations, and incoming news of a technological breakthrough in England. Such disturbances all occurred during the collegial months. Why did they not lead to profound change within Bureau operations? Because the Bureau had developed procedures that enabled the four intendants to handle such inputs, whether routine in nature or of crisis proportions in their threat to the ongoing equilibrium of the bureaucratic procedures and to the psychological balance of the bureaucrats themselves.

An administration reveals itself in the day-by-day conduct of business and also in the handling of crisis. Petitions for aid to establish a factory were routine. The intendants handled them through a rational, information-gathering, information-appraising, cause-and-effect analysis that impersonally balanced costs against benefits and applied policies for each industry that had been tested for years against industrial reality. The operation of the collegial Bureau in this analysis was regular, incessant, and intelligent, its only systemic shortcoming being the failure to follow up a grant and discover whether the prospected quality and benefits did indeed materialize. This lack of an automatic, systematic follow-up procedure tended to cushion the intendants from knowledge of their failures, and hence led them to have a more favorable opinion of their own work than was justified by reality. With self-satisfied intendants of commerce in control, continuity of operational procedures was apt to prevail.

The massive mutiny by many artisans against the enforcement of Necker's intermediate system of regulations was a crisis of legitimacy, not simply for the four intendants but for the administrative monarchy of the Old Regime as well. For centuries, ever since Hugh Capet, the chief problem of French kings had been to get themselves obeyed. They had resolved the problem by negotiating bargains with the upper classes, the towns, and the provinces, by elaborating the machinery of a centralized administration, by building instruments of forcible coercion (the royal army, constabulary, and judiciary), and by creating a mystique of royalty. Yet their hold on the French people was always tenuous; an example of sustained disobedience might prove contagious; the massive mutiny of craftsmen in some areas threatened the security of all royal authority. Yet throughout this crisis of disobedience the four intendants kept their cool; they repeatedly sought information (feedback) from their inspectors of manufactures about how the new regulations were faring in the outlying provinces; while maintaining the principles of Necker's reform, they adjusted the details of its enforcement to the circumstances of a locality; coolly, calmly, soothingly they explained, elucidated, cajoled, and only in the last resort called upon the coercive power of the Farmers General, the royal constabulary, and the judiciary. The modern terms—"output" (the regulations), continuous "feedback input," continuous adjustments to continuous feedback—give the method of their operation. Their own favorite word, *concilier* (to conciliate, negotiate, adjust), gives its spirit. Thus peaceably, persuasively the intendants together and without the leadership of any dominant personality moved French industrial policy from rigid mercantilism toward greater freedom. Their success was a triumph of quiet reasonableness. It was also a justification of the total Bureau: its physical facilities, its organizational structure, its network of information-gathering, information-processing agents, and its rational decision making through group discussion. With success came satisfaction, and a continuance of methods already in use.

A second phenomenon of crisis proportions was still brewing: the technological breakthrough occurring in England in cotton spinning, the manufacture of iron and steel, and steam power. Here the information-gathering procedures of the total Bureau worked only imperfectly. Industrial espionage and *émigré* English workmen had informed the intendants of the use of coke, the methods of *acier cémenté*, the flying shuttle, Hargreaves's spinning jenny, Arkwright's water frame, and Watt's basic steam engine, and these had been transferred to France. But word had not yet reached them of the latest devices: the perfected steam engine, Cort's puddling and rolling process, Crompton's magical "mule." So the four intendants could believe they were doing all right. With the Bureau's encouragement French industry, they thought, was ahead in silks and plate glass; it was catching up in paper, chemicals, copper, glassware, and cotton textiles (Hargreaves's jenny, Arkwright's water frame), use of coke, and *acier cémenté*; soon it would reach English perfection in *acier fondu* and break through in the synthetic manufacture of soda. Since the Bureau's procedures had not discovered the latest British triumphs, the complacent intendants were undisturbed by British developments, their psychological balance was not upset, change in the bureaucratic system was not provoked, and massive continuity prevailed throughout the Bureau.

And yet despite the dramatic irony of the widening divergence between what was happening in Great Britain and what the Bureau thought was happening, we must recognize that this lapse was a defect in execution and not in structure and principle. In principle and in practice the collegial Bureau was open to innovation and responded positively and creatively to news of changes in the outside world. Indeed it continued as a viable operation only because it was so open and responsive to outside changes. Changes in three areas, it seems, chiefly moved the intendants into action: changes in technology, as these were mediated to the Bureau by petitioners, roving and sedentary inspectors of manufactures, foreign workmen, and industrial spies; changes in science, as mediated by the Bureau's consultant scientists and the younger inspectors of manufactures; and, most fundamentally, improvements in transportation, which enlarged and varied the market for French goods and led some French manufacturers to demand greater freedom from regulation. To this demand the four intendants had responded by loyally implementing Necker's intermediate system, a major advance into a more liberal regime and a considerable alteration of the laws the Bureau was administering. Change usually did not occur when a proposal from the Bureau was blocked by the implacable opposition of some outside agency, such as the Farmers General (as with Guyton de Morveau's soda manufactory) or the Ministry of War, which had other concerns than the promotion of industry.

Though during these twenty-nine months the collegial Bureau had itself innovated no new major strategies (that seemed to have been the function of a dominating personality), it had sturdily, intelligently operated and maintained and thus continued the institutional achievements of the past, in a spirit of rational inquiry, openness to innovation, and willingness to secure ever freer opportunities for private economic initiatives.

From our data we have thus offered answers to two of the questions with which we opened this inquiry: What were the characteristics and qualities of this segment of the French royal administration? During these twenty-nine months, what of the administration continued, and why, and what changed, and why? There remains the third question: What were the interrelations of the administrators and the French people?

Here our knowledge is more complete on how the administrators related to the administered than vice versa, and our reflections on the relationship between the two groups must lie in the realm of surmise. From my reading of the manuscript evidence it seems to me that by now the intendants of commerce thought of themselves as professional civil servants who *managed* from above the king's subjects for the long-term prosperity of the kingdom and of the royal revenue. In the encouragement of private initiatives and in the formulation of new regulations they prudently researched the situation and conferred with those involved. They expected obedience to decrees of general import. Yet they were often understanding of local and individual complaints, and adapted policies to local situations. Nevertheless, their position was nearly always that of a manager who impersonally operated at a certain distance to secure enforcement of royal procedures and policies.

The response of the king's subjects varied. Consultant scientists, who understood the processes and promise of rational analysis of evidence, loyally cooperated with the intendants of commerce. Enterprising private entrepreneurs schemed how to utilize the royal administration to promote their own pecuniary ambitions. Some craftsmen, as at Sedan and Valenciennes, welcomed the regulations that protected and furthered their interests. Craftsmen elsewhere, as at Lyons, Nîmes, and Laval, regarding the regulations as onerous, wasteful of time and money, and even obstructive to profitable endeavor, protested, evaded, outwitted, and openly disobeyed direct commands. The royal administration, however well-intentioned, might then be considered an adversary and even an enemy. Between the managers at the center of legal authority and power and the subordinate subjects the relationshihp was not necessarily one of automatic obedience to royal command. Rather there was often a gray zone of stalling and negotiation, with always the lurking possibility of successful defiance of any royal order. However, more research on the local level, especially at Lyons, Nîmes, and Laval, is needed here.

Appendix:
A Partial List of Outgoing Dispatches on the Subject of the New Regulations Sent out by the Four Intendants of Commerce during the Early Months of 1782

Circular from Joly de Fleury to all the intendants of all the généralités, January 9. What do the principal fabricants of woolens in your *généralité* think of a proposed special decree instituting a new array of penalties against theft, by workmen within the shop, of the waste fag-ends from the manufacturing process? (F12* 156)

Montaran to Caryu, inspector of manufactures at Bayonne, January 16. The fabricants of woolens in the provinces of Béarn and Bigorre may follow their ancient custom of presenting their cloth to the *gardes jurés* after fulling and then selling it before finishing. However, do not publicize this adaptation to local usage lest the modification be requested by craftsmen in other localities. (F12* 130)

Montaran to Charles François Hyacinthe Esmangart, intendant of the généralité of Caen, January 17. Brown, the inspector of manufactures at Caen, reports that the fabricants of fustian in a canton within his jurisdiction are so exercised by the rigorous judgment of the Caen *bureau de visite* that condemned their cloth, already stamped as *réglée* but found to be one inch too narrow, to be cut up and the pieces returned to the fabricants—a decision well within the prescription of the new regulations—that they threaten to take their cloth to be inspected elsewhere. Brown suggests that a new *bureau de visite* be established in the canton's chief village. What do you think of his suggestion? (F12* 130)

To Brunet, inspector of manufactures at Alençon, January 27, in reply to two questions. (1) How many seals does a piece of cloth (*réglée*) acquire? Apparently three: one, provisional, as it is taken from the loom; a second after fulling; and a third after finishing (*apprêt*). (2) How many *bureaux de visite* should there be in the neighborhood of Lisieux? The wholesale merchants of Lisieux wish only the one, in that town, so that they can control the output of the rural fabricants of the neighboring seventy to eighty parishes; the fabricants of the distant parishes complain of the loss of time that the long trips to Lisieux entail. The Bureau of Commerce sides with the fabricants and recommends the establishment of two additional bureaus; then these fabricants will have no pretext for evading inspection and fixation of the first, provisional seal. (F12* 156)

To Monseigneur the duc de Bouillon, January 29. No, we are very sorry but the firm of Sieur Ribouleau and Company of Evreux may not stamp your coat of arms on one side of the seal attached to its pieces of cloth. To permit the firm to do that would encourage other firms to imprint their particular stamp and thus restore the confusion that the new regulations were designed to remove by requiring of each type of manufacture a uniform seal.

Joly de Fleury to Claude de Chazerat, intendant of the généralité of Auvergne, January 29. With respect to the fabricants of the different *bureaux de visite* of your *généralité* who have refused to assemble in order to name the *gardes jurés* from among their number, it must be recalled that exercise of the functions of *garde juré* is a public obligation from which no fabricant may exempt himself. Hence, following the example of your predecessors in similar circumstances, issue an ordinance that shall compel them to fulfill their duties. Jubié, the inspector of manufactures of your *généralité*, recommends that since during the winter, snow closes the roads to the *bureau de visite* at Apchou(?), it be transferred to another, more approachable town. What is your opinion? (F12* 130)

To Thiroux de Crosne, intendant of the généralité of Rouen, January 30. Fees from the "droit de marque des étoffes" collected by the *gardes jurés* and *préposés* of the *généralité* of Rouen and not expended in maintaining the local *bureaux de visite* should be deposited with Sieur Le Carpentier, receiver of the "droit de marque à la halle de Rouen," to be credited to the account of the Caisse du Commerce. (F12* 156)

Montaran to Sieur de la Geniere, inspector of manufactures at Castres. In response to a query, outlines the fiscal and accounting procedures prescribed by the new regulations for the deposit by the *gardes jurés* and *préposés* of collected fees and fines in the Caisse du Commerce. (F12* 130)

Montaran to Paul Esprit Marie de la Bourdonnaye de Blossac, intendant of Poitou (Poitiers), February 1. The nine-article decree issued by the intendant for the establishment of a *bureau de visite* at Fontenai le Comte is to be corrected article by article for conformity to the new regulations. For example, articles 1–3 violate the provision that a *bureau* staffed by *gardes jurés* must not have a *préposé*; domiciliary visits of inspection by *gardes jurés* are to be undertaken only with certain safeguards; fabricants who find it more convenient to take their cloth to another *bureau* than that of Fontenai le Comte may do so. (F12* 130)

Montaran to François Pierre Du Clozel de la Chabrerie, intendant of the généralité of Tours, February 3. De Tournay, inspector of manufactures of Tours, reports that within his district the *gardes jurés* elected by the fabricants from among themselves do not know how to conduct a *bureau de visite*, do not keep accounts, do not maintain the register of transactions, do not draft the *procès-verbaux*, and in nineteen instances out of twenty do not know how to write. Hence, except at Maur, he has used paid *préposés* at all his *bureaux* and he recommends that the same policy be followed at Maur. What do you think? (F12* 130)

Montaran to Marie Pierre Charles Meulan d'Ablois, intendant of the généralité of Montauban, February 3. The inspector of manufactures at Montauban reports that you have deferred the establishment of *bureaux de visite* within your *généralité*, pending the clarification of administrative policy. Permit me to observe that such *bureaux* have already been established in most of the *généralités* of the kingdom; accelerate their establishment in yours; if a few fabricants object, we shall confer about appropriate measures of enforcement. (F12* 130)

Montaran to Brisson, inspector of manufactures at Lyons, February 3. With respect to bleachers of cloth who are disregarding the new regulations, try first "the voice of persuasion" to bring them into line before menacing them with a new law inflicting penalties proportionate to their crime. With regard to the crime of false or forged marks, confer with the intendant of the *généralité* concerning the severity to be applied. (F12* 130)

Montaran to François Marie Bruno d'Agay de Mutigney, intendant of the généralité of Picardy (Amiens), February 4. Your proposals for the establishment of *bureaux de visite* at St. Quentin, Amiens, and Abbeville are subject to several observations and corrections. The persons elected *gardes jurés* of St. Quentin are neither merchants nor fabricants as the new regulations prescribe; if necessary appoint a *préposé*. It is astonishing that a commercial-industrial town the size of Amiens cannot provide *gardes jurés*; insist by a vis-à-vis confrontation that the fabricants elect these officers at once. (If they persist in disobedience, "you may go so far as to make them fear on the part of the Royal Council proofs of its discontent.") If they still stubbornly refuse, appoint a paid *préposé*. Abbeville does not need the proposed subinspector of manufactures to conduct its *bureau de visite*. If the inspector of manufactures at Amiens, Roland de la Platière, who has talent and intelligence, did his duty in routine inspections of fabricants, the subinspectorship would be unnecessary. Appoint a simple *préposé* instead. (F12* 130)

Montaran to a M. de Villeraux, February 5. Firms designated *Manufactures Royales* do not have to pass their products through a *bureau de visite*. They may, as before, attach their own seal, subject always to visits of the local inspector of manufactures. (F12* 130)

Joly de Fleury to Thiroux de Crosne, intendant of the généralité of Rouen, February 5. Establish, as you suggest, a M. Richard as a "commis de marque" at Bolbec with an annual salary of 600 livres, even though the normal procedure would be to have him nominated by the *gardes jurés*. (F12* 130)

To Brown, inspector of manufactures for the généralité of Caen, February 10, in response to questions raised by the fabricants of woolens of the town of Vire. If cloth is to merit the stamp of *réglée* it must have the number of threads in the warp prescribed by the table for that *généralité*. However, if it has fewer threads it still may be registered and marketed under the *libre* category. Waste wool from manufacturing operations may be used in weaving new cloth to be sold in the *libre* classification. Blue thread may not replace red in the border of the cloth. This time the fullers who rebelled will be forgiven "de grâce," but on the next occasion they will be punished. Every fabricant is eligible to vote for the *gardes jurés*, but to be rated a fabricant he must possess a loom; hence simple weavers, fullers, and shearers without looms are excluded from the electoral assembly. (F12* 156)

To Messieurs Les Maîtres Gardes Drapiers de Darnetal, February 12. The borders of *espagnolettes lisses* may retain the colors prescribed by old regulations since these were unchanged in the new, but the borders of twilled material and ratteens must change to the new since that is the way they will be distinguished in commerce. The letter *R* may be embroidered on the cloth if the other required marks are likewise embroidered. A narrow band of cloth may be woven to lengths of 80 to 90 ells instead of 50 to 55, provided each segment into which it is cut is indicated by a transverse bar of another color and by the letter *R*. The borders of cloth of the *libre* category must conform to the regulations and not to the wishes of the consumer; do not worry, he will buy the cloth if its quality and price are right. (F12* 156)

Montaran to Tribert, inspector for linens and batistes at St. Quentin, February 16. The merchants and fabricants of St. Quentin allege that performance of the functions of *garde juré* is incompatible with the effective prosecution of their business, and they name two *préposés* to conduct the *bureau de visite* at a joint annual salary of 750 livres. This action is contrary to sound administration and the new regulations. Only the Royal Council can appoint a *préposé*; only one is needed for a *bureau de visite*; and his salary should not exceed 600 livres. You should see to it that these principles are observed during the coming year. (F12* 130)

Montaran to Cornuau, inspector of manufactures at Limoges, February 20. My compliments on the fine work you are doing to establish the new regime within your inspectorate. Would you now send the *procès-verbal* of the assembly of the fabricants of Limoges, gathered to elect the *gardes jurés* from among their number? (F12* 130)

To Le Marchant, subinspector of manufactures at St. Simphorien de Lay, February 24. Do not invent a special mark for the fabricants of your district; conform to the one the new regulations prescribe. (F12* 156)

Montaran to all the inspectors of manufactures within his department, February 26. Since the current mark applied to woolen cloth before finishing stains and spoils the products, the intendant sends his inspectors the recipe for the mixing of a new liquid that will mark the cloth without spoiling it. (F12* 130)

Montaran to Libour, subinspector of manufactures at Laval, February 26. Investigate and report on two separate cases of Laval fabricants who protest that their cloth, which the *bureau de visite* of Laval has seized for violation of the new regulations, actually conforms to the new rules. (F12* 130)

Joly de Fleury to all intendants of the généralités, February 27. To simplify and safeguard the fiscal administration of all the *généralités*, a single collector is being set up in Paris to receive for the Caisse du Commerce the fees and fines collected by the *gardes jurés* and *préposés* at their *bureaux de visite*. (F12* 130)

To Brown, inspector of manufactures for the généralité of Caen, March 1, in reply to several queries. (1) Who pays for the one-sol "droit de marque" and the seal? The fabricant pays the one-sol duty, but the *bureau de visite* furnishes the lead seal. (2) In view of their daily work at the *bureau*, are the elected *gardes jurés* exempt from payment of the one-sol duty? No, they must pay like everyone else. (3) How shall stockings be marked? With oil, black smoke, or ink? After comparative tests the chemist Macquer of the Academy of Sciences recommends ink. (4) How shall Sieur Boullay, fabricant of Caen, be prevented from passing off, as his own, stockings knitted in the villages of Picardy, especially since we still await the new regulations for marking *bonneterie*? In accord with the decree of October 25, 1781 let the Picardy weavers affix to every dozen stockings a small provisional seal bearing the name of the fabricant and of his village; let M. Boullay remove this seal, substitute the usual mark made in ink, and after "finishing" the stockings affix a seal with "bonneterie" on one side and "Picardy" on the other. These measures will check smuggling and fraud. (F12 156)

Blondel and Montaran to Roland de la Platière, inspector of manufactures at Amiens, March 1. Exasperated beyond endurance by Roland's casual attitude toward the implementation of the new regulations, the two intendants write jointly to dress him down in a long (ten-page) dispatch for placing *bureaux de visite* in villages where they do not belong, for failing to place them in villages where they do belong, for placing two bureaus in Abbeville when one would do, for failure to inspect fabricants in their shops, for failure to seek the support of police officers, judges of manufactures, and the intendant of the *généralité* in correcting disobedient fabricants, and for submitting disorganized, wandering, uninformative reports that reflect the "anarchy" that reigns in his inspectorate with respect to the enforcement of the new regulations. (F12* 130)

Montaran to Agay de Mutigney, intendant of the généralité of Amiens, March 6. In completion of the St. Quentin case (see above, February 16), the intendant is ordered to choose an intelligent *préposé* for the *bureau de visite* of St. Quentin and arrange to pay him approximately 600 livres. His commission will be forwarded from Paris, all in accord with the principle of a sound administration. (F12* 130)

Montaran or Joly de Fleury to Goy, inspector of manufactures at Rouen (March 6), to Pajot de Marcheval and Du Clozel, intendants respectively of the généralités of Dauphiny (March 28) and of Tours (March 31), and to Goy again (March 28). Reviews of cases involving violations of the new regulations. If the breach is a first offense and apparently committed inadvertently by some poor, obscure artisan, treat leniently and "de grâce" remit the fine while continuing to enforce the regulation. If the violation is repetitive and deliberate, crack down on the violator and make a "severe example" lest his disobedience prove contagious and dangerous. (F12* 130)

Joly de Fleury to Louis Bénigne François Bertier de Sauvigny and Claude de Chazerat, intendants respectively of Paris (March 6) and of Auvergne (March 27), and Montaran to Thiroux de Crosne of Rouen (March 6) and

Esmangart of Caen (March 12). Detailed discussions of where *bureaux de visite* are to be located within each *généralité* in the light of established criteria for their siting (near either a center of production or a center of sale, but in either instance to be convenient to the manufacturing craftsmen). (F12* 130)

To Brunet, inspector of manufactures at Alençon, March 14. Severely rebukes the inspector of manufactures for siding with the wholesale merchants of gowns (*frocs*) of Lisieux in their disputes with the fabricants (craftsmen) within and without the town. In general the Bureau of Commerce is disposed to side with fabricants rather than with merchants because the latter are less likely to need protection. Iterates the order of January 27 (see above) to establish two new *bureaux de visite* for the convenience of the rural fabricants. If *gardes jurés* are unavailable, hire *préposés* at an annual salary of 250 livres. If necessary to keep the peace, divide the *bureau de visite* at Lisieux into bureaus, one served by the *gardes jurés* of the fabricants for cloth manufactured within the town and the other by the *gardes jurés* of the merchants for cloth manufactured without. Cloth in the *réglée* category shall pay one sol for the provisional seal upon being taken from the loom and two sols for the definitive seal after fulling; cloth in the *libre* category may in some instances omit the first provisional seal. (F12* 156)

To Brunet again, March 19. Vigorously rebukes the inspector, who forgot that manufacturers do not have to fabricate cloth according to the standards set down for the *réglée* category. They are free do present deviant goods in the *libre* classification. Since most fabricants at Nogent-le-Rotrou will probably do just that, a *préposé* is not necessary. (F12* 156)

To Thiroux de Crosne, intendant of Rouen, March 21. Since a day laborer ("homme de peine") is needed to move the machine marking the cloth, pay him 100 livres a year from the proceeds of the "droit de marque." (F12* 156)

And so, in this way the dispatches concerning the implementation of the new regulations continued to go out during the winter, spring, and early summer of 1782, before tapering off in August and September.

Notes

Chapter 1. The Administrative Context

1. J. F. Bosher, *French Finances 1770–1795: From Business to Bureaucracy*, p. 48.

2. For the names and ostensible schedules see *Almanach royal* (1781); for a realistic correction see Michel Antoine, *Le Conseil du Roi sous le règne de Louis XV*, pp. 135, 138–139, 303, 328, and J. F. Bosher, *French Finances 1770–1795: From Business to Bureaucracy*, pp. 35, 40.

3. Anne Buot de L'Epine, "Les bureaux de la guerre à la fin de l'Ancien Régime"; Jean-Claude Devos, "Le Secrétariat d'Etat à la Guerre et ses bureaux"; Prince de Montbarey, *Mémoires autographes de M. le Prince de Montbarey*, I; for a description of the bureaus in the Department of Foreign Affairs see Jean Baillou, *Les affaires étrangères et le corps diplomatique français*, vol. I: *De l'Ancien Régime au Second Empire*, pp. 92–140, Camille-Vincent Piccioni, *Les premiers commis des affaires étrangères au XVIIe et au XVIIIe siècles*, and M. J.-P. Samoyault, *Les bureaux du Secrétariat de l'Etat aux Affaires Etrangères sous Louis XV*; on the character of the *premier commis* see J. F. Bosher, "The *premiers commis des finances* in the Reign of Louis XVI," Roland Mousnier, "La fonction publique en France au début du seizième siècle à la fin du dix-huitième siècle."

4. For a description of the Controller General's Department see Bosher, *French Finances*, pp. 47–66.

5. Georges Pagès, *La monarchie d'Ancien Régime en France*, p. 161. For the intendants of the *généralité*, their *premiers commis*, and their subdelegates during the reign of Louis XVI see, for example, A. Antoine, *Les subdélégués de l'intendance, spécialement en Franche-Comté, dans la seconde moitié du XVIIIe siècle*; Michel Antoine, "La notion de subdélégation dans la monarchie d'Ancien Régime"; Pavel Nikolaevich Ardashev, *Les intendants de province sous Louis XVI*; Maurice Bordes, *L'administration provinciale et municipale en France au XVIIIe siècle*, pp. 116–159; idem, "Un intendant éclairé de la fin de l'Ancien Régime: Claude François Bertrand de Boucheporn"; idem, "Les intendants éclairés à la fin de l'Ancien Régime"; Charles Dartigue-Peyrou, *Dupré de Saint-Maur et le problème de corvées: le conflit entre l'intendant de Guyenne et le parlement de Bordeaux, 1776–1785*; F. Dumas, *La généralité de Tours au XVIIIe siècle: administration de l'intendant Du Cluzel (1766–1783)*; François-Xavier Emmanuelli, *Pouvoir royal et vie régionale en Provence au déclin de la monarchie: psychologie, pratiques administratives, defrancisation de l'intendance d'Aix 1745–1790*, II, 645–861; E. Esmonin, "Les intendants du Dauphiné des origines à la Révolution"; Henri Fréville, *L'intendance de Bretagne (1689–1790)*, III, 325–327, 335–337; idem, "Notes sur les subdélégués généraux et subdélégués de Bretagne au XVIIIe siècle"; Vivian R. Gruder, *The Royal Provincial Intendants: A Governing Elite in Eighteenth-Century France*; L. Guérin, *L'intendant de Cypierre et la vie économique de l'Orléanais 1760–1785*; Marie-Claire Guyonnet, *Jacques de Flesselles, intendant de Lyon (1768–1784)*; M. Lhéritier, "Histoire des rapports de la Chambre de Commerce de Bordeaux avec les intendants, le parlement et les jurats de 1705 à 1791," 6 (1913), pp. 63, 144; Louis Legrand, *Sénac de Meilhan et l'intendance du Hainaut et du Cambrésis sous Louis XVI*, pp. 128–129, 146–148; Georges Livet, *Les intendants d'Alsace et leur oeuvre, 1648–1789*; Roger de Lurion, *M. de Lacoré, intendant de Franche-Comté (1761–1784)*; M. Palanque, "Le dernier intendant de la généralité d'Auch:

Claude-François Bertrand de Boucheporn (1741–1794)"; M. Piquard, "Charles André de Lacoré, intendant de Franche-Comté 1761–1784"; J. Planel-Arnoux, "Premières recherches sur l'administration d'Esmangart, intendant de la généralité de Caen 1775–1783"; J. A. de Rotours, "Le dernier intendant de la généralité d'Alençon."

6. *Almanach royal* (1781); Michel Antoine, *Le gouvernement et l'administration sous Louis XV*, pp. 3, 32, 64, 74, 102.

7. "Compte rendu par M. Tolozan des différents objets qui concernent son département, envoyé à M. de Villedeuil, Contrôleur Général des Finances, le 13 mai 1787," F12 657. These perquisites and functions may have given Tolozan a slight preeminence among the four intendants. However, from the archival evidence it seems to me that Necker as director of finances was his own central economic-industrial strategist. Under his two noninnovating successors from 1781 to 1783, the controllers general Joly de Fleury and d'Ormesson, when the collegial Bureau seemed to run itself, Tolozan shared his eminent influence with the two Montarans, *père et fils*, who were his seniors in the Bureau. Only with the controller general Calonne (1783–1787) does Tolozan attain a dominant position in an essentially collegial-bureaucratic operation. This is also the opinion of Claude Perroud, editor of the *Lettres de Madame Roland*. For a differing view that gives Tolozan a dominant position from 1777 see Charles Coulston Gillispie, *Science and Polity in France at the End of the Old Regime*, pp. 388–390.

8. *Almanach royal* (1781); Antoine, *Le gouvernement et l'administration sous Louis XV*, pp. 73, 185–186, 238; Léon Biollay, *Etudes économiques sur le XVIIIe siècle: le pacte de famine; l'administration du commerce*, pp. 468–469; Ministère de l'Instruction Publique et des Beaux-Arts, *Conseil de Commerce et Bureau du Commerce, 1700–1791: inventaire analytique des procès-verbaux*, ed. Bonnassieux and Lelong, pp. xix–xx, lxi; Marie Jeanne Phlipon Roland de la Platière, *Lettres de Madame Roland, 1780–1793*, II, 617–624.

9. The pay of an intendant of commerce in any given year is difficult to estimate, because several received supplements on an individual basis. In 1781 an intendant's regular salary was 6,000 livres; he also received 3,000 for his office expenses. A chief clerk was paid approximately 2,400 livres, a *rédacteur* 1,700 to 2,000, a copyist and a keeper of the register and files 1,400, the office boy 720. In 1781 Bruyard, former chief clerk of the two Trudaines, was receiving a pension of 4,200 livres; three other clerks retired with an annual pension of 2,000 livres (Biollay, *Etudes économiques*, pp. 468–471, 480).

10. "My good friend, all of these people are not such devils" (Madame Roland to Roland, Paris, April 20, 1784, *Lettres de Madame Roland, 1780–1793*, I, 353.

11. In Paris the "Six Corps Marchands" nominated six candidates; from that list the crown chose one; in other towns the chambers of commerce each nominated three persons. In 1781 the "Députés des Villes et des Colonies pour le Commerce" were by order of appointment Marion (Paris, 1746), Lhéritier de Brutelle (San Domingo and the Windward Isles, 1761), Du Bergier (Bordeaux, 1763), Jolly de Pontadeuc (Saint-Malo, 1766), Drouet (Nantes, 1771), Rostagny (Marseilles, 1772), Montferrier (Languedoc, 1776), Deschamps (Rouen, 1777), Tournachon (Lyons, 1779), De Tortenne (La Rochelle, 1781), Hardy de Merville (Flanders, Hainaut, and Cambrésis, 1781), Boyetet (Bayonne, 1781), two Farmers General (Guadeloupe). On the deputies see Léon Biollay, *Etudes économiques*, pp. 381–428; J. F. Bosher, "French Administration and Public Finance in Their European Setting," p. 575; Jean-Auguste Brutails, "Etudes sur la Chambre du Commerce de Guienne," pp. 285–287, 332–333; John G. Clark, *La Rochelle and the Atlantic Economy during the Eighteenth Century*, pp. 11–13; Joseph Fournier, *La Chambre de Commerce de Marseille et ses représentants à Paris, 1599–1875*; V. Labracque-Bordenave, "Histoire des députés de Bordeaux au conseil de commerce, au comité national, est à l'agence commerciale à Paris, 1700–1793"; M. Lhéritier, "Histoire des rapports de la Chambre de Commerce de Bordeaux avec les intendants, le parlement et les jurats de 1705 à 1791," 6 (1913), p. 57; Ernest Pariset, "La Chambre de Commerce de Lyon au dix-huitième siècle: étude faite sur

les registres de ses délibérations," pp. 4, 14–15, 91, 96–97, 149–150, 157–158; Maurice Quénet, "Un exemple de consultation dans l'administration monarchique au XVIIIe siècle: les Nantais et leurs députés au Conseil de Commerce"; Thomas J. Schaeper, *The French Council of Commerce 1700–1715: A Study of Mercantilism after Colbert*, pp. 6, 21–22, 25, 73–74, 81, 258.

12. The edict of August 13, 1669, establishing the inspectors of manufactures and describing the machinery of enforcement, is found in Charles W. Cole, *Colbert and a Century of French Mercantilism*, II, 418–426. See also Franc Bacquié, *Un siècle d'histoire de l'industrie: les inspecteurs des manufactures sous l'Ancien Régime, 1669–1791*, pp. 6–7, 20, 24; Biollay, *Etudes économiques*, pp. 425–447; J. Hayem, "Les inspecteurs des manufactures et le mémoire de l'inspecteur Tribert sur la généralité d'Orléans," pp. 284; Thomas J. Schaeper, *The French Council of Commerce*, pp. 155, 164.

13. This is a hypothetical model, followed only if the Bureau of Commerce found it necessary to give the petition a full treatment. Sometimes the procedure was abridged.

14. Herbert A. Simon, Donald W. Smithburg, and Victor A. Thompson, *Public Administration*, pp. 252–253.

Chapter 2. The Story

1. Technically Joly de Fleury, while performing the functions of controller general, was "administrateur général de finances" from May 21, 1781 to March 6, 1783; he was appointed "ministre d'Etat" on June 4, 1781. See Michel Antoine, *Le gouvernement et l'administration sous Louis XV: dictionnaire biographique*, p. 122.

2. Joly de Fleury to Brunet, November 27, 1781, F12* 156.

3. D'Ormesson to the intendant of Brittany, October 8, 1783.

4. By the spring of 1782 the Bureau of Commerce still had to issue a clean-up decree (April 18) ordering the *généralités* that had not instituted their *bureaux de visite* to do so at once. Roland de la Platière, *Encyclopédie méthodique*, II, xxx–xxxi.

5. The decree is printed in Roland de la Platière, *Encyclopédie méthodique*, II, xxix–xxx.

6. Joly de Fleury to Thiroux de Crosne, June 19, 1781, F12* 156.

7. "Mémoire des Marchands Fabriquands et Faisant Fabriquer les étoffes de soye de Nismes," July 6, 1781, in chemise, "1779; Mémoire des fabriquants en soye de Nismes . . . ," F12 1438. On the situation in Nîmes see Parker, *The Bureau of Commerce in 1781*, pp. 24–25, 32, and Léon Dutil, "L'industrie de la soie à Nîmes jusqu'en 1789," pp. 328–331, 335.

8. Joly de Fleury to Perrin de Cipierre, September 25, 1781, F12* 156.

9. Joly de Fleury to Thiroux de Crosne, October 10, 1781, ibid.

10. To Brunet, November 27, 1781, ibid.

11. Joly de Fleury to Thiroux de Crosne, November 28, 1781, ibid.

12. To Brown, November 29 and also December 30, 1781, ibid.

13. To Lepage, November 30, 1781, ibid.

14. To Boisroger, December 6 and December 7, 1781, ibid.

15. To Messieurs les Gardes Jurés de la fabrique d'Elbeuf, December 19, 1781, ibid. Elbeuf appears again on January 3, 1783 in a letter to Lazowsky. The *gardes jurés* of Elbeuf had asked that cloth manufactured at Orcival and inspected at Elbeuf be stamped Orcival rather than Elbeuf. The four intendants said no, since each piece of cloth already carried the name of the originating fabrique, and to stamp every piece of cloth with the names of multitudinous originating towns would cause endless confusion.

16. Two letters of Joly de Fleury, dated January 1, 1782, to the bishop of Uzès and to the comte de Périgord, ibid.

17. For the story of the gradual installation of the machinery of enforcement in a single *généralité*, that of Provence, see Emmanuelli, *Pouvoir royal et vie régionale en Provence au déclin de la monarchie*, II, 81 and n. 89. Perhaps a sense of the continuing flow of the correspondence of the four Paris intendants of commerce on the new regulations can be communicated simply by a list of their outgoing dispatches on the subject during the early months of 1782: see the Appendix.

18. "Procès Verbal de Tournée du Sieur Vaugelade pour l'année 1782 dans la Généralité de Poitiers," Poitiers, January 14, 1782, F12 650.

19. "Mémoire [from Goy] sur les Bureaux de Toilerie établis dans la Ville et Généralité de Rouen, et sur le Commerce de ses Fabriques en conséquence de la tournée générale que l'Inspecteur des Manufactures vient d'y faire," 1782, ibid.

20. Montaran to Vaugelade, April 26, 1782, F12* 130.

21. On Crommelin see the excellent account in Philippe Guignet, *Mines, manufactures et ouvriers du Valenciennois au XVIIIe siècle*, pp. 85–107; see also idem, "L'histoire du travail dans le Valenciennois au XVIIIe siècle."

22. Montaran to Sénac de Meilhan, April 23, 1782, quoted in Guignet, *Mines, manufactures, et ouvriers du Valenciennois*, pp. 104–105; on Sénac de Meilhan's enlightened and "philanthropic" administration of his intendancy for the benefit of the administered, see Louis Legrand, *Sénac de Meilhan et l'intendance du Hainaut et du Cambrésis sous Louis XVI*, pp. 127–150.

23. Montaran's letter to Crommelin reads in part: "il n'a été en thèse générale que de dispenser les toiles de modes de toute règle attendu les inconvénients qui en resulteraient pour la plupart des fabricants et en thèse particulière que de reserver à ceux que voudraient s'accréditer et se distinguer par une fabrication plus parfaite la faculté d'y parvenir . . . en obtenant la marque du règlement" (quoted in Guignet, *Mines, manufactures, et ouvriers du Valenciennois*, p. 95 n. 66).

24. Gita May, *Madame Roland and the Age of Revolution*, p. 109.

25. Claude Perroud, "Appendice G: Les arts et le dictionnaire des manufactures," in Marie Jeanne (Phlipon) Roland de la Platière, *Lettres de Madame Roland, 1780–1793*, II, 625.

26. Quoted in ibid., pp. 625–626. Panne is a soft fabric, resembling velvet, but with a longer, looser nap and a smooth, lustrous finish. Sometimes urban textile craftsmen used their control of the *gardes-jurés* to impose long delays at the local *bureau de visite* upon rival rural artisans and to inflict upon them unreasonable and unjustifiable fines, over the repeated protests of the royal inspectors of manufactures (see Jean Claude Perrat, "Recherches sur l'analyse de l'économie urbaine au XVIIIe siècle," p. 364).

27. "Observations sur l'état des fabriques et du commerce de Picardie, faites dans ma tournée, commencée le 22 Juillet et finie 7 Aoust 1781," F12 650.

28. Montaran to Roland de la Platière, March 3, 1782, F12 650.

29. Roland de la Platière to Montaran, August 27, 1782, F12 650. Bruyard's comment and the decision are in F12 650. From 1756 to 1783 Bruyard also supervised the collection of import and export statistics of French foreign commerce (Michel Beaud, "Le bureau de la balance du commerce (1781–1791)," p. 358).

30. Roland de la Platière, *Encyclopédie méthodique*, II, xxx–xxxi.

31. Montaran to the inspectors of his department, May 13, 1782, F12* 130.

32. Chemise, "1782; Les Sindics Jurés Gardes de la grande fabrique de Lyon demandent que les étoffes de leur fabrique soient affrancies . . . ," F12 1441. The petition was perhaps a response to the royal decree of April 18, 1782.

33. Joly de Fleury to Thiroux de Crosne, April 16, 1782, F12* 156.

34. "Avis des Députés du Commerce sur la demande en cassation d'un arrêt du Parlement de Rouen . . . ," July 16, 1782, F12 727.

35. This statement assumes that the register of letters of the controller general and the

four intendants with respect to the new regulations (found in F12* 156) is complete, a hazardous assumption. By months, the number of new regulations was: June (1781), 1; July, 0; August, 0; September, 1; October, 1; November (last four days), 4; December, 4; January (1782), 5; February, 3; March, 8; April, 5; May, 4; June, 0; July, 6; August, 2; September, 1; October, 0; November, 0. (Decisions in cases of individual violations were not counted in this tabulation.) The figures do seem to indicate a tapering off.

36. Joly de Fleury to Perrin de Cypierre, September 24, 1782, F12* 156.

37. An additional motivation: cloth in the *libre* category did not have to receive a provisional seal as it was taken off the loom, and hence was not charged the initial one-sou duty. It received a seal after fulling and paid a duty then (to Lepage, July 16, 1782, ibid.).

38. Goy, "Mémoire sur les Bureaux de Toilerie établis dans la Ville et Généralité de Rouen, et sur le Commerce de ses Fabriques en Conséquence de la tournée générale que L'Inspecteur des Manufactures vient d'y Faire" (1782), and Bruyard's comment on the "Mémoire," F12 650.

39. Joly de Fleury to Perrin de Cypierre, September 24, 1782, F12* 156.

40. "Journal de l'inspecteur des manufactures sur sa tournée dans les Bureaux établis pour la visite des toiles dans le Poitou commencée le 2 septembre, 1782," F12 650.

41. Biollay, *Etudes économiques sur le XVIIIe siècle*, pp. 470–472. Biollay's statements on the dates of Valioud's promotion to chief and his assumption of the position of Tolozan's *premier commis* are not clear.

42. André Rémond, *John Holker: manufacturier et grand fonctionnaire en France au XVIIIe siècle 1719–1786*, pp. 100–101.

43. Franc Bacquié, *Un siècle d'histoire de l'industrie: les inspecteurs des manufactures sous l'Ancien Régime, 1669–1791*, p. 379.

44. The fact that inspectors of manufactures recruited their sons into the inspectorate also indicated a strong morale. In 1783 the *Almanach Royal* (pp. 270–272) reported six such father-son situations: Bruté, inspector of manufactures at Montauban (Montauban); Bruté *fils*, subinspector at Lodève (Languedoc). Coprez, subinspector at Rouen (Upper Normandy); Coprez *fils*, *élève de manufactures* at Elbeuf (Upper Normandy). Holker, inspector general for foreign manufactures at Rouen; Holker *fils*, *adjoint*. Tribert, inspector for linens at St. Quentin (Picardy); Tribert *fils*, subinspector at Morlaix (Brittany). Tricou, inspector at S. Chinia and S. Pons (Languedoc); Tricou *fils*, *élève* at Nîmes (Languedoc). Watier, inspector at Nantes (Brittany); Watier *fils*, *élève* at Alençon (Middle Normandy).

45. Born at Dijon in 1755, Lansel had been an *avocat* at the parlement of Dijon (Bacquié, *Les inspecteurs des manufactures*, pp. 82–83; Woronoff, *L'industrie sidérurgique en France*, p. 40 n. 41).

46. Montaran to the Prévôt des Marchands de Lyon, October 26, and Joly Fleury to the Prévôt, December 4, 1782, F12* 130.

47. Montaran to the intendant of Auvergne, December 12, 1782, ibid.

48. George T. Matthews, *The Royal General Farms in Eighteenth-Century France*, pp. 132, 138, 140, 207.

49. Joly de Fleury to the intendant of Auvergne, January 8, 1783, F12* 130.

50. Montaran to Vilevault, January 9, 1783, ibid. However, marked and unmarked cloth could still freely travel down a road until it met the first checkpoint of the Farmers General. Thus unmarked goods circulating locally would escape the back-up surveillance of the Farmers General (Emmanuelli, *Pouvoir royal et vie régionale en Provence au déclin de la monarchie*, II, 817; see also II, 827).

51. Joly de Fleury to the intendant of Languedoc, January 15 and 16, 1783, F12* 130.

52. Montaran to Flesselles, intendant of Lyons, May 28, 1783, F12* 130.

53. The story of the "effervescence" in Lyons and some of its background and resolution is told in the following dispatches of Montaran, all of 1783 and in F12* 130; to Chaix,

préposé, July 1, 21, August 23, September 20, 23; to Brisson, inspector of manufactures, August 2; to the intendant of Lyons, August 14; to Vilevault, August 23, September 3, 15. Pierre Léon remarks that the merchants of Lyons, protecting the "secret of their business," fought "the establishment in their town of any inspection of manufactures worthy of the name" (*Papiers d'industriels et de commerçants lyonnais: Lyon et le grand commerce au XVIIIe siècle*, p. xxiii).

54. François Lebrun, *Histoire des pays de la Loire: Orléanais, Touraine, Anjou, Maine*, p. 253 (the translation is somewhat abridged); see also Léon, *Papiers d'industriels et de commerçants lyonnais*, p. xxiii.

55. In his dispatches Montaran reiterated that this was a monarchy that governs tactfully in accordance with the law and the procedures of a sound administration. See Montaran to Jubié, inspector of manufactures at Auvergne, April 16; to Huet de Vaudour, April 16; to the intendant of Tours, July 16, 1783, F12* 130.

56. The story of Libour and the "fermentation" in Laval is told in the following dispatches of Montaran, all of 1783 and in F12* 130: to Huet de Vaudour, inspector of manufactures at Tours, January 17, April 14, 16, May 6, June 11, September 13, 15, 28; to the intendant of Tours, March 8; to Gentil, *subdélégué général* of the intendant of Tours, August 29, September 8; to Libour, May 17, August 14, 22, 29, September 8; to Vilevault, August 14, September 16; to Chaix, now subinspector of manufactures of Laval, October 16, November 5. See also d'Ormesson to the intendant of Tours, September 24, 1783, F12* 130.

57. Montaran to Vilevault, September 16, 1783, F12* 130.

58. The letters are registered in F12* 167. The letter of d'Ormesson to Jullien, October 7, 1783, is in F12* 156.

59. D'Ormesson to Jullien, October 7, 1783, F12* 156.

60. D'Ormesson to the keeper of the seals, May 7, 1783, ibid.

61. See, for example, the following instances of reduction of fine or other moderation of penalty: Joly de Fleury to the intendant of Rouen, May 15 (nos. 10,838, 10,839), June 19, July 10 (nos. 10,888, 10,895, 10,899, 10,903), September 11 (nos. 10,950, 10,951, 10,952, 10,953), October 18, October 30 (nos. 10,983, 10,985, 10,986), December 30, 1782; Joly de Fleury to the intendant of Auch, July 31, 1782; d'Ormesson to the intendant of Rouen, May 21 (nos. 11,137, 11,139, 11,140), June 27, July 9, October 25, 1783, F12* 130.

62. D'Ormesson to the intendant of Rouen, May 21 (nos. 11,135, 11,136), July 9, 1783, F12* 130.

63. Joly de Fleury to the intendant of Rouen, October 30, 1782; to the intendant of Montauban, February 27, 1783, F12* 130.

64. "Avis des Deputés du Commerce sur la demand des Srs. Le Blond et Paire, fabriquans à Rouen d'être affranchis de la marque et du plomb pour les toileries et passementeries destinés pour la traite," F12 721.

65. "Avis des Deputés du Commerce sur la demande des Passementiers de Rouen d'être affranchis du plomb de teinture," May 27, 1783, and d'Ormesson to the intendant of Rouen, July 9, 1783, in chemise, "1782, 1783; Pièces relatives à Bourgeois l'Aîné, Fabricant passementier à Rouen, demandant que les étoffes mêlées de soie et coton soient dispensées du plomb de teinture," F12 1449.

66. D'Ormesson to Thiroux de Crosne, August 26, 1783, F12* 156.

67. D'Ormesson to the intendants of the provinces, October 7, 1783, F* 156; Roland de la Platière, *Encyclopédie méthodique*, II, xxiii.

68. Tolozan to Colonia, March 28, 1784, F12 1396.

69. D'Ormesson to the intendant, June 13 and July 18, 1783, registered in F12* 167. The fabricants of Elbeuf also requested that a foreigner not be received into the guild until

he had worked at his trade for six years; nor should a master receive an apprentice who had not worked the same length of time. These requests, too, were turned down by the Bureau.

70. See, for example, the minutes of the Bureau session of May 15, 1783, referring to the discussion during the session of December 12, 1782, F12* 106.

71. Minutes of the session of the Bureau of Commerce, May 15, 1783, F12* 106.

72. Minutes of the session of the Bureau of Commerce, July 24, 1783, F12* 106. On July 29, 1783, the controller general (d'Ormesson) instructed the intendants of the frontier provinces to order the arrest and imprisonment for "quelques temps" of all workers seeking to leave the kingdom without a passport from the intendant or commandant of the province (F12* 156). On the same day he wrote the minister of war, Ségur (July 27, 1783, ibid.), to instruct the commandants of the frontier provinces to do the same. Also on the same day d'Ormesson informed Saint-Priest of the Bureau's thinking on the subject of the emigration of workers and of the measures the Bureau was taking (ibid.).

73. D'Ormesson to Saint-Priest, July 3, and to the Farmers General, July 3, 1783, F12* 156. Concern with smuggling of looms abroad had surfaced in February, 1783, when Vergennes, the secretary for foreign affairs, had forwarded to Joly de Fleury a letter from de Pio, chargé d'affaires of the Kingdom of Naples, requesting permission to export from France two looms for knitting silk stockings that he had built in Paris for the service of his king. The Bureau of Commerce agreed with Vergennes: departure from the regulation that prohibited the export of looms, tools, and machines used in French manufactures would "set a dangerous example." Hence the controller general denied de Pio's request (Joly de Fleury to Vergennes, February, 1783, ibid.). Even a disposition to do a personal favor to a fellow Bourbon monarch must yield to the inclination to regard all other countries as economic enemies and to hug close any technological superiority.

74. D'Ormesson to Saint-Priest, October 7, 1783, ibid.

75. Circular of the controller general to the intendants of the provinces, October 7, 1783, ibid.

76. The history of Tolozan's search for information is sketched in the minutes of the Bureau's session of December 18, 1783, F12* 106. A document in the search is the controller general's circular to the intendants of Orléans, Bourges, Bretagne, Languedoc, Soissons, Metz, Lorraine, Alsace, Limoges, Poitou, La Rochelle, and Bordeaux, April 15, 1783 (F12* 156), reiterating a request for information about the problem of theft and its relation to the export of woolen waste abroad.

77. A detailed description of these encouragements to industry is found in Parker, *The Bureau of Commerce*, pp. 47–69.

78. The reader interested in having the story of a particular industry in uninterrupted sequence can still find it by consulting the appropriate industrial entry in the index.

79. The relevant documents in this case are in chemise, "1781 à 1783; Arrêt du 7. Janvier 1783 qui Permet à M. Le Comte D'Artois de Faire établir une verrerie au lieu dit Forêt L'Abbaye . . . ," F12 1488A.

80. On the problem of deforestation in France during the 1780s, on the royal response, and specifically on the forested appanage of the comte D'Artois see Michel Devèze, "Les forêts françaises à la veille de la Révolution de 1789," esp. pp. 242, 255, and P. M. Bondois, "Le développement de la verrerie française au XVIIIe siècle," p. 346 n. 257; also Edward A. Allen, "Deforestation and Fuel Crisis in Pre-revolutionary Languedoc, 1720–1789"; Paul W. Bamford, "French Forest Legislation and Administration 1660–1789"; David Bruce Young, "Forests, Mines, and Fuel: The Question of Wood and Coal in Eighteenth-Century France."

81. For the history of these two firms see the references in note 82 below and also "Mémoire pour le Sieur Joseph Esnard, entrepreneur de la verrerie de Pierrebénite," in chemise, "1778; Les Sieurs Esnard, Entrepreneurs de la Verrerie de Pierre Bénite, et le Robichon,

de celle de Givors près Lyon, demandent que l'Arrêt rendu en faveur de la Demoiselle Bouvier, le 16 Avril 1778 . . . ," F12 1488B; also Bondois, "Le développement de la verrerie française au XVIIIe siècle," p. 334, and François-Georges Dreyfus, "L'industrie de la verrerie en Bas-Languedoc de Colbert à la révolution industrielle du XIXe siècle," p. 63.

82. Flesselles to Necker, Lyons, November 21, 1788, and also an untitled administrative summary that opens "Dans le mois de février 1778 la Demoiselle Bouvier de Lyon . . ." in chemise, "1778; La Demoiselle Eléonore Bouvier supplie Sa Majesté . . . ," F12 1488B.

83. "Précis pour les sieurs Robichon, entrepreneurs de la verrerie Royale de Givors, en Lyonnaise, contre la dame La Palun, ci-devant connue sous le nom de demoiselle Bouvier," "Résumé de l'affaire," "Arrêt du 26 Avril 1785," in chemise, "1786; sur l'opposition formée par les Sieurs Robichon Frères . . . à deux arrêts obtenus par la demoiselle Bouvier . . . ," F12 1488B; Bondois, "Le développement de la verrerie française au XVIIIe siècle," pp. 348–349.

84. Colonia to Des Forges, June 22, 1781, in chemise, "1782; Defréjard, Père et Fils, demandent l'autorisation de rétablir les verreries au village de Longchamp, Généralité de Dijon," F12 1489A.

85. Dupré de St. Maur to Colonia, Paris, July 9, 1781, in chemise, "1782; Arrêt du Conseil du 9 Avril 1782, qui permet aux Sieurs Guiraud et de Montmarillon d'établir une verrerie . . . ," F12 1487.

86. Morize to Tolozan, Evreux, June 27, 1781, F12 1453A.

87. Vandermonde to Colonia, July 10, 1783, and Tolozan to Vandermonde, February 21, 1784, F12 1453A.

88. Valioud to Guillaume, Paris, January 8, 1793, F12 1498A.

89. "Avis des Deputés du Commerce sur le Mémoire donné par la Ferme Générale, sur le tartre et cendres de Gravelle," June 17, 1782, F12 721.

90. Administrative summary of the Stoucard affair, F12 1308.

91. Vergennes to Joly de Fleury, August 30, 1781, in chemise, "1781; M. de Vergennes envoye une lettre de M. de la Salle de Lyon . . . ," F12 1444B.

92. Montaran to M. l'Intendant de Provence, October 12, 1781, in chemise, "1781; Le Sieur Jean Joseph Gaspard D'audouard demande . . . ," F12 1486.

93. La Tour to Montaran, Aix, December 28, 1781, in ibid.

94. François-Xavier Emmanuelli, *Pouvoir royal et vie régionale en Provence au déclin de la monarchie*, II, 786–787; on the intendant La Tour see Edouard Baratier, *Histoire de la Provence*, pp. 371–373.

95. On the work of these two chemists see John J. Beer, "Eighteenth-Century Theories on the Process of Dyeing"; L. J. M. Coleby, *The Chemical Studies of P. J. Macquer*, pp. 52–59, 85–110, 115–116, 121–124; Parker, *The Bureau of Commerce in 1781*, pp. 97, 104–105, 120–121; and W. A. Smeaton, "Pierre Joseph Macquer," *Dictionary of Scientific Biography*, VIII, 618–624.

96. Macquer to Tolozan, Paris, August 13, 1779, in chemise, "Culture et industrie de la Garance, 1747–1779," F12 655.

97. Macquer to Montaran, Paris, January 17, 1782, ibid.

98. Dufour to Tolozan, January 20, 1782, in chemise, "1782; arrêt du Conseil du 26. février 1782 qui déboute M. le Comte de Melfort . . . ," F12 1486. In summarizing the views of the preceding intendant, Dufour, it may be assumed, adopted them as his own before proceeding to his own line of argument.

99. Parker, *The Bureau of Commerce in 1781*, pp. 157–158.

100. On Guyton's life and career see Evan M. Melhado, "Oxygen, Phlogiston, and Caloric: The Case of Guyton"; and several articles by W. A. Smeaton: "The Contributions of P.-J. Macquer, T. O. Bergman and L. B. Guyton de Morveau to the Reform of Chemical Nomenclature"; "Louis Bernard Guyton de Morveau," *Dictionary of Scientific Biography*,

V, 600–604; "L. B. Guyton de Morveau (1737–1816): A Bibliographic Study"; "Guyton de Morveau and Chemical Affinity"; "Guyton de Morveau's Course of Chemistry in the Dijon Academy"; and "Guyton de Morveau and the Phlogiston Theory."

101. Smeaton, "Guyton de Morveau," *Dictionary of Scientific Biography*, V, 600.

102. Guyton de Morveau to the controller general, Dijon, February 16, 1782, F12 1507.

103. Marginal note on Guyton de Morveau's letter of February 16, 1782, ibid.

104. Colonia to Guyton de Morveau, March 9, 1782, in dossier on the Bullion-Morveau affair, ibid. On the chemistry and industrial technology of Guyton's processes see John Graham Smith, *The Origins and Early Development of the Heavy Chemical Industry in France*, pp. 200–202, and Charles C. Gillispie, "The Discovery of the Leblanc Process," pp. 156–157.

105. Quoted in Joseph Fayet, *La Révolution française et la science 1789–1795*, p. 296. For his services to the administration Vandermonde received annually from the administration a gratification of 2,000 livres as well as a pension of the same amount (Léon Biollay, *Etudes économiques sur le XVIIIe siècle*, p. 477). See also André Doyon and Lucien Liaigre, "L'Hôtel de Mortagne après la mort de Vaucanson," pp. 5–17; idem, *Jacques Vaucanson, mécanicien de génie*, p. 383; Dominique de Place, "Le sort des Ateliers de Vaucanson (1783–1791) d'après un document nouveau"; and Phillip S. Jones, "Alexandre-Théophile Vandermonde," *Dictionary of Scientific Biography*, XIII, 571–572.

106. "Mémoire et Propositions de G. Villard, pour introduire la connaissance et l'usage de sa mécanique sur les soyes dans les filatures et moulinages du Royaume," and a note for Villard, Paris, February 26, 1782, in F12 1449; "Mémoire pour Sieur George Villard" in chemise, "1782; Le Sieur Villard sollicite la commission accordée au Sieur Vaucanson pour le travail des soyes," F12 1453B.

107. The correspondence is in chemise, "1782; Arrêt du Conseil du 9 avril 1782, qui permet aux Sieurs Guiraud et de Montmarillon d'établir une verrerie en Verres blancs . . . ," F12 1487; on the intendant of Bordeaux, Dupré de Saint-Maur, who was characterized by his historian, Dartigue-Payrou, as "honest, disinterested, liberal, enamored of working for the development of the public good," see Maurice Bordes, "Les intendants éclairés à la fin de l'Ancien Régime," pp. 60–62.

108. Joly de Fleury to MM. les Sindics de la chambre de commerce de Normandie, April 10, 1782, F12* 156.

109. Chemise, "1782; demande de la Demoiselle D'Auxon et Compagnie d'Abbeville d'établir dans cette commune une manufacture de savon blanc, égal au savon de Marseille," F12 1505.

110. Charles C. Gillispie, *Science and Polity in France*, pp. 463–464.

111. Report of Berthollet, "sur les fers et aciers préparés par le procédé de M. de la Place," June 30, 1785, F12 1305A.

112. Diderot, *Pictorial Encyclopedia*, vol. I, plates 86–100.

113. Denis Woronoff, *L'industrie sidérurgique en France pendant la Révolution et l'Empire*, p. 349.

114. On the history of the file industry, vital to the French economy, see chemise, "1788, Vaucher, horloger, inventeur d'une machine à tailler les limes, demande une gratification qui le mette à même de perfectionner son invention . . . ," F12 1325A.

115. This outline of manufacturing procedures is based on K. C. Barraclough, "The Origins of the British Steel Industry," pp. 623–629; J. R. Harris, "The Diffusion of English Metallurgical Methods to France in the Eighteenth Century"; Louis Gueneau, "L'usage industriel de la houille au XVIIIe siècle"; René Tresse, "Contribution à l'histoire d'une technique agricole: le développement de la fabrication des faux en France de 1785 à 1827 et ses conséquences sur la pratique des moissons," p. 343; Woronoff, *L'industrie sidérurgique en France*, pp. 349–351.

116. On the 1779 tests see Gillispie, *Science and Polity in France*, pp. 463–471.

117. "Mémoire," Tolozan to Joly de Fleury, July 12, 1782, and Tolozan to Blondel, March 17, 1792, in chemise, "1792; Le Ministre de l'Intérieur, prie M. Blondel, de donner en communication au Sieur de la Place, chimiste, les pièces qui existent dans les Bureaux de l'ancienne administration du commerce . . . ," F12 1305A. That Joly de Fleury did not transmit the documents in question to De La Place is inferred from the fact that ten years later, in 1792, the latter is still petitioning to have them. Since Tolozan, Necker, Joly de Fleury, and a succession of clerks observed the principle of confidentiality, it seems just to refer to it as a Bureau policy.

118. J. R. Harris, *Industry and Technology in the Eighteenth Century: Britain and France*, pp. 16–17; see also idem, "The Rolt Memorial Lecture 1984: Industrial Espionage in the Eighteenth Century," p. 135.

119. Joly de Fleury to the duc de Guisnes, July 4, and Montaran to the duc de Guines, July 16, 1782, F12* 130.

120. Macquer's report on the "Procédés proposés par M. de Morveau . . . ," Paris, July 31, 1782, F12 1507.

121. Macquer's report, September 5, 1782, and marginal comment, September 8, 1782, presumably by Montaran, in chemise, "1791; Le Sieur Dino Stéphanopoli, Corse, propose . . . ," F12 1330; Montaran's referral of the case to Macquer is in his letter dated July 13, 1782, F12* 130.

122. Gillispie, *Science and Polity in France*, p. 65. See also Robert P. Multhauf, "The French Crash Program for Saltpeter Production, 1776–1794"; Carleton E. Perrin, "Of Theory Shifts and Industrial Innovations: The Relations of J. A. C. Chaptal and A. L. Lavoisier," pp. 525–530; and Smith, *The Origins and Early Development of the Heavy Chemical Industry in France*, pp. 27–28, 198–99, 225. Authorities differ concerning the quality of French saltpeter, even under the Régie. In the 1780s Chaptal, a contemporary chemist, found it variable.

123. Montaran to d'Ormesson, July 22, 1782, F12* 130; "Mémoire du Sieur Lapenne, et avis de M. Dormesson, et de M. l'Intendant de Languedoc sur sa demande: Extrait," F12 1507; and Joly de Fleury to Saint-Priest, intendant de Languedoc, December 30, 1782, F12 1507 (also in F12* 130). The sources conflict as to the sequence of the Bureau's actions: whether in July, upon the receipt of Lapenne's petition, it dispatched inquiries concurrently to the intendant of Languedoc and to the *Régisseurs* of the Compagnie des Poudres; or whether in July it wrote first to the intendant and then, upon the receipt of his August 26 report, to the *Régisseurs* through d'Ormesson. I have followed the sequence indicated in the December letter to the intendant rather than the clerk's possibly mistaken summary of the history. On Lapenne's enterprise see also Smith, *Origins and Early Development of the Heavy Chemical Industry in France*, pp. 16, 52.

124. "Journal de l'inspecteur des manufactures sur sa tournée dans les Bureaux établis pour la visite des toiles dans le Poitou commencée le 2 september, 1782," F12 650.

125. Letter of Goy, Rouen, November 12, 1782, enclosing the "Procès Verbal de Tournée de Sieur Goy, Inspecteur des Manufactures à Rouen, pour l'année 1782," ibid.

126. "Inspection des Manufactures d'Etoffes du Poitou, Semestre de Juillet 1782— Comparé avec la même de 1781," ibid.

127. Bruyard's commentary on Goy's memoir, ibid.; in his *Encyclopédie méthodique* (II, 264) Roland de la Platière warns his readers against facile acceptance of Old Regime statistics as precisely accurate. Their accuracy varies from official to official.

128. Goy, "Mémoire" (1782), F12 650.

129. On the Rouen commercial-industrial "miracle" see Jean-Pierre Bardet, *Rouen aux XVIIe et XVIIIe siècles*, pp. 183–207.

130. Joly de Fleury to M. de Morveau, "ancien avocat général au Parlement de Dijon,"

Paris, November 6, 1782, F12 1507; see also "Mémoire pour le Sieur De Morveau," ibid.

131. M. P. Crosland, "Jean Antoine Chaptal," *Dictionary of Scientific Biography*, III, 199.

132. Homer E. Le Grand, "Chemistry in a Provincial Context: The Montpellier Société royale des sciences in the Eighteenth Century," p. 92. On Chaptal's many chemical-industrial experiments and manufacturing operations see, in general, idem, "Theory and Application: The Early Chemical Work of J. A. C. Chaptal"; Gillispie, "The Natural History of Industry"; Perrin, "Of Theory Shifts and Industrial Innovations: The Relations of J. A. C. Chaptal and A. L. Lavoisier," pp. 511–525; and Robert Tinthoin, "Chaptal créateur de l'industrie chimique de France."

133. Chaptal to Joly de Fleury, Montpellier, November 22, 1782, in chemise, "1782; Le Sieur Chaptal, Professeur de Chymie à Montpellier annonce qu'il a découvert avec M. de Castelvieil le secret de faire des bouteilles de laver . . . ," F12 1486.

134. Montaran to Coster, December 19, 1782, ibid.

135. The evidence concerning the administrative discussion of Chaptal's request for permission to naturalize Spanish barilla on French beaches is contradictory. In chronological series the dispatches may be arranged as follows:

Before October 30, 1782. Chaptal, through a M. de Joubert, asks Joly de Fleury for permission to cultivate several leagues of beach; Joly de Fleury writes Saint-Priest for information.

October 30. Saint-Priest to Joly de Fleury, giving requested information.

November 14. Joly de Fleury to Saint-Priest, authorizing Saint-Priest to issue an ordinance giving Chaptal permission.

November 22. Chaptal writes Joly de Fleury directly, requesting permission once again.

December 1. Joly de Fleury to Chaptal, answering about bottles and tin but not about permission to cultivate the beaches; the administrative summary states that the "Bureau de Ministre" sent this letter.

December 2. Chaptal's letter of November 22 is referred to Montaran.

December 4. Notation indicating the letter is to go to the indendants' Comité on that day.

December 10. Another notation indicating the letter is to go to the intendants' Comité on that day.

December 11. Notation by Montaran to his *premier commis* or a *rédacteur*: prepare me a letter for M. Coster, saying that the "Ministre" asked me to inquire about the concession to Chaptal. [But why did the minister, that is, Joly de Fleury, ask Montaran to look into the matter when he had signed a letter to Saint-Priest according the permission? Did the bureau of Joly de Fleury not inform him? Or was Montaran using the word *ministre* as a euphemism for *Comité*?]

December 19. Montaran to Coster (who seems to be a member of Joly de Fleury's bureau), asking for information.

December 24. Coster to Montaran, giving history of correspondence of Joly de Fleury with Saint-Priest.

Why did Joly de Fleury's bureau (or perhaps Joly de Fleury) cut in and take it upon themselves to handle Chaptal's permission instead of referring it to the four intendants? The reason is unknown. However, Saint-Priest was an intendant of a *généralité* who insisted on dealing directly with the controller general and his bureau; he usually ignored the four intendants, and they had to accept this disregard. Also, in this instance, the issue probably seemed simple and easily handled, and the minister's bureau may have wished to expedite the affair. The incident seems to suggest that Joly de Fleury did not always know what his office was doing.

The documents are interesting also for showing how an intendant of commerce worked within his own office. A letter comes in to the controller general's office; it is referred to the intendant in charge; he brings it to the Comité, which instructs him what to do; he sketches the guidelines for a letter incorporating the instructions; a *rédacteur* fleshes them out; his draft is probably revised by the intendant, copied by the *expéditionnaire*, and sent out. In this instance the intendant's guidelines (December 11) for the *rédacteur* read: "Me faire préparer une lettre pour M. Coster par laquelle je lui manderai que le ministre m'a chargé de lui faire passer une note relative à la concession demandé par le Sieur Chaptal. Lui observer que ce particulier paraisse très favorable à raison des découvertes utiles qu'il a déjà fait et des soins qu'il se donne pour perfectionner différentes branches d'industrie très intéressantes, et que le ministre m'a paru penser de même." The final letter of Montaran to Coster (December 19) reads: "Le Ministre, à qui j'ai parlé, Monsieur, de la concession des plages incultes qu'a demandée le Sieur Chaptal professeur de Chimie de la province de Languedoc pour y naturaliser la soude d'Espagne, m'a chargé de vous faire passer une note relative à cet objet. Je m'empresse d'autant plus volontiers de remplir ses intentions à cet égard, qu'il me semble que le Sieur Chaptal mérite beaucoup de considération, à raison des découvertes utiles qu'il a déjà faites, et des soins qu'il se donne pour perfectionner différentes branches d'industie très intéressantes. J'avais l'honneur de vous prévenir que le Ministre m'a paru penser de même, et être disposer à le [regarder?] favorablement."

136. Parker, *The Bureau of Commerce in 1781*, pp. 74–81.

137. The "Avis" for 1782 are in F12 721. This paragraph is a summary of the opinions dealing with tariff rates.

138. "Avis des Députés du Commerce sur un Mémoire présenté au Ministre par les Marchands Merciers de Lyon," October 8, 1782, ibid.

139. "Avis des Députés du Commerce sur un Mémoire de MM. les Fermiers Généraux relative aux tresses et lacets, en pièces, de fil teint, venant de l'étranger," January 13, 1784, F12 722.

140. See, for example, "Avis des Députés du Commerce sur la demande du Sieur Link, relative aux treillis, en réponse à un Mémoire de la ferme générale," December 24, 1782, F12 721.

141. "Mémoire sur un Projet de Lettres Patentes Relatives aux Déclarations pour la Perception des Droits du Roy," December 7, 1782, ibid.

142. Montaran to the intendant of Grenoble, January 12, 1782, F12* 130; "Mémoire," September 28, 1784, F12 1303.

143. Blondel to Le Roy, February 21, 1792, in the dossier on S. Rivey, F12 1446.

144. See the documents in chemise, "1782; les Srs. Lambert et Boyer demandent un privilège exclusif de 30 ans pour vendre à Paris et dans tout le Royaume des Cristaux, Emaux, et Cendre bleu de leur composition: ils se proposent de former leur établissement à Paris . . . ," F12 1486.

145. The decree is in ibid.; also in chemise, "1782; Gratification en faveur des Srs. Lambert et Boyer, Entrepreneurs . . . ," F12 1489B.

146. Joly de Fleury to the intendant of Languedoc, December 30, 1782, F12 1507; also in F12* 130.

147. Lapenne might have been somewhat consolé if he had known that his illustrious contemporary, Benjamin Franklin, seeking in Paris a cargo of saltpeter for the new American republic, likewise became entangled in the toils of the Régie des Poudres and the Farmers General, despite his high connections (see Claude-Anne Lopez, "Saltpetre, Tin and Gunpowder: Addenda to the Correspondence of Lavoisier and Franklin").

148. See above, pp. 000–000.

149. The decree of the Conseil d'Etat is found in chemise, "1781 à 1783; Arrêt du 7. Janvier 1783 qui Permet à M. Le Comte D'Artois de Faire établir une verrerie au lieu dit Forêt L'Abbaye . . . ," F12 1488A.

150. Allen, "Deforestation and Fuel Crisis in Pre-revolutionary Languedoc, 1720–

1789," p. 463 n. 17; Bamford, "French Forest Legislation and Administration 1660–1789," p. 107.

151. *Almanach Royal* (1783), p. 213.

152. "Ormesson d'Amboile (Henri-François de Paule Lefèvre d')," *Biographie universelle*, VI, 151.

153. He secretly transferred 6 million livres from the Caisse d'Escompte to the royal treasury, a secret that became known within twenty-four hours and undermined the credit of both the Caisse and the treasury. Without warning he canceled the lease of the Farmers General with the view of converting their operations into a *régie*, an action that brought down upon his head all those who were profiting from the lucrative lease. He also placed the customs records of the Farmers General at the disposition of Guillaume-François Mahy de Cormeré, chief of the "Bureau pour la Refonte des Traites," which was studying the proposal to abolish the internal customs duties the Farmers General collected. (Bosher, "Guillaume-François Mahy de Cormeré," pp. 239–240.)

154. Documents on the Priqueleur foundry are found in chemise, "1780; Priqueleur, fabricant de Carre d'aciers pour le bout des clefs de montres et autres pièces d'horlogerie . . . ," F12 1325A, and in another chemise in F12 1303; the favorable recommendation of the intendant Lacoré accorded with his policy throughout his intendancy (1761–1784) to encourage industry and commerce in a province that was largely agricultural (see Piquard, "Charles-André de Lacoré, intendant de Franche-Comté (1761–1784)," pp. 15–19.

155. Flesselles to Colonia, March 24, 1783, in chemise, "1783, 1784; Lettres et mémoires des Srs. Glaesner et Prudhomme, horlogers à Lyons . . . ," F12 1325A.

156. Colonia to Glaesner, May 1, and to M. l'abbé de St. Hilaire, July 16, 1783, in ibid.

157. Guyton de Morveau to d'Ormesson, Dijon, April 5, 1783, in Morveau-Bullion chemise, F12 1507; Vilevault to Tolozan, Paris, April 18, 1783, in ibid.

158. Smith, *Origins and Early Development of the Heavy Chemical Industry in France*, pp. 202–203.

159. Memoir of Hollenweger, April, 1783, in chemise, "1782 [*sic*: the date should be 1783]; Mémoire pour Le S. Hollenweger, cidevant élève de Fabrique de la Manufacture Royale des Glaces . . . ," F12 1507.

160. The decree is found in the Morveau-Bullion chemise, F12 1507.

161. Guyton de Morveau to d'Ormesson, Dijon, October 18, 1783, in ibid.

162. Register of the receipt of Hollenweger's petition, its referral to Macquer, and the receipt of Macquer's report, F12* 167; marginal comment on the letter of Tolozan to Guyton de Morveau, November 19, 1783, in Morveau-Bullion chemise, F12 1507; on the chemistry of Hollenweger's process see Gillispie, "The Discovery of the Leblanc Process," pp. 156–157; and Smith, *Origins and Early Development of the Heavy Chemical Industry in France*, pp. 58, 202–204.

163. The decree is found in F12* 30, 111.

164. Guyton de Morveau to d'Ormesson, Dijon, October 18, 1783, in Morveau-Bullion chemise, F12 1507; "Mémoire pour le Sr. De Morveau," in ibid.

165. Tolozan to Guyton de Morveau, November 19, 1783, in ibid.

166. "Mémoire pour le Sr. De Morveau," in ibid. This letter is curious, for in July, 1783 Macquer had assured Tolozan that Hollenweger's method "infinitely surpasses all that has been devised to the present on this subject and . . . would alone merit a privilege or a distinguished award" (quoted in Smith, *Origins and Early Development of the Heavy Chemical Industry in France*, p. 58). Macquer seems to have been talking out of two sides of his mouth.

167. "Mémoire pour le Sr. De Morveau"; De Bertrand to Tolozan, Paris, January 30, 1787, in Morveau-Bullion chemise, F12 1507; "Copie du Rapport fait au Comité d'Instruction publique par la Commission de l'Instruction publique concernant le Citoyen Malherbe, en date du 6 le ventôse an 3," F12 1508.

168. Marginal comment on letter from Guyton de Morveau to Tolozan, Dijon, May 3, 1788, in Morveau-Bullion chemise, F12 1507; "Mémoire pour le Sr. De Morveau," in ibid. It is important to note that Guyton suspended operations not because of the threat of the Hollenweger rivalry but because of the obduracy of the Farmers General. For a different chronology see Gillispie, "The Discovery of the Leblanc Process," p. 157.

169. To Colonia, undated and unsigned letter, in the Morveau-Bullion chemise, F13 1507.

170. "Notes des branches d'industrie de méchaniques et des procédés qui ont été établis, ou qui se sont perfectionnées pour raison desquels il a été accordé des secours ou récompenses dans le Département de M. de Tolozan . . . ," F12 1559. The date of the decision to subsidize the publication of Dambourney's journal is not given. It may have been taken in 1784 or 1785 rather than 1783.

171. Devin de Gallande to Vandermonde, February 21, 1784, in chemise, "1781; M. Morize de la Société d'Agriculture d'Evreux présente à l'administration du commerce un projet de tour à tirer la soye," F12 1453A.

172. Vandermonde to Colonia, July 10, 1783, in ibid.

173. "Notes des branches d'industrie, des méchaniques et des procédés qui ont été établis, ou qui se sont perfectionnées pour raison desquels il a été accordé des secours ou récompenses dans le Département de M. Tolozan, . . . ," F12 1559; see a note on Le Turc for "M. de Tolozan," 20 July 1784, F12 677c (reference supplied by J. R. Harris).

174. J. R. Harris, "The Rolt Memorial Lecture 1984: Industrial Espionage in the Eighteenth Century," p. 131.

175. Parker, *The Bureau of Commerce in 1781*, p. 112; Charles Schmidt, "Les débuts de l'industrie cotonnière en France 1760–1806," p. 267.

176. Parker, *The Bureau of Commerce in 1781*, pp. 112–113; Schmidt, "Les débuts de l'industrie cotonnière en France," pp. 272–275.

177. Holker to d'Ormesson, May 27, 1783, F12 1338; the letter was referred first to Tolozan on May 29 and then to Montaran on July 14 (see ibid., and F12* 167).

178. Holker to d'Ormesson, May 27, 1783, F12 1338.

179. Report of the Bureau consultatif des arts et manufactures, 8 prairial an 7, F12 1413; report of the Bureau des arts to the minister of the interior, Paris, 14 prairial an 7, ibid. Other initiatives in textiles during the d'Ormesson administration included the grant on May 13 of an annual pension of 600 livres to a M. Merlin, "marchand fabriquant de velours," for depositing his secret process of dyeing silk cloth black, with the chemist Berthollet as commissioner of the Bureau of Commerce (the deposit was effectuated June 22, 1784) (Tolozan to Blondel, January 27, 1792, F12 1454). During June, July, and August, 1783, there was a sustained correspondence between Roland de la Platière, the intendants of commerce, and Vandermonde about a locksmith who had allegedly invented better machines for making the metal teeth of carding equipment (F12* 167). On December 18, 1782, Joly de Fleury had granted Sieur Rivey, the Lyons inventor of intricate knitting looms, an annual pension of 300 livres; on October 28, 1783, d'Ormesson doubled it to 600 (chemises concerning Rivey are in F12 1446).

180. Parker, *The Bureau of Commerce in 1781*, pp. 110, 137, 175.

181. Guy Richard, "Les fonderies de Romilly-sur-Andelle et les débuts de la métallurgie non ferreuse en Haute-Normandie (1782–1850)"; see also Henry Hamilton, *The English Brass and Copper Industries to 1800*, p. 281; J. R. Harris, "Copper and Shipping in the Eighteenth Century"; idem, *The Copper King: A Biography of Thomas Williams of Llanidan*, pp. 8, 45–50; A. H. John, "War and the English Economy, 1700–1763"; see also "Notes des branches d'industrie, des méchaniques et des procédés qui ont été établis, ou qui se sont perfectionnées pour raison desquels il a été accordé des secours ou récompenses dans le Département de M. Tolozan, . . . ," F12 1559.

182. Castries to d'Ormesson, Versailles, June 2, 1783, F12 1308; "Mémoire du S. Leca-

mus de Lemare," and marginal comments on it concerning the decisions of the four intendants of commerce, ibid.

183. Tolozan to Vilevault, July 3, 1783; "Mémoire [of the Farmers General]," July 21, 1783; Vilevault to Tolozan, Paris, August 12, 1783; F12 1308.

184. Tolozan to Thiroux de Crosne, July 3, 1783, and April 12, 1784, F12 1308.

185. La Chaussade was the example of a firm that with government aid was developed by private initiative before being sold to the royal government. Founded in 1720 by Jacques Masson, a Parisian banker, it was developed from 1741 by his son-in-law Pierre Babaud de la Chaussade. By 1769 it comprised ten forges fabricating 1,400 milliers of wrought iron, two blast furnaces producing 1,800 milliers of cast iron, three forges for the production of anchors, another forge with seven tilt-hammers, 6,400 acres of forest, 300 acres of meadow, the total valued at 2,243,000 livres. The navy, by periodic contracts, took most of the product. Thus by the contract of 1752, renewed in 1756, the firm was to supply all the iron requested by the naval arsenals of Brest and Le Havre; the renewal of 1762 extended the contract for six years and to all the ports. In peacetime the Company of the Indies was another major customer. In 1781 the government purchased the firm for 2.5 million livres and appointed its former executive officer to operate. On La Chaussade see chiefly Paul W. Bamford, *Privilege and Profit: A Business Family in Eighteenth-Century France*, and "Entrepreneurship in Seventeenth and Eighteenth Century France: Some General Conditions and a Case Study"; also Charles Ballot, *L'introduction du machinisme dans l'industrie française*, pp. 427–428; Bertrand Gille, *Les origines de la grande industrie métallurgique en France*, pp. 181–186; chemise, "1775; M. de Sartines envoye et recommande un mémoire du Sr. Lauchassade, propriétaire de Forges en Nivernais, par lequel il se plaint de ne pouvoir soutenir la concurrence avec les ancres étrangères . . . ," F12 1302.

186. Report of Berthollet "sur les fers et aciers préparés par le procédé de M. de La Place," June 30, 1785, F12 1305A.

187. On Sanche and Amboise see J. H. Harris, "The Diffusion of English Metallurgical Methods to France in the Eighteenth Century"; and Woronoff, *L'industrie sidérurgique en France*, p. 352.

188. Report of Macquer, Paris, July 26, 1783, on the "Acier fin présenté par M. Sanche," F12 656.

189. "Mémoire," September 28, 1784, F12 1303.

190. Flesselles to Colonia, Lyons, October 18, 1783, in chemise, "1783; Le S. Palle, demande la titre de manufacture royale . . . ," F12 1318.

191. Ségur to d'Ormesson, Versailles, September 29, 1783, F12 1309.

192. D'Ormesson to Ségur, October 28, 1783, F12 1309.

193. Dupré de Saint Maur to Colonia, Bordeaux, October 4, 1783, and Arrêt of November 18, 1783, in chemise, "1783 à 1786; Pièces relatives au S. Darchambault," F12 1308.

194. Laubréaux to d'Ormesson, Paris, October 23, 1783, and Arrêt of December 30, 1783, F12 1308. The machine seems to have been a kind of mold; Labréaux was not excused from paying the customary fees of mastership.

195. "Mémoire du S. Mayere Openheim [sic], négociant anglais," and Tolozan to Thiroux de Crosne, October 11, 1783, in chemise, "1784; arrêt du 4. Mai 1784 permet aux Srs. Mercier Père et Mayer Openheim [sic] d'établir . . . une manufacture de cristal blanc, façon et qualité d'Angleterre . . . ," F12 1489B; see also Bondois, "Le développement de la verrerie française au XVIIIe siècle," pp. 347–348; and R. B. Prosser, *Birmingham Inventors and Inventions*, p. 139.

196. Bacquié, *Les inspecteurs des manufactures*, p. 37.

197. "Extrait des Registres du Conseil de Monseigeur Comte d'Artois," Versailles, June 8, 1784, F12 1479.

198. On a case-by-case basis they sometimes aided in securing a guild mastership for

mature candidates who had not passed through the regular apprentice-journeyman route or who could not pay the fee but had demonstrated competence during their working careers. See, for example, Montaran to the intendant of Bordeaux, October 18 (nos. 146–168), November 4 (nos. 169–170), and November 23, 1781, F12* 130. Meanwhile the intendant of Provence, La Tour, was in 1781–1782 obliging the *passementiers* of Aix to receive without an apprenticeship the manufacturer Antoine Perron. La Tour's historian Emmanuelli (see *Pouvoir royal et vie régionale en Provence au déclin de la monarchie*, II, 742) suggests that this case "epitomizes the policy of all the directing officials of the epoch who try to clear the way for the new industrial structures."

199. D'Ormesson to Saint-Priest, intendant of Languedoc, October 8, 1783, F12* 130.
200. Montaran to Tribou *fils*, September 9, 1783, F12* 130.

Chapter 3. The Yield in Conclusions and Reflections

1. The incident also illustrates a growing trend in the Bureau to reward faithful civil servants by according the inheritance of their office to their sons. Thus a royal decree of July 26, 1783, granted to Sieur Abeille *fils* the survivance of Sieur Abeille *père*, including the permanent secretaryship of the Bureau of Commerce. (The decree was read at the August 26, 1783 session of the Bureau; see F12* 106 for that date.) In June, 1783, the advisory deputies of commerce had solicited for one of the number, Marion *père*, the favor of passing on his office to his son, Marion *fils* (F12* 106, September 2, 1784). At the close of d'Ormesson's term of office this request was still being discussed.

2. Michel Antoine, *Le Conseil du Roi sous le règne de Louis XV*, p. 542.
3. James Grier Miller, *Living Systems*, p. 16.
4. Robert A. Freitas, Jr., "A General Theory of Living Systems," *Analog Science Fiction/Science Fact*, Spring 1980, p. 64. This article summarizes Miller's book.

Bibliography

This is both an updated bibliography for *The Bureau of Commerce in 1781 and Its Policies with Respect to French Industry* (1979) and a bibliography for this volume.

Primary Sources

MANUSCRIPT

All references are to registers or cartons in the Archives Nationales.

F1a 3, 4
F1b I2, 3(2), 5, 6
F2b I*, 531, 532
F12* 78, 80, 106, 130, 131, 132, 133, 138, 139, 156, 164, 165, 166, 167, 168, 169, 170
F12 650, 651, 652, 655A, 656, 657, 658B
F12 721, 722, 723, 724
F12 1300, 1302, 1303, 1304, 1305A, 1306, 1307, 1308, 1309, 1316, 1317, 1318, 1321–1322, 1323, 1325A, 1325B, 1327, 1329, 1330, 1338, 1339, 1340, 1341, 1343A, 1389–1390, 1396
F12 1430–1431, 1433, 1434, 1435, 1436, 1437, 1438, 1439, 1440, 1441, 1442, 1443, 1444A, 1444B, 1445, 1446, 1447A, 1447B, 1448A, 1448B, 1449, 1450, 1451, 1452, 1453A, 1453B, 1454, 1479, 1486, 1487, 1488B, 1489A, 1489B, 1490, 1491, 1498A, 1498B
F12 1502, 1505, 1506, 1507, 1508, 1559
F12 1639A, 1640

PRINTED

Almanach royal. 1781. Mis en ordre publié et imprimé par d'Houry, Imprimeur—Libraire de Monseigneur le Duc d'Orléans.

———. 1790. Mis en ordre et publié par Debure, gendre de feu M. D'Houry; De l'Imprimerie de la Veuve D'Houry et Debure, l'Imprimeurs—Libraires de Duc d'Orléans.

———. 1792. A Paris, De l'Imp. de Testu, successeur de la Veuve D'Houry.

Bibliothèque Nationale. Division des Manuscrits. Collection Joly de Fleury. Vol. 1732, "Communauté d'Arts et Métiers: Paris." Vol. 1733, "Corporations des métier de Paris." Vol. 1729, "Communautés d'arts et métiers: affaires générales, II: 1763–1788." Vol. 1730–1731, "Communautés d'arts et métiers: provinces, I: A–L; II, L–V."

Chaptal de Chanteloup, Jean Antoine Claude. *Chimie appliquée aux arts*. 4 vols. Paris: Deterville, 1807.

———. *De l'industrie françoise*. 2 vols. Paris: A. A. Renouard, 1819.

———. *Mes souvenirs sur Napoléon*. Paris: E. Plon, Nourrit et Cie, 1893.

Colbert. *Lettres, instructions, et mémoires.* Vol. 2, *Finances, impôts, monnaies, industrie, commerce.* Edited by Pierre Clément. Paris: Imprimerie Impériale, 1863.

Costaz, Claude Anthelme. *Histoire de l'administration en France de l'agriculture, des arts utiles, du commerce, des manufactures, des subsistances, des mines et des usines.* 2 vols. Paris: Mme Huzard, 1832.

———. *Mémoire sur les moyens qui ont amené le grand développement que l'industrie française a pris depuis vingt ans, suivi de la législation relative aux fabriques, aux ateliers, aux ouvriers, et aux découvertes dans les arts.* Paris: Firmin Didot, 1816.

Desmarest, Nicholas. "Art de fabriquer le papier." *Encyclopédie méthodique: arts et métiers méchaniques,* 5:463–592. Paris: Chez Panckoucke, 1788.

———. "Second mémoire sur la papeterie. . . ." *Histoire de l'Académie Royale des Sciences, Année MDCCLXXIV.* Paris: De l'Imprimerie Royale, 1778.

Diderot, Denis. *A Diderot Pictorial Encyclopedia of Trades and Industry; Manufacturing and the Technical Arts in Plates Selected from "L'Encyclopédie, ou Dictionnaire raisonné des sciences des arts, et des métiers."* Edited by Charles Coulston Gillispie. 2 vols. New York: Dover Publications, 1959.

"Fayencerie (Art de la)." *Encyclopédie méthodique: arts et métiers mécaniques,* 2:506–528. Paris: Chez Panckoucke, 1783.

France. Commission d'histoire économique et sociale de la Révolution française. *Le commerce: instruction, recueil de textes et notes.* Edited by Charles Schmidt. Paris: Imprimerie Nationale, 1912.

———. *L'industrie: instruction, recueil de textes et notes.* Edited by Charles Schmidt. Paris: Imprimerie Nationale, 1910.

Gaudin, duc de Gaëte. *Mémoires, souvenirs, opinions et écrits.* Paris: Baudouin, 1826.

Grignon, Pierre Clément. *Mémoires de physique sur l'art de fabriquer le fer, d'en fondre et forger des canons d'artillerie; sur l'histoire naturelle, et sur divers sujets particuliers de physique et d'économie.* Paris: n.p., 1775.

Hellot, Jean, P. J. Macquer, and Le Pileur D'Apligny. *The Art of Dyeing Wool, Silk, and Cotton.* Translated from the French. London: Printed for R. Baldwin, 1789.

Jars, Gabriel. *Voyages métallurgiques, ou Recherches et observations sur les mines et forges de fer, la fabrication de l'acier, celle du fer-blanc, et plusieurs mines de charbon de terre, faites depuis l'année 1757 jusques et compris 1769, en Allemagne, Suède, Norwège, Angleterre, et Ecosse. . . .* 3 vols. Lyon: Chez G. Regnault, 1774–1781.

Journal des arts et manufactures. Paris, 1795–1797.

[Macquer, Pierre-Joseph]. *Dictionnaire raisonné universel des arts et métiers, contenant l'histoire, la description, la police des fabriques et manufactures de France et des pays étrangers: ouvrage utile à tous les citoyens. Nouvelle édition, corrigée et considérablement augmentée d'après les mémoires et les procédés des artistes.* Revue et mise en ordre par M. l'Abbé Jaubert, de l'Académie Royale des Sciences de Bordeaux. 5 vols. Paris: Chez P. Fr. Didot jeune, 1773.

Molinier, A. *Inventaire de la collection Joly de Fleury.* Paris: Alphonse Picard, 1931.

Montbarey, Prince de. *Mémoires autographes de M. le Prince de Montbarey.* 3 vols. Paris: Alexis Eymery, 1826.

Necker, Jacques. *De l'administration des finances de la France.* Paris: n.p., 1784.

———. "Eloge de Jean-Baptiste Colbert." *Oeuvres complètes de M. Necker,* 15:3–126. Publiées par M. le baron de Staël. Paris: Ches Treuttel et Würtz, 1821.

Réaumur, René Antoine Ferchault de. *Réaumur's Memoirs on Steel and Iron: A Translation from the Original Printed in 1722.* Translated by Anneliese Grünhaldt Sisco. Chicago: University of Chicago Press, 1956.

Roland de la Platière, Jean Marie. *Encyclopédie méthodique: manufactures, arts et métiers.* 3 vols. Paris: Chez Panckoucke, 1784–1790.

Roland de la Platière, Marie Jeanne (Phlipon). *Lettres de Madame Roland, 1780–1793.* Publiées par Claude Perroud. 2 vols. Paris: Imprimerie Nationale, 1900–1902.

Sénac de Meilhan, Gabriel. *Considérations sur l'esprit et les moeurs, choisies, introduites, et commentées par Fernand Caussey.* Paris: E. Sansot et Cie, n.d.

———. *Considérations sur les richesses et de luxe. Nouvelle édition, corrigée et augmentée.* Amsterdam and Paris: Chez la Veuve Valade, 1789.

———. *Du gouvernement, des moeurs, et des conditions en France, avant la Révolution, avec le caractère des principaux personnages du règne du Louis XVI.* Hamburg: B. G. Hoffman, 1795.

"Sucre." *Encyclopédie méthodique: arts et métiers mécaniques*, 7:596–717. Paris: Chez Panckcoucke, 1790.

Tolozan, Jean François de [and Béchet]. *Mémoire sur le commerce de la France et de ses colonies.* Paris: Moutard, 1789.

Turgot, Anne-Robert-Jacques. "Eloge de Gournay." *Oeuvres*, 1:262–291. Paris: Guillaumin, 1844.

Vandermonde, [N.], [Claude Louis] Berthollet, and [Gaspard] Monge. "Mémoire sur le fer, considéré dans ses différens états métalliques." *Histoire de l'Académie Royale des Sciences, Année MDCCLXXXVI.* Paris: De l'Imprimerie Royale, 1788.

Voltaire. *Philosophical Letters.* Translated by Ernest Dilworth. Indianapolis and New York: Bobbs-Merrill, 1961.

Secondary Works

Adams, Thomas M. "From Old Regime to New Business, Bureaucracy, and Social Change." *Business History Review* 55 (1981), 41–61.

Agulhon, Maurice. *La vie sociale en Provence intérieure au lendemain de la Révolution.* Bibliothèque d'histoire révolutionnaire, ser. 3, no. 12. Paris: Société des Etudes Robespierristes, 1970.

Aldrich, Robert. "Late-Comer or Early-Starter? New Views on French Economic History." *Journal of European Economic History* 16 (Spring 1987), 89–100.

Allen, Edward A. "Deforestation and Fuel Crisis in Pre-Revolutionary Languedoc, 1720–1789." *French Historical Studies* 13 (1984), 455–473.

Antoine, A. *Les subdélégués de l'intendance, spécialement en Franche-Comté, dans la seconde moitié du XVIIIe siècle.* Verdun: Imprimerie Moderne (Ch. Galland), 1929.

Antoine, Michel. *Le Conseil du Roi sous le règne de Louis XV.* Geneva: Librairie Droz, 1970.

———. *Le gouvernement et l'administration sous Louis XV: dictionnaire biographique.* Paris: Editions du Centre National de la Recherche Scientifique, 1978.

———. "La notion de subdélégation dans la monarchie d'Ancien Régime." *Bibliothèque de l'Ecole des Chartes* 132 (1974), 267–287.

———, and Yvonne Lanhers. *Les archives d'Ormesson.* Paris: Imprimerie Nationale, 1960.

Ardashev, Pavel Nikolaevich. *Les intendants de province sous Louis XVI.* Translated by Louis Jousserandot. Paris: F. Alcan, 1909.

Armstrong, John A. "Old Regime Administrative Elites: Prelude to Modernization in France, Prussia, and Russia." *Revue internationale des sciences administratives* 38 (1972), 21–40.

Arnauné, Auguste. *Le commerce extérieur et les tarifs de douane.* Paris: Félix Alcan, 1911.

Artz, Frederick B. *The Development of Technical Education in France, 1500–1850.* Cambridge: Harvard University Press, 1966.

―――. "L'éducation technique en France au XVIIIe siècle (1700–1789)." *Revue d'histoire moderne* 13 (September 1938), 361–407.

―――. "L'enseignement technique en France pendant l'époque révolutionnaire, 1789–1815." *Revue historique* 194 (1946), 257–286, 385–407.

Aubry, Paul V. *Monge, le savant ami de Napoléon Bonaparte: 1746–1818.* Paris: Gauthier-Villars, 1954.

Aykroyd, Wallace R. *The Story of Sugar.* Chicago: Quadrangle Books, 1967.

Azimi, Vida. "La discipline administrative sous l'Ancien Régime." *Revue historique du droit français et étranger* 65 (January–March 1987), 45–70.

―――. *Un modèle administratif de l'Ancien Régime: les commis de la Ferme générale de la Régie générale des aides.* Paris: C.N.R.S., 1987.

Bacquié, Franc. *Un siècle d'histoire de l'industrie. Les inspecteurs des manufactures sous l'Ancien Régime, 1669–1791: étude historique et anecdotique d'après des documents inédits.* Toulouse: E. B. Soubiron, 1927.

Baehrel, R. *Une croissance: la Basse-Provence rurale, fin du XVIe siècle-1789; essai d'économie historique statistique.* Ecole Pratique des Hautes Etudes, VIe section, Centre de Recherches Historiques; Démographie et sociétés, 6. Paris: S.E.V.P.N., 1961.

Baillou, Jean. *Les affaires étrangères et le corps diplomatique français.* Vol. 1, *De l'Ancien Régime au Second Empire.* Paris: Editions du Centre National de la Recherche Scientifique, 1984.

Baker, Keith Michael. "Scientism at the End of the Old Regime: Reflection on a Theme of Professor Charles Gillispie." *Minerva* 25 (Spring–Summer 1987), 21–34.

Ballot, Charles. *L'introduction du machinisme dans l'industrie française.* Paris: F. Rieder, 1923.

Bamford, Paul W. "Entrepreneurship in Seventeenth and Eighteenth Century France: Some General Conditions and a Case Study." *Explorations in Entrepreneurial History* 9 (1957), 204–213.

―――. *Forests and French Sea Power, 1660–1789.* Toronto: University of Toronto Press, 1956.

―――. "French Forest Legislation and Administration 1660–1789." *Agricultural History* 29 (1955), 97–107.

―――. *Privilege and Profit: A Business Family in Eighteenth-Century France.* Philadelphia: University of Pennsylvania Press, 1988.

―――. "The Transfer of Technology between France and Britain during the Eighteenth Century: Comment." *Proceedings (1984) of the Consortium on Revolutionary Europe,* pp. 83–86. Athens, Ga.: Consortium on Revolutionary Europe, 1986.

Baratier, Edouard. *Histoire de la Provence.* Toulouse: Privat, 1969.

Baratin, H.-L. *Organisation et méthodes dans l'administration publique.* Paris: Berger-Levrault, 1961.

Bardet, Jean-Pierre. *Rouen aux XVIIe et XVIIIe siècles: les mutations d'un espace social.* Paris: Société d'Edition d'Enseignement Supérieur, 1983.

Barker, T. C., and J. R. Harris. *A Merseyside Town in the Industrial Revolution: St. Helens 1750–1900*. Liverpool: Liverpool University Press, 1954.

Barnard, Chester I. *The Functions of the Executive*. Cambridge: Harvard University Press, 1938.

Barraclough, K. C. "The Origins of the British Steel Industry." *The Metallurgist and Materials Technologist* 5 (December 1973), 623–619.

―――. *Steelmaking before Bessemer*. Vol. 1, *Blister Steel: The Birth of an Industry*. Vol. 2, *Crucible Steel: The Growth of Technology*. London: The Metals Society, 1984.

Baud, Paul. *L'industrie chimique en France: étude historique et géographique*. Paris: Masson et Cie, 1932.

―――. *Une industrie d'état sous l'Ancien Régime: l'exploitation de Salines de Tarentaise*. Paris: M. Rivière, 1937.

―――. "Les origines de la grande industrie chimique en France." *Revue historique* 174 (1934), 1–18.

Beaud, Michel. "Le bureau de la balance du commerce (1781–1791)." *Revue d'histoire économique et sociale* 42 (1964), 357–377.

Beer, John J. "Eighteenth-Century Theories on the Process of Dyeing." *Isis* 51 (1960), 21–30.

Belmonte, Jean-François. "Les manufactures de drap fin en France au XVIIe siècle et au XVIIIe siècle." *Revue de l'art* 65 (1984), 26–38.

Belorgey, Gérard. *Le gouvernement et l'administration de la France*. Paris: A. Colin, 1967.

Benoit, Bruno. "Trévoux et ses tireurs d'or et d'argent." *Revue d'histoire moderne et contemporaine* 33 (1986), 374–402.

Bensaud-Vincent, Bernadette. "Une mythologie révolutionnaire dans la chimie française." *Annals of Science* 40 (1983), 187–196.

Bergeron, Louis. *Les capitalistes en France (1780–1814)*. Paris: Editions Gallimard, 1978.

Berges, Ruth. *From Gold to Porcelain: The Art of Porcelain and Faïence*. New York and London: Thomas Yoseloff, 1963.

Bertrand, Joseph. *L'Académie des Sciences et les académiciens de 1666 à 1793*. Paris: J. Hetzel, 1869.

Biollay, Léon. *Etudes économiques sur le XVIIIe siècle: le pacte de famine; l'administration du commerce*. Paris: Guillaumin, 1885.

Birch, A. "Foreign Observers of the British Iron Industry during the Eighteenth Century." *Journal of Economic History* 25 (1955), 23–33.

Birn, Raymond. "Deconstructing Popular Culture: The *Bibliothèque Bleue* and Its Historians." *Australian Journal of French Studies* 23 (January–April 1986), 31–47.

Bodiguel, Jean-Luc, and Marie Christine Kessler. *L'administration française*. Paris: Armand Colin, 1970.

Boehm, Klaus. *The British Patent System: Administration*. London: Cambridge University Press, 1967.

Boissonade, P. "Trois mémoires relatifs à l'amélioration des manufactures de France sous l'administration des Trudaines (1754)." *Revue d'histoire économique et sociale* 7 (1914–1919), 56–86.

Bond, Gordon C. "Political Articulation and Alignment: Late Enlightenment [in France] to 1791." *Proceedings of the Annual Meeting of the Western Society for French History* 8 (1980; published 1981), 276–278.

Bondois, Paul-M. "Les centres sucriers français au XVIIIe siècle." *Revue d'histoire économique et sociale* 19 (1931), 27–76.

———. "Le développement de la verrerie française au XVIIIe siècle." *Revue d'histoire économique et sociale* 23 (1936–1937), 237–261, 333–361.

———. "L'industrie sucrière en France au XVIIIe siècle." *Revue d'histoire économique et sociale* 19 (1931), 316–346.

———. "Le privilège exclusif au XVIIIe siècle." *Revue d'histoire économique et sociale* 21 (1933), 140–189.

Bonin, Hubert. "La Révolution française a-t-elle bloqué la croissance économique?" *Histoire* 77 (1985), 98–100.

———. "La sidérurgie française de 1789 à 1815." *L'information historique* 48 (1986), 21–22.

Bonnassieux, Pierre. *Les assemblées representatives du commerce sous l'Ancien Régime*. Paris: Berger-Levrault, 1883.

Bordes, Maurice. *L'administration provinciale et municipale en France au XVIIIe siècle*. Paris: Société d'Edition d'Enseignement Supérieur, 1972.

———. "Une grande circonscription administrative du XVIIIe siècle: l'intendance d'Auch." *L'information historique* 24 (1962), 1–14.

———. *D'Etigny et l'administration de l'intendance d'Auch (1751–1767)*. 2 vols. Auch: Frédéric Cocharaux, 1957.

———. "Un intendant éclairé de la fin de l'Ancien Régime: Claude François Bertrand de Boucheporn." *Annales du Midi*, n.s., 74 (1962), 177–194.

———. "Les intendants de Louis XV." *Revue historique* 223 (1960), 45–62.

———. "Les intendants de province aux XVIIe et XVIIIe siècles." *L'information historique* 3 (1968), 107–120.

———. "Les intendants éclairés à la fin de l'Ancien Régime." *Revue d'histoire économique et sociale* 39 (1961), 57–83.

Bosher, J. F. "Current Writing on Administration and Finance in Eighteenth-Century France." *Journal of Modern History* 53 (1981), 73–83.

———. "French Administration and Public Finance in Their European Setting, 1763–1793." *The New Cambridge Modern History*, 8:565–591. Edited by A. Goodwin. Cambridge: Cambridge University Press, 1965.

———. *French Finances 1770–1795: From Business to Bureaucracy*. Cambridge: Cambridge University Press, 1970.

———. "Guillaume-François Mahy de Cormeré et la réforme officielle sous l'Ancien Régime." *Annali della Fondazione Italiana per la Storia Amministrativa* 3 (1966), 236–253.

———. "Jacques Necker et l'état moderne." *Rapport de la Société Historique du Canada* (1963), 162–175.

———. "The *premiers commis des finances* in the Reign of Louis XVI." *French Historical Studies* 3 (1964), 475–494.

———. *The Single Duty Project: A Study of the Movement for a French Customs Union in the Eighteenth Century*. London: The Athlone Press, University of London, 1964.

Bossenga, Gail. "Economic Privilege and Government Regulation: Guilds, Public Officials, and the Bourgeoisie in Lille, 1700–1820." *Proceedings of the Western Society for French History* 11 (1983): 222–230.

———. "From *corps* to Citizenship: The *Bureaux des Finances* before the French Revolution." *Journal of Modern History* 58 (1986): 610–642.

Bouchard, Georges. *Guyton-Morveau: chimiste et conventionnel (1737–1816)*. Paris: Librairie Académique Perrin, 1938.

———. *Un organisateur de la victoire, Prieur de la Côte-d'Or [membre du Comité de salut public]*. Paris: R. Clavreuil, 1946.

Bouchary, Jean. *L'eau à Paris à la fin du XVIIIe siècle: la Compagnie des Eaux de Paris et l'entreprise de l'Yvette*. Paris: M. Rivière et Cie, 1946.

Bourdon, Jean. *La législation du consulat et de l'empire*. Rodez: Carrère, 1942.

Bourgin, Hubert, and Georges Bourgin. *L'industrie sidérurgique en France au début de la Révolution*. Paris: Imprimerie Nationale, 1920.

Bouteron, Marcel. "Le fonctionnement du Conseil du Roi Louis XVI, expliqué par un de ses secrétaires, B.-F. Balzac." In *Etudes sur l'histoire administrative et sociale de l'Ancien Régime*, 39–51. Edited by Georges Pagès. Paris: Félix Alcan, 1938.

Bouvier-Ajam, Maurice, and Gilbert Mury. *Les classes sociales en France*. 2 vols. Paris: Editions Sociales, 1963.

Boyer de Sainte-Suzanne, Emile Victor Charles. *L'administration sous l'Ancien Régime: les intendants de la généralité d'Amiens (Picardy et Artois)*. Paris: n.p., 1865.

Braudel, Fernand, and Ernest Labrousse. *Histoire économique et sociale de la France*. 4 vols. Paris: Presses Universitaires de France, 1970–ca. 1982. Vol. 2, *Des derniers temps de l'âge seigneurial aux préludes de l'âge industriel (1660–1789)*.

Brongniart, Alexandre. *Traité des arts céramiques ou des poteries, considérées dans leur histoire, leur pratique et leur théorie*. Paris: Béchet jeune, 1844.

Brunot, André, and R. Cocquand. *Le corps des ponts et chaussées*. Paris: Editions du Centre National de la Recherche Scientifique, 1982.

Brutalis, Jean-Auguste. "Etudes sur la Chambre du Commerce de Guienne." *Actes de l'Académie Nationale des Sciences, Belles-lettres et Arts de Bordeaux* 55 (1893), 255–350.

Buot de l'Epine, Anne. "Les bureaux de la guerre à la fin de l'Ancien Régime." *Revue historique de droit française et étranger*, ser. 4, 54 (1976), 533–558.

Burns, Tom, and S. B. Saul, eds. *Social Theory and Economic Change*. London: Tavistock Publications, 1967.

Burton, William. *A General History of Porcelain*. 2 vols. London, New York, Toronto, and Melbourne: Cassell, 1921.

Butel, P. *La croissance commerciale bordelaise dans la second moitié du XVIIIe siècle*. 5 vols., with 2 vols. notes and appendixes. Lille: Université de Lille III, 1973.

———. "L'économie maritime française au XVIIIe siècle." *Vierteljahrschrift für Sozial- und Wirtschaftsgeschichte* 62 (1975), 289–308.

Camboulives, Catherine. "Jean-Baptiste Nudy de Mauléon, ou l'esprit d'entreprise à la veille de la Révolution." *Revue d'histoire moderne et contemporaine* 27 (1980), 258–269.

Cameron, Rondo. "The Diffusion of Technology as a Problem in Economic History." *Economic Geography* 51 (1975), 217–230.

———. "A New View of European Industrialisation." *Economic History Review* 28 (1985), 1–23.

———. "Was England Really Superior to France?" *Journal of Economic History* 46 (1986), 1031–1043.

———, with the assistance of Franklin F. Mendels and Judith F. Ward. *Essays in French Economic History*. Translation series. Homewood, Ill.: published for the American Economic Association by R. D. Irwin, 1970.

Caritey, J. "Politique, administration et administrateurs." *Revue administrative* 12 (1959), 260–267, 367–373, 476–483, 609–619.

Carrière, Charles. *Négociants Marseillais au XVIIIe siècle: contribution à l'étude des économies maritimes*. 2 vols. Marseille: Institut Historique de la Provence, 1973.

Catherine, Robert. *Le fonctionnaire français; droit, devoirs, comportement: introduction à une déontologie de la fonction publique*. Paris: Albin Michel, 1961.

———, and Guy Thuillier. *Introduction à une philosophie de l'administration*. Paris: Armand Colin, 1969.

Cavanaugh, Gerald. "Peasants, Office Holders, and Bureaucrats: The Articulation of Liberalism in Old Regime France." *Proceedings of the Annual Meeting of the Western Society for French History, 1980* 8 (1981), 254–264.

Chaplain, J. M. "Avoir ce qui manque aux autres: la manufacture de draps fins van Robais d'Abbeville au 18e siècle au milieu local." *Mouvement social* 125 (1983), 13–24.

———. *La chambre des tisseurs: Louviers, cité drapière, 1680–1840*. Seyssel: Champ Vallon, 1984.

Chapman, S. D., and S. Chassagne. *European Textile Printers in the Eighteenth Century: A Study of Peel and Oberkampf*. London: Heinemann Educational, 1981.

Chapuisat, Edouard. *Necker (1732–1804)*. Paris: Librairie du Receuil Sirey, n.d.

Charles, Rollo. *Continental Porcelain of the Eighteenth Century*. London: Ernest Benn, 1964.

Charleston, Robert J., ed. *World Ceramics: An Illustrated History*. London: P. Hamlyn, [1968].

Chassagne, Serge. "La diffusion rurale de l'industrie cotonnière en France (1750–1850)." *Revue du Nord* 61 (January–March 1979), 97–114.

———. *La manufacture de toiles imprimées de Tournemine-les-Angers (1752–1820)*. Publications de l'Institut Armoricain de Recherches Historiques de Rennes, no. 10. Paris, 1971.

———. *Oberkampf: un entrepreneur capitaliste au siècle des lumières*. Paris: Aubier Montaigne, 1980.

Chaussinard-Nogaret, Guy. *Les financiers de Languedoc au XVIIIe siècle*. Paris: S.E.V.P.E.N., 1970.

———. *Une histoire des élites 1700–1848: recueil de textes présentés et commentés*. Paris and La Haye: Mouton, 1975.

Chevalier, Jean. *Le Creusot, berceau de la grande industrie française*. Paris: Dunod, 1935.

———. "La mission de Gabriel Jars dans les mines et usines britanniques en 1764." *Transactions of the Newcomen Society* 26 (1947–1949), 57–68.

Chinault, Jules. *La Chambre de Commerce de Toulouse du XVIIIe siècle: esquisse historique*. Toulouse: Mémoires de l'Académie de Législation, 1956.

Choulguine, A. "L'organisation capitaliste de l'industrie existait-elle en France à la veille de la Révolution (l'installation et l'entreprise industrielles)?" *Revue d'histoire économique et sociale* 10 (1922), 184–218.

Church, Clive H. *Revolution and Red Tape: The French Ministerial Bureaucracy, 1770–1850*. New York: Oxford University Press, 1981.

———. "The Social Basis of the French Central Bureaucracy under the Directory 1795–1799." *Past and Present*, no. 36 (April 1967), 59–72.

Cilleuls, Alfred des. *Histoire et régime de la grande industrie en France aux XVIIe et XVIIIe siècles*. Paris: V. Giard and E. Brière, 1898.

Clark, John G. *La Rochelle and the Atlantic Economy during the Eighteenth Century*. Baltimore and London: The Johns Hopkins University Press, 1981.

Clément, Pierre. *Histoire du système protecteur en France depuis le ministère de Colbert jusqu'à la Révolution de 1848*. Paris: Guillaumin, 1854.

Clow, Archibald, and Nan L. Clow. *The Chemical Revolution: A Contribution to Social Technology*. London: The Batchworth Press, 1962.

Cole, Arthur H., and George B. Watts. *The Handicrafts of France, as Recorded in the Descriptions des arts et métiers, 1761–1788*. Kress Library of Business and Economics, Publication no. 8. Cambridge, Mass., 1952.

Cole, Charles W. *Colbert and a Century of French Mercantilism*. 2 vols. New York: Columbia University Press, 1939.

———. *French Mercantilism 1683–1700*. New York: Columbia University Press, 1943.

Coleby, Leslie James Moger. *The Chemical Studies of P. J. Macquer*. London: G. Allen & Unwin, 1938.

Conant, James Bryant, ed. *Harvard Case Histories in Experimental Science*, 1, case 2, *The Overthrow of the Phlogiston Theory: The Chemical Revolution of 1775–1789*. Cambridge: Harvard University Press, 1957.

Conturié, P. M. J. *Histoire de la Fonderie Nationale de Ruelle (1750–1940) et des anciennes fonderies de canons de fer de la marine*. 2 vols. Paris: Imprimerie Nationale, 1951.

Coornaert, Emile. *Un centre industriel d'autrefois: la draperie-sayetterie d'Hondschoote (XIV–XVIIIe siècles)*. Paris: Presses Universitaires de France, 1930.

———. *Les compagnonnages en France du moyen âge à nos jours*. Paris: Les Editions Ouvrières, 1966.

———. *Les corporations en France avant 1789*. 3rd ed. Paris: Gallimard, 1941.

Coulaudon, A. *Chazerat, dernier intendant de la généralité de Riom et province d'Auvergne, 1774–1789*. Thèse pour le doctorat, la Faculté de Droit de l'Université de Poitiers. Paris: Jouve, 1932.

Courtecuisse, Maximilien. *La manufacture de draps fins, Vanrobais aux XVIIe et XVIIIe siècles*. Paris: A. Picard, 1920.

Courthéoux, Jean-Paul. "Observations et idées économiques de Réaumur." *Revue d'histoire économique et sociale* 35 (1957), 347–369.

Cox, Warren E. *The Book of Pottery and Porcelain*. 2 vols. New York: Crown, 1944.

Crafts, N. F. R. "Industrial Revolution in England and France: Some Thoughts on the Question 'Why Was England First?'" *Economic History Review*, ser. 2, 30 (1977), 429–441.

Croix, Charles. "Claude-Michel Faussabry, subdélégué de l'intendant de Hainaut 1722–1783." *Mémoires de la Société Archéologique et Historique de l'Arrondissement d'Avesnes* 19 (1955), 47–60.

Crosland, M. P. "Jean Antoine Chaptal." *Dictionary of Scientific Biography* 3:198–203. Edited by Charles Coulston Gillispie. New York: Charles Scribner's Sons, 1971.

Crouzet, François. "Angleterre et France au XVIIIe siècle: essai d'analyse comparée de deux croissances économiques." *Annales: économies, sociétés, civilisations* 21 (1966), 254–291.

———. *De la supériorité de l'Angleterre sur la France: l'économique et l'imaginaire, XVIIe–XXe siècles*. Paris: Librairie Académique Perrin, 1985.

———. "The Sources of England's Wealth: Some French Views in the Eighteenth Century." In *Shipping, Trade and Commerce: Essays in Memory of Ralph Davis*. Leicester: Leicester University Press, 1981.

Crozier, Michel. *Petits fonctionnaires au travail: compte-rendu d'une enquête sociologique effectuée dans une grande administration publique parisienne*. Travaux du Centre d'Etudes Sociologiques. Paris: Centre National de la Recherche Scientifique, 1955.

———. *Le phenomène bureaucratique: essai sur les tendances bureaucratiques des systèmes d'organisation modernes et sur leurs relations en France avec le système social et culturel*. Paris: Editions de Seuil, 1963.

Dagnaud, G. *L'administration centrale de la marine sous l'Ancien Régime*. Nancy and Paris, 1913.

Dakin, Douglas. *Turgot and the Ancien Régime in France*. London: Methuen, 1939.

Dalby, Michael T., and Michael S. Werthman. *Bureaucracy in Historical Perspective*. Glenview, Ill.: Scott Foresman, 1971.

Dardel, Pierre. *Commerce, industrie et navigation à Rouen et au Havre au XVIIIe siècle*. Fécamp: L. Durand, 1966.

———. *Les manufactures de toiles peintes et serges imprimées à Rouen et à Bolbec aux XVIIe et XVIIIe siècles*. Rouen: Fayard, 1940.

———. *Navires et marchandises dans les ports de Rouen et du Havre au XVIIIe siècle*. Paris: S.E.V.P.E.N., 1963.

Darnton, Robert. "In Search of the Enlightenment: Recent Attempts to Create a Social History of Ideas." *Journal of Modern History* 43 (1971), 113–132.

———. *The Great Cat Massacre and Other Episodes in French Cultural History*. New York: Basic Books, 1984.

Dartigue-Peyrou, Charles. *Dupré de Saint-Maur et le problème des corvées: le conflit entre l'intendant de Guyenne et le parlement de Bordeaux, 1776–1785*. Mont-de-Marsan: Editions J. Lacoste, 1936.

Daumas, Maurice. *L'archéologie industrielle en France*. Paris: R. Laffont, 1980.

———. *Les instruments scientifiques aux XVIIe et XVIIIe siècles*. Paris: Presses Universitaires de France, 1953.

———. *Lavoisier, théoricien et expérimentateur*. Paris: Presses Universitaires de France, 1955.

Dauterman, Carl Christian. *Sèvres*. London: Studio Vista, 1969.

Daviet, Jean-Pierre. "Saint-Gobain et l'industrie de la glace: l'innovation dans un vieux secteur." *Histoire économique et sociale* 2 (1987), 235–262.

Degros, M. "L'administration des consulats sous la Révolution (1789–1799)." *Revue d'histoire diplomatique* 96 (1982), 68–111.

Delmaire, B., A. Derville, and Louis Trénard. "Recherches, travaux, et publications en histoire régionale, 1969–1973." *Revue du Nord* 57 (1975), 195–220.

Delorme, Suzanne. "Une famille de grands commis de l'état: les Trudaine." *Revue d'histoire des sciences* 3 (1950), 101–109.

Delsalle, Paul. "Les entreprises textiles de Tourcoing (XVIIe–XXe siècle)." *Revue du Nord* 69 (October–December 1987), 751–766.

Depitre, Edgard. "Les prêts au commerce et aux manufactures de 1740 et 1789." *Revue d'histoire économique et sociale* 7 (1914–1919), 196–217.

———. *La toile peinte en France au XVIIe et au XVIIIe siècles: industrie; commerce; prohibitions*. Paris: Librairie des Sciences Politiques et Sociales, 1912.

Depors, H. *Recherches sur l'état de l'industrie des cuirs en France pendant le XVIIIe siècle et le début du XIXe siècle*. Paris: Imprimerie Nationale, 1932.

Déroche, Henri. *Les mythes administratifs: essai de sociologie phénoménologique*. Paris: Presses Universitaires de France, 1966.

Devèze, Michel. "La crise forestière en France dans la première moitié du XVIIIe siècle et les suggestions de Vauban, Réaumur, Buffon." In *Actes du quatre-vingt-huitième Congrès National des Sociétés Savantes: Clermont-Ferrand, 1963)*, pp. 595–616. Paris: Imprimerie Nationale, 1964.

———. "Les forêts françaises à la veille de la Révolution de 1789." *Revue d'histoire moderne et contemporaine* 13 (1966), 241–272.

Devos, Jean-Claude. "Le Secrétariat d'Etat à la Guerre et ses bureaux." *Revue historique des armées* 162 (March 1986), 88–98.

Dewerpe, Mann, and Yves Gaulupeau. *La fabrique des prolétaires: les ouvriers de la manufacture d'Oberkampf à Jouy-en-Josas, 1760–1815*. Paris: Presses de l'Ecole Normale Supérieure, 1990.

Deyon, Pierre. *Histoire de la Picardie*. Toulouse, 1974.

———. "Le mouvement de la production textile à Amiens au XVIIIe siècle." *Revue du Nord* 44 (1962), 200–211.

———, and Philippe Guignet. "The Royal Manufactures and Economic and Technological Progress in France before the Industrial Revolution." *Journal of European Economic History* 9 (1980), 611–632.

Dickinson, H. W. "History of Vitriol Manufacture in England." *Transactions of the Newcomen Society* 18 (1907–1908).

———. *James Watt: Craftsman and Engineer*. Cambridge: Cambridge University Press, 1936.

———. *Matthew Boulton*. Cambridge: Cambridge University Press, 1937.

———. *A Short History of the Steam Engine*. Cambridge: Cambridge University Press, n.d.

Dine, Henri. *Un intendant de Poitiers sous Louis XVI: Boula de Nanteuil 1746–1816, sa famille, ses amis*. Vol. 1. Paris: by the author, 1962.

Dolléans, Edouard. *Histoire du travail*. 2nd ed. Paris: Les Editions Domat-Montchrestien, 1943.

Donaghay, Marie. "The Transfer of Technology between France and Britain during the Eighteenth Century: Comment." *Proceedings (1984) of the Fourteenth Consortium on Revolutionary Europe*. Athens, Ga.: Consortium on Revolutionary Europe, 1986.

Dornic, François. *L'industrie textile dans le Maine et ses débouchés internationaux (1650–1815)*. Le Mans: Editions Pierre-Belon, 1955.

Doyon, André. "Une société par actions en Dauphiné à la fin du XVIIIe siècle: la Compagnie Royale des Aciers." *Revue d'histoire de la sidérurgie* 5 (1964), 53–70.

———. *Jacques Vaucanson, mécanicien de génie*. Preface by Bertrand Gille. Paris: Presses Universitaires de France, 1966.

———, and Lucien Liaigre. "L'Hôtel de Mortagne après la mort de Vaucanson, 1782–1837." *Histoire des entreprises*, no. 11 (May 1963), 5–35.

Drago, Roland. *Cours de science administrative rédigé d'après les notes et avec l'autorisation de Roland Drago*. Paris: Les cours de la droit, 1968.

Dreyfus, François-Georges. "L'industrie de la verrerie en Bas-Languedoc de Colbert à la révolution industrielle du XIXe siècle." *Annales du Midi* 63 (1951), 43–70.

Duchêne, Albert. *La politique coloniale de la France: le ministère des colonies depuis Richelieu*. Paris: Payot, 1928.

Dumas, F. *La généralité de Tours au XVIIIe siècle: administration de l'intendant Du Cluzel (1766–1783)*. Tours: S. Péricat, 1894.

Durand, Charles. *Les auditeurs au Conseil d'Etat de 1803 à 1814*. Aix-en-Provence: La Pensée Universitaire, 1958.

———. *Etudes sur le Conseil d'Etat napoléonien*. Paris: Presses Universitaires de France, 1949.

———. *Le fonctionnement du Conseil d'Etat napoléonien*. Gap: Imprimerie Louis-Jean, 1954.

Durand, Yves. *Les Fermiers Généraux au XVIIIe siècle*. Paris: Presses Universitaires de France, 1971.

Durouvray, Edmond. "Comment Joly de Fleury devint ministre des finances." *Feuilles d'histoire* 6 (1911), 392–396.

Dutil, Léon. *L'état économique du Languedoc à la fin de l'Ancien Régime (1750–1789)*. Paris: Hachette, 1911.

———. "L'industrie de la soie à Nîmes jusqu'en 1789." *Revue d'histoire moderne* 10 (1908), 318–343.

Egret, Jean. *Necker, ministre de Louis XVI (1776–1790)*. Paris: Honoré Champion, 1975.

Emmanuelli, François-Xavier. *Pouvoir royal et vie régionale en Provence au déclin de la monarchie: psychologie, pratiques administratives, defrancisation de l'intendance d'Aix 1745–1790*. 2 vols. Lille: Service de réproduction des thèses, Université de Lille III, 1974.

Emsley, Clive. "La maréchaussée à la fin de l'Ancien Régime: note sur la composition du corps." *Revue d'histoire moderne et contemporaine* 33 (1986), 622–644.

Engrand, Charles. "Concurrences et complémentarités des villes et des campagnes: les manufactures picardes de 1700 à 1815." *Revue du Nord* 61 (1979), 61–81.

———. "Pauperisme et condition ouvrière dans la seconde moitié du XVIIIe siècle." *Revue d'histoire moderne et contemporaine* 29 (July 1983), 376–410.

Eriksen, Svend, and Geoffrey de Bellaigre. *Sèvres Porcelain: Vincennes and Sèvres, 1740–1800*. Translated by R. J. Charleston. New York: Harper & Row, 1987.

Escoube, Pierre. "Sénac de Meilhan, grand administrateur de l'Ancien Régime." *Revue administrative* 35 (1982), 129–142.

———. "Un Versaillais méconnu: Sénac de Meilhan (1736–1803)." *Revue de l'histoire de Versailles et de Seine-et-Oise* 63 (1978), 15–35.

Esmonin, E. "Les intendants du Dauphiné des origines à la Révolution." *Annales de l'Université de Grenoble* 34 (1923), 37–90.

Faure, E. *La disgrâce de Turgot*. Paris: Gallimard, 1961.

Fayet, Joseph. *La Révolution française et la science 1789–1795*. Paris: M. Rivière, 1960.

Fenaille, Maurice. *Etat-général des tapisseries de la manufacture des Gobelins depuis son origine jusqu'à nos jours, 1600–1900*. 5 vols. Paris: Imprimerie Nationale, Hachette, 1903–23.

Feuer, Lewis S. *The Scientific Intellectual: The Psychological and Sociological Origins of Modern Science*. New York: Basic Books, 1963.

Feuilloley, Paul. "De l'intendant au préfet: une page d'histoire administrative de l'Eure." *Revue administrative* 11 (1958), 467–471.

Forster, Robert. *The House of Saulx-Tavanes, Versailles and Burgundy, 1700–1803*. Baltimore: The Johns Hopkins University Press, 1971.

———. *The Nobility of Toulouse in the Eighteenth Century*. Studies in Historical and Political Science, ser. 78, no. 1. Baltimore: The Johns Hopkins University, 1960.

Fourest, Henry-Pierre. *L'oeuvre des faïenciers français du XVIe à la fin du XVIIIe siècle*. Paris: Librairie Hachette, 1966.

Fournier, Joseph. *La Chambre de Commerce de Marseille et ses représentants à Paris, 1599–1875*. Marseilles: Barlatier, 1910.

Fox-Genovese, Elizabeth. *The Origins of Physiocracy: Economic Revolution and Social Order in Eighteenth-Century France*. Ithaca: Cornell University Press, 1976.

Franklin, Alfred. *Dictionnaire historique des arts, métiers et professions*. Paris: H. Welter, 1906.

Frémy, Elphège. *Histoire de la Manufacture royale des glaces de France au XVIIe et au XVIIIe siècles*. Paris: Plon-Nourrit, 1909.

French, Sidney J. *Torch and Crucible: The Life and Death of Antoine Lavoisier*. Princeton: Princeton University Press, 1941.

Fréville, Henri. *L'intendance de Bretagne (1679–1790): essai sur l'histoire d'une intendance en Pays d'Etats au XVIIIe siècle*. 3 vols. Rennes: Plihon, 1953.

———. "Notes sur les subdélégués généraux et subdélégués de l'intendance de Bretagne au XVIIIe siècle." In *Etudes sur l'histoire administrative et sociale de l'Ancien Régime*, 122–162. Edited by Georges Pagès. Paris: Félix Alcan, 1938.

Garden, Maurice. *Lyon et les lyonnais au XVIIIe siècle*. Paris: Les Belles Lettres, 1970.

Garnault, E. *Le commerce rochelais au XVIIIe siècle, d'après les documents composant les anciennes archives de la Chambre de Commerce de La Rochelle*. 5 vols. La Rochelle: Imprimerie de Veuve Mareschal et E. Martin, 1887–1900.

Garnier, Edouard. *The Soft Porcelain of Sèvres, with an Historical Introduction*. New York: Scribner's, 1891; London: J. C. Nimmo, 1892.

Gayot, Gérard. "Les entrepreneurs au bon temps des privilèges: la Draperie Royale de Sedan au XVIIIe siècle." *Revue du Nord* 67 (1985), 413–445.

———. "La longue insolence des tondeurs de draps dans la manufacture de Sedan au XVIIIe siècle." *Revue du Nord* 63 (1981), 105–134.

Géneau, G. "La législation forestière sous l'Ancien Régime: l'ordonnance de 1669." *Revue des eaux et forêts* 80 (1942), 157–168, 257–269, 344–358, 512–520.

Gide, Charles, and Charles Rist. *Histoire des doctrines économiques*. Vol. 1, *Des physiocrates à J. Stuart Mill*. 7th ed. Paris: Librairie du Recueil Sirey, 1959.

Gille, Bertrand. *Documents sur l'état de l'industrie et du commerce de Paris et du département de la Seine (1778–1810), publiés avec un étude sur les essais d'industrialisation de Paris sous la Révolution et l'Empire*. Paris: Imprimerie Municipale, 1963.

———. "L'enquête sur les bois de 1783." In *Actes du quatre-vingt-huitième Congrès des Sociétés Savantes: Clermont-Ferrand, 1963*, pp. 627–646. Paris: Imprimerie Nationale, 1964.

———. *Les forges françaises en 1772*. Affaires et gens d'affaires, 22. Paris: S.E.V.P.E.N., 1960.

———. *Les origines de la grande industrie métallurgique en France*. Paris: Editions Domat-Montchrestien, 1947.

———. *Les sources statistiques de l'histoire de France: des enquêtes du XVIIe siècle à 1870*. Geneva: Librairie Droz, 1964.

Gillispie, Charles Coulston. "The Discovery of the Leblanc Process." *Isis* 48 (1957), 152–170.

———. *The Edge of Objectivity: An Essay in the History of Scientific Ideas*. Princeton: Princeton University Press, 1960.

———. "The *Encyclopédie* and the Jacobin Philosophy of Science." In *Critical Problems in the History of Science*, edited by Marshall Clagett, 255–289. Madison: University of Wisconsin Press, 1959.

———. *Lazare Carnot Savant: A Monograph Treating Carnot's Scientific Work*. Princeton: Princeton University Press, 1971.

———. "The Liberating Influence of Science in History." In *Aspects of American Liberty, Philosophical, Historical, and Political*. Memoirs of the American Philosophical Society 118 (1977), 37–46.

———. "The Natural History of Industry." *Isis* 48 (1957), 398–407.

———. *Science and Polity in France at the End of the Old Regime*. Princeton: Princeton University Press, 1980.

Gillmor, C. Stewart. *Coulomb and the Evolution of Physics and Engineering in Eighteenth-Century France*. Princeton: Princeton University Press, 1971.

Godechot, Jacques. "La Commission d'Histoire Economique et Sociale de la Révolution française." *Annales historiques de la Révolution française* 55 (July 1984), 314–333.

Goubert, Pierre. *L'Ancien Régime*. Vol. 1, *La société*. Vol. 2, *Les pouvoirs*. Paris: Armand Colin, 1968, 1973.

Gouher, Pierre. *L'intendance de Caen 1636–1789: étude de géographie historique*. Thesis, 3e Cycle Lettres, Caen, 1966.

Gournay, Bernard. *Introduction à la science administrative: les administrations publiques dans les sociétés contemporaines*. Cahiers de la Fondation Nationale des Sciences Politiques, 139. Paris: Armand Colin, 1966. New ed., Paris: Presses de la Fondation Nationale des Sciences Politiques, 1978.

Granger, A. "Essai sur la législation forestière de 1789 à 1827." *Revue des eaux et forêts* 82 (1943), 453ff.

Gras, Louis Joseph. *Essai sur l'histoire de la quincaillerie et petite métallurgie . . . à Saint-Etienne et dans la région stéphanoise comparée aux régions concurrentes*. Saint-Etienne: J. Thomas, 1904.

Grassé, Pierre-P. *La vie et l'oeuvre de Réaumur (1683–1757)*. Paris: Presses Universitaires de France, 1962.

Grémion, Catherine. "Vers une nouvelle théorie de la décision?" *Sociologie de travail* 11 (1969), 463–471.

Gruder, Vivian R. *The Royal Provincial Intendants: A Governing Elite in Eighteenth-Century France*. Ithaca: Cornell University Press, 1968.

Gueneau, Louis. *L'organisation du travail à Nevers aux XVIIe et XVIIIe siècles (1660–1790)*. Paris: Librairie Hachette, 1919.

———. "L'usage industriel de la houille au XVIIIe siècle." In *Mémoires et documents pour servir à l'histoire du commerce et de l'industrie en France*, ser. 8, 321–334. Edited by Julien Hayem. Paris: Hachette, 1924.

Guérin, L. *L'intendant de Cypierre et la vie économique de l'Orléannais 1760–1785*. Mayenne: Imprimerie Floch, 1938.

Guerlac, Henry. *Lavoisier—The Crucial Year: The Background and Origin of His First Experiments on Combustion in 1772*. Ithaca: Cornell University Press, 1961.

———. "Some French Antecedents of the Chemical Revolution." *Chymia* 5 (1959), 73–112.

Guignet, Philippe. "Adaptations, mutations, et survivances proto-industrielles dans le textile du Cambrésis et du Valenciennois du XVIIIe au début du XXe siècle." *Revue du Nord* 61 (1979), 27–60.

———. "L'histoire du travail dans le Valenciennois au XVIIIe siècle." *L'information historique* 39 (1977), 84–87.

———. *Mines, manufactures, et ouvriers du Valenciennois au XVIIIe siècle: contribution à l'histoire du travail dans l'ancienne France*. New York: Arno Press, 1977.

Guillerme, André. "From Lime to Cement: The Industrial Revolution in French Civil Engineering (1770–1850)." *History and Technology* 3, no. 1 (1986), 25–85.

Guimbaud, Louis. *Un grand bourgeois au XVIIIe siècle: Auget de Montyon (1733–1820) d'après des documents inédits*. Paris: Emile-Paul, 1909.

Guitard, E. "L'industrie des draps en Languedoc et ses protecteurs sous l'Ancien Régime." In *Mémoires et documents pour servir à l'histoire du commerce et de l'industrie en France*, ser. 1, 9–34. Edited by J. Hayem. Paris: Hachette, 1911.

Gullickson, Gay. "The Sexual Division of Labor in Cottage Industry and Agriculture in the Pays de Caux Auffay 1750–1850." *French Historical Studies* 12 (Fall 1981), 179–190.

———. *The Spinners and Weavers of Auffay: Rural Industry and Sexual Division of Labor in a French Village*. Cambridge: Cambridge University Press, 1987.

Guttery, D. R. *From Broad-Glass to Cut Crystal: A History of the Stourbridge Glass Industry*. London: Leonard Hill, 1956.

Guttman, Oscar. "The Early Manufacture of Sulphuric Acid and Nitric Acid." *Journal of the Society of Chemical Industry* 20 (1901), 5–7.

Guyonnet, Marie-Claire. *Jacques de Flesselles, intendant de Lyon (1768–1784)*. Lyon: Imprimeries réunies, 1956.

Haber, L. F. *The Chemical Industry during the Nineteenth Century: A Study of the Economic Aspect of Applied Chemistry in Europe and North America*. Oxford: Clarendon Press, 1958.

Hahn, Roger. *The Anatomy of a Scientific Institution: The Paris Academy of Science, 1666–1803*. Berkeley and Los Angeles: University of California Press, 1971.

———. "The Application of Science to Society: The Societies of Arts." *Studies on Voltaire and the Eighteenth Century* 24/27 (1963), 829–836.

———. *L'hydrodynamique au XVIIIe siècle: aspects scientifiques et sociologiques*. Paris: Palais de la Découverte, 1964.

Hamilton, Henry. *The English Brass and Copper Industries to 1800*. London: Longmans, Green, 1926.

Haney, Lewis H. *History of Economic Thought*. 3rd ed. New York: Macmillan, 1936.

Harris, J. R. "Attempts to Transfer English Steel Techniques to France in the Eighteenth Century." In *Business and Businessmen: Studies in Business, Economic and Accounting History Presented to F. E. Hyde*, edited by Sheila Marriner, pp. 199–233. Liverpool: Liverpool University Press, 1978.

———. *The British Iron Industry 1700–1850*. London: Macmillan Educational, 1988.

———. "Copper and Shipping in the Eighteenth Century." *Economic History Review*, ser. 2, 19 (1966), 550–568.

---. *The Copper King: A Biography of Thomas Williams of Llanidan*. Liverpool: Liverpool University Press, 1964.

---. "The Diffusion of English Metallurgical Methods to France in the Eighteenth Century." *French History* 2 (1988), 22–44.

---. *Essays in Industry and Technology in the Eighteenth Century: England and France*. Hampshire: Variorum, 1992.

---. "The First British Measures against Industrial Espionage." In *Industry and Finance in Early Modern History*, edited by I. Blanchard, A. Goodman, and J. Newman, pp. 205–225. Stuttgart: F. Steiner, 1992.

---. "First Thoughts on Files." *Tools and Trades: Journal of the Tool and Trade History Society* 3 (1985), 27–35.

---. *Industry and Technology in the Eighteenth Century: Britain and France*. Printed inaugural lecture, University of Birmingham, 1972.

---. "Michael Alcock and the Transfer of Birmingham Technology to France before the Revolution." *Journal of European Economic History* 15 (1986), 7–58.

---. "Movements of Technology between Britain and Europe in the Eighteenth Century." In *International Technology Transfer: Europe, Japan, and the United States*, edited by D. Jeremy, pp. 9–30. Aldershot: Edward Elgar, 1991.

---. "The Rise of Coal Technology." *Scientific American* 231 (1974), 92–97.

---. "The Rolt Memorial Lecture 1984: Industrial Espionage in the Eighteenth Century." *Industrial Archaeology Review* 7 (1985), 127–138.

---. "Saint-Gobain and Ravenhead." In *Great Britain and Her World 1750–1914: Essays in Honour of W. O. Henderson*, edited by Barrie M. Ratcliffe, pp. 27–70. Manchester: Manchester University Press, 1975.

---. "Skills, Coal and British Industry in the Eighteenth Century." *History* 61 (1976), 167–182.

---. "The Technological Factor in the Transfer of Technology between France and Great Britain during the Eighteenth Century." In *Proceedings (1984) of the Fourteenth Consortium on Revolutionary Europe*, pp. 59–67. Athens, Ga.: Consortium on Revolutionary Europe, 1986.

---. "Technological Transfer between England and France in the Eighteenth Century: The Case of the Hardware Industry." In *History and Sociology of Technology: Proceedings of the 24th Annual Meeting of the Society for the History of Technology*, 287–298. Milwaukee, Wis.: Milwaukee Public Museum, 1981.

---. "The Transfer of Technology between Britain and France and the French Revolution." In *The French Revolution and British Culture*, edited by Ceri Crossley and Ian Small, pp. 156–186. Oxford and New York: Oxford University Press, 1989.

---, and C. Pris. "The Memoirs of Delaunay Deslandes." *Technology and Culture* 17 (1976), 201–216.

Harris, Robert D. *Necker and the Revolution of 1789*. Lanham, Md.: University Press of America, 1986.

---. *Necker: Reform Statesman of the Ancien Régime*. Berkeley and Los Angeles: University of California Press, 1979.

Havard, Henry, and Marius Vachon. *Les Manufactures nationales: les Gobelins, la Savonnerie, Sèvres, Beauvais*. Paris: Georges Decaux, 1889.

Hayem, J. "Les inspecteurs des manufactures et le mémoire de l'inspecteur Tribert sur la généralité d'Orléans." In *Mémoires et documents pour servir à l'histoire du commerce et de l'industrie en France*, ser. 2, 227–286. Edited by J. Hayem. Paris: Hachette, 1912.

———. "Le mémoire de Tribert sur la généralité d'Orléans." In *Mémoires et documents pour servir à l'histoire du commerce et de l'industrie en France*, ser. 1, 2:258ff. Edited by J. Hayem. Paris: Hachette, 1912.

Heady, Ferrell. *Public Administration: A Comparative Perspective*. 3rd ed., rev. New York and Basel: Marcel Dekker, 1984.

Henderson, W. O. *Britain and Industrial Europe 1750–1870: Studies in British Influence on the Industrial Revolution in Western Europe*. 2nd ed. London: Leicester University Press, 1965.

Hunt, Lynn, and George Sheridan. "Corporatism, Association, and the Language of Labor in France, 1750–1850." *Journal of Modern History* 58 (1986), 813–844.

Hunter, Dard. *Papermaking: The History and Technique of an Ancient Craft*. 2nd ed. New York: A. A. Knopf, 1947.

Hutteau d'Origny, Antoine-François, Vicomte de. *Des institutions commerciales en France: histoire du Bureau de Commerce et du Conseil Royal des Finances et du Commerce*. Paris: E. Dentu, 1857.

Isoré, Jacques. "De l'existence des brevets d'invention en droit français avant 1791." *Revue historique du droit français et étranger*, ser. 4, 16 (1937), 94–130.

Jacoby, Henry. *The Bureaucratization of the World*. Translated by Eveline Kanes. Berkeley: University of California Press, 1973.

Jacquemart, Albert, and Edmond Le Blant. *Histoire artistique, industrielle, et commerciale de la porcelaine*. Paris: J. Techner, 1862.

Jarrett, Derek. *The Begetters of Revolution: England's Involvement with France, 1759–1789*. Totowa, N.J.: Rowman and Littlefield, 1973.

John, A. H. "War and the English Economy, 1700–1763." *English Historical Review*, ser. 2, 7 (1955), 329–344.

Jolly, Pierre. *Calonne, 1734–1802*. Paris: Plon, 1949.

———. *Dupont de Nemours, soldat de la liberté*. Paris: Presses Universitaires de France, 1956.

Jones, Phillip S. "Alexandre-Théophile Vandermonde." *Dictionary of Scientific Biography*, 13:571–572. Edited by Charles Coulston Gillispie. New York: Charles Scribner's Sons, 1976.

Jouvencel, Henri de. *Le contrôleur général des finances sous l'Ancien Régime*. Thèse droit. Paris: L. Larose, 1901.

Kaplan, Steven L. "Réflexions sur la police du monde de travail, 1700–1791." *Revue historique* 261 (1979), 17–77.

———, and C. Koepp, eds. *Work in France: Representations, Meaning, Organization and Practice*. Ithaca: Cornell University Press, 1986.

Kaplow, Jeffry. *Elbeuf during the Revolutionary Period: History and Social Structures*. Baltimore: The Johns Hopkins University Press, 1963.

Kessler, Marie-Christine. *Le Conseil d'Etat*. Paris: Armand Colin, 1968.

Kingary, W. D., ed. *Ceramics and Civilization*. Vol. 1, *From Ancient Technology to Modern Science*. Columbus, Oh.: American Ceramic Society, 1985.

Labraque-Bordenave, V. "Histoire des députés de Bordeaux au Conseil de Commerce, au Comité National, et à l'Agence Commerciale à Paris, 1700–1793." *Actes de l'Académie Nationale des Sciences, Arts et Belles-lettres de Bordeaux*, ser. 3, 51 (1889), 277–466.

Labrousse, Camille Ernst. *La crise de l'économie française à la fin de l'Ancien Régime et au début de la Révolution*. Paris: Presses Universitaires de France, 1943.

———. *Esquisse du mouvement des prix et des revenus en France au XVIIIe siècle*. 2 vols. Paris: Librairie Dalloz, 1933; Paris: Editions des Archives Contemporaines, 1984.

———, Pierre Léon, Pierre Goubert, Jean Bouvier, Charles Garrière, and Paul Harsin. *Histoire économique et sociale de la France*. Vol. 2, *Des derniers temps de l'âge seigneurial aux préludes de l'âge industriel, 1660–1789*. Paris: Presses Universitaires de France, 1970.

Lacour-Gayet, Robert. *Calonne: financier, réformateur, contre-révolutionnaire 1734–1802*. Paris: Hachette, 1963.

———. "La première année de Calonne au Contrôle Générale." *Académie des Sciences Morales et Politiques: comptes rendus et revue des travaux* (1962, 2e semestre), 80–93.

Launay, Louis de. *Un grand français: Monge, fondateur de l'Ecole Polytechnique*. Paris: Editions Pierre Roger, 1933.

Lavaquery, E. *Necker: fourrier de la révolution, 1732–1804*. Paris: Librairie Plon, 1933.

Lebrun, François. "Les grandes enquêtes statistiques des XVIIe et XVIIIe siècles sur la généralité de Tours (Maine, Anjou, Touraine)." *Annales de Bretagne* 72 (1965), 338–345.

———. *Histoire des pays de la Loire: Orléanais, Touraine, Anjou, Maine*. Toulouse: Privat, 1972.

———. "Les intendants de Tours et d'Orléans aux XVIIe et XVIIIe siècles." *Annales de Bretagne* 78 (1971), 287–305.

Lebrun, P. *L'industrie de la laine à Verviers pendant le XVIIIe et le début du XIXe siècle: contribution à l'étude des origines de la révolution industrielle*. Liège: Faculté de philosophie et lettres, 1948.

Leet, Don R., and John A. Shaw. "French Economic Stagnation, 1700–1960: Old Economic History Revisited." *Journal of Interdisciplinary History* 8 (1978), 531–544.

Lefebvre, Georges. Review of Frances Acomb, *Anglophobia in France (1763–1789)*. In *Annales historiques de la Révolution française* 29 (1952), 332–336.

LeGrand, Homer E. "Chemistry in a Provincial Context: The Montpellier Société Royale des Sciences in the Eighteenth Century." *Ambix* 29 (1982), 88–105.

———. "The 'Conversion' of C. L. Berthollet to Lavoisier's Chemistry." *Ambix* 22 (1975), 58–69.

———. "Theory and Application: The Early Chemical Work of J. A. C. Chaptal." *British Journal for the History of Science* 17 (1984), 31–46.

Legrand, Louis. *Sénac de Meilhan et l'intendance de Hainaut et du Cambrésis sous Louis XVI*. Valenciennes: J. Giard, 1868.

Le Guin, Charles A. *Roland de la Platière: A Public Servant in the Eighteenth Century*. Transactions of the American Philosophical Society, n.s., 56, part 6. Philadelphia: American Philosophical Society, 1966.

Leicester, Henry M. *The Historical Background of Chemistry*. New York: John Wiley & Sons, 1956.

Lemay, Pierre. "Berthollet et l'emploi du chlore pour le blanchiment des toiles." *Revue d'histoire de la pharmacie* 3 (1932), 79–86.

———, and Ralph Oesper. "Claude-Louis Berthollet." *Journal of Chemical Education* 34 (1946), 158–165, 230–236.

Léon, Antoine. *La Révolution française et l'éducation technique*. Bibliothèque d'histoire révolutionnaire, ser. 3, no. 8. Paris: Société des Etudes Robespierristes, 1968.

Léon, Pierre. *La naissance de la grande industrie en Dauphiné*. 2 vols. Paris: Presses Universitaires de France, [1953].

———. *Les techniques métallurgiques dauphinoises au dix-huitième siècle*. Paris: Hermann, 1961.

———. "Tradition et machinisme dans la France du XVIIIe siècle." *L'information historique* 17 (1955), 5–14.

———, ed. *Papiers d'industriels et de commerçants lyonnais: Lyon et le grand commerce au XVIIIe siècle*. [Lyon]: Centre d'Histoire Economique et Sociale de la Région Lyonnaise, n.d.

Lepetit, Bernard. *Chemins de terre et voies d'eau: réseaux de transports et organization de l'espace en France 1740–1840*. Paris: Ecole des Hautes Etudes en Sciences Sociales, 1984.

Leroux, André. "Les industries textiles dans la Bourgogne d'Ancien Régime." *Annales de Bourgogne* 43 (1971), 5–33.

Levasseur, Emile. *Histoire des classes ouvrières et de l'industrie en France avant 1789*. 2nd ed. 2 vols. Paris: Arthur Rousseau, 1901.

Levin, A. "Venel, Lavoisier, Fourcroy, and the Idea of Scientific Revolution: The French Political Context and the Central Pattern of Conceptualization of Scientific Change." *History of Science* 22 (1984), 303–320.

Lévy-Bruhl, Henri. "Une enquête sur le régime des entreprises en 1761: liberté ou monopole?" *Revue d'histoire économique et sociale* 21 (1933), 140–189.

———. *Un projet de code de commerce à la veille de la révolution: le projet Miromesnil (1778–1789)*. Paris: Imprimerie Nationale, 1932.

Lhéritier, Michel. "Histoire des rapports de la Chambre de Commerce de Bordeaux avec les intendants, le parlement, et les jurats, de 1705 à 1791." *Revue historique de Bordeaux et du département de la Gironde* 5 (1912), 73–104, 192–205, 256–268, 328–345, 400–418; 6 (1913), 56–70, 123–146.

Lhomer, Jean. *Un homme politique lorrain: François de Neufchâteau (1750–1828), d'après des documents inédits*. Paris: Berger-Levrault, 1913.

Linant de Bellefonds, X. "Les techniciens anglais dans l'industrie français au XVIIIe siècle." Thesis, Doctorat en droit, Paris, 1971.

Lintilhac, Eugène. *Figures du passé: Vergniaud, le drame des Girondins*. Paris: Hachette, 1920.

Lipson, Ephraim. *A Short History of Wool and Its Manufacture, Mainly in England*. Cambridge: Harvard University Press, 1953.

Livet, Georges. *Les intendants d'Alsace et leur oeuvre, 1648–1789*. Paris: Belles Lettres, 1948.

Locke, Robert. "French Industrialization: The Roehl Thesis Reconsidered." *Explorations in Economic History* 18 (1981), 415–433.

Logette, Aline. "La régie générale au temps de Necker et de ses successeurs (1777–1786)." *Revue historique de droit français et étranger*, ser. 4, 60 (1982), 415–446.

Logié, P. *Les institutions du commerce à Amiens au XVIIIe siècle*. Amiens: Chez l'auteur, 1951.

Lomuller, Louis Marie. *Guillaume Ternaux, 1763–1833, créateur de la première intégration industrielle français: histoire économique et industrielle de la France de la fin du XVIIIe au début du XIXe siècle*. Paris: Editions de la Cabro d'Or, 1978.

Long, Marceau. "Réflexions sur l'évolution de l'administration français." *Canadian Public Administration/Administration publique du Canada* 24 (1981), 272–294.

Longfellow, David L. "Silk Weavers and the Social Struggle in Lyon during the French Revolution, 1789–1794." *French Historical Studies* 12 (1981), 1–40.

Lopez, Claude-Anne. "Saltpetre, Tin and Gunpowder: Addenda to the Correspondence of Lavoisier and Franklin." *Annals of Science* 16 (1960), 83–94.

Lurion, Roger de. *M. de Lacoré, intendant de Franche-Comté (1761–1784)*. Extract from the *Bulletin de l'Académie des Sciences, Belles-lettres et Arts de Besançon* (1897). Besançon, 1898.

Lutfalla, Michael. "Necker, ou la révolte de l'économie politique circonstancielle contre le despotisme des maximes générales." *Revue d'histoire économique et sociale* 51 (1973), 578–586.

Lüthy, Herbert. *La Banque Protestante en France, de la révocation de l'Edit de Nantes à la Révolution*. 2 vols. Paris: S.E.V.P.E.N., 1959–1961.

Lynch, K. A. "French Historical Demography: Theory and Practice." *Journal of Family History* 11 (1986), 303–309.

McCann, H. Gilman. *Chemistry Transformed: The Paradigmatic Shift from Phlogiston to Oxygen*. Norwood, N.J.: Ablex, 1978.

McClellan, James E., III. "The Académie Royale des Sciences, 1699–1793: A Statistical Portrait." *Isis* 72 (1981), 541–567.

McCloy, Shelby. *French Inventions of the Eighteenth Century*. Lexington: University of Kentucky Press, 1952.

Mandrou, R. *La France aux XVIIe et XVIIIe siècles*. Paris: Presses Universitaires de France, 1967.

Marczewski, J. "Some Aspects of the Economic Growth of France, 1660–1958." *Economic Development and Cultural Change* 9 (1961), 369–386.

Marion, Marcel. *Dictionnaire des institutions de la France aux XVIIe et XVIIIe siècles*. Paris: Auguste Picard, 1923.

———. *Histoire financière de la France depuis 1715*. 6 vols. Paris: A. Rousseau, 1914–1931.

Markovitch, Tihomir. "La croissance industrielle sous l'Ancien Régime." *Annales: économies, sociétés, civilisations* 31 (1976), 644–655.

———. "L'évolution industrielle de la France au XVIIIe siècle." *Revue d'histoire économique et sociale* 53 (1975), 266–288.

———. *Histoire des industries françaises*. Vol. 1, *Les industries lainières de Colbert à la Révolution*. Geneva: Librairie Droz, 1976.

———. "La Révolution industrielle: le cas de la France." *Revue d'histoire économique et sociale* 52 (1974), 115–125.

———. "Le triple tricentenaire de Colbert: l'enquête, les règlements, les inspecteurs." *Revue d'histoire économique et sociale* 49 (1971), 305–324.

Martin, Daniel W. "Déjà vu: French Antecedents of American Public Administration." *Public Administration Revue* 47 (July–August 1987), 297–303.

Martin, Germain. *Les associations ouvrières au XVIIIe siècle*. Paris: A. Rousseau, 1900.

———. *La grande industrie en France sous le règne de Louis XV*. Paris: Fontemoing, 1900.

———. *L'industrie et le commerce du Velay aux XVIIe et XVIIIe siècles*. Le Puy: Imprimerie Régis Marchessou, 1900.

———. *Le tissage du ruban à domicile dans les campagnes du Velay*. Etudes historiques et économiques sur le Velay, fasc. no. 1. Paris: Librairie de la Société du Recueil Sirey, 1913.

Masson, Frédéric. *Le Département des Affaires Etrangères pendant la Révolution*. Paris: E. Plon, 1877.

Masson, Paul. *Histoire du commerce français du Levant au XVIIIe siècle*. Paris: Hachette, 1911.

Mathias, Peter. *The First Industrial Nation: An Economic History of Britain 1700–1914*. New York: Charles Scribner's Sons, 1969.

———. "Skills and the Diffusion of Innovations from Britain in the Eighteenth Century." *Transactions of the Royal Historical Society*, ser. 5, 25 (1975), 93–113.

———, ed. *Science and Society 1600–1900*. Cambridge: Cambridge University Press, 1972.

———, and Patrick O'Brien. "Taxation in Britain and France, 1715–1810: A Comparison of the Social and Economic Incidence of Taxes Collected for the Central Government." *Journal of European Economic History* 5 (1976), 601–650.

Mathieu, Georges. "Notes sur l'industrie du Bas-Limousin dans la seconde moitié du XVIIIe siècle." In *Mémoires et documents pour servir à l'histoire du commerce et de l'industrie en France*, ser. 1, 35–72. Paris: Hachette, 1911.

Matthews, George T. *The Royal General Farms in Eighteenth-Century France*. New York: Columbia University Press, 1958.

May, Gita. *Madame Roland and the Age of Revolution*. New York and London: Columbia University Press, 1970.

Melhado, Evan M. "Oxygen, Phlogiston, and Caloric: The Case of Guyton." *Historical Studies in the Physical Sciences* 13 (1983), 311–334.

Merton, Robert K. "Science, Technology and Society in Seventeenth-Century England." *Osiris* 4 (1938), 360–632.

———, Ailsa P. Tray, Barbara Hockey, and Hanan C. Selvin, eds. *Reader in Bureaucracy*. Glencoe, Ill.: The Free Press, 1952.

Metzger, H. *Les doctrines chimiques en France, au début du XVIIe siècle à la fin du XVIIIe siècle*. 2nd ed. Paris: Librairie Scientifique et Technique Albert Blanchard, 1969.

Meyerson, Emile. *De l'explication dans les sciences*. Paris: Payot, 1927.

Miller, James Grier. *Living Systems*. New York: McGraw-Hill, 1978.

Ministère de l'Instruction Publique et des Beaux-arts. Archives Nationales. *Inventaire analytique des procès-verbaux du Conseil de Commerce et Bureau de Commerce, 1790–1791*. By Pierre Bonnassieux. Introduction and table by Eugène Lelong. Paris: Imprimerie Nationale, 1900.

Molinier, Alain. *Stagnations et croissance: le Vivarais aux XVIIe–XVIIIe siècles*. Paris: Ecole des Hautes Etudes en Sciences Sociales, 1985.

Morineau, Michel. "L'alimentation en Europe du XIVe au XVIIIe siècle." *Revue d'histoire économique et sociale* 54 (1976), 258–265.

———. "Budgets populaires en France au XVIIIe siècle." *Revue d'histoire économique et sociale* 50 (1972), 449–481.

———, and Charles Carrière. "Draps de Languedoc et commerce du Levant au XVIIIe siècle." *Revue d'histoire économique et sociale* 46 (1968), 108–121.

Mosser, Françoise. *Les intendants des finances au XVIIIe siècle: les Lefèvre d'Ormesson et le Département des Impositions, 1715–1777*. Geneva: Droz, 1978.

Mourlot, Félix. *La fin de l'Ancien Régime et les débuts de la Révolution dans la généralité de Caen (1787–1790)*. Paris: Au siège de la Société, 1913.

———. "Les quatre derniers intendants de la généralité de Caen: Fontette, Esmangard, Feydeau de Brou (1783–1787), Coudrès de Launay." *Congrès des Sociétés Savantes*, session of 6 April 1904. *Journal Officiel*, April 1904, 2183.

Mousnier, Roland. *Le Conseil du Roi, de Louis XII à la Révolution*. 1st ed. Paris: Presses Universitaires de France, 1970.

———. "La fonction publique en France du début du seizième à la fin du dix-huitième siècle." *Revue historique* 261 (1979), 323–335.

———. *The Institutions of France under the Absolute Monarchy, 1598–1789: Society and State*. Translated by Brian Pearce. Chicago: University of Chicago Press, 1979.

———. *La plume, la faucille et le marteau: institutions en France du moyen âge à la Révolution*. Paris: Presses Universitaires de France, 1970.

———. *Progrès scientifique et technique au XVIIIe siècle*. Paris: Librairie Plon, 1958.

Multhauf, Robert P. "The French Crash Program for Saltpeter Production, 1776–1794." *Technology and Culture* 12 (1971), 163–181.

Murphy, Antoine. "Le développement des idées économiques en France (1750–1756)." *Revue d'histoire moderne et contemporaine* 33 (1986), 521–541.

Musson, Albert Edward, ed. *Science, Technology, and Economic Growth in the Eighteenth Century*. London: Methuen, 1972.

———, and Eric Robinson. "Science and Industry in the Late Eighteenth Century." *Economic History Review* 13 (1960–61), 222–244.

———. *Science and Technology in the Industrial Revolution*. Toronto: University of Toronto Press, 1969.

Néraud, J. *Les intendants de la généralité de Berry*. Thèse pour le doctorat, la Faculté de Droit de l'Université de Paris. Paris: Editions de la Vie Universitaire, 1922.

Neville, Roy G. "'Observations sur la mine de fer de Bagory,' (1767), an unpublished manuscript by P.-J. Macquer." *Chymia* 8 (1962), 89–96.

Nigeon, R. *Etat financier des corporations parisiennes d'arts et métiers au XVIIIe siècle*. Paris: Les Editions Rieder, 1934.

O'Brien, Patrick, and Caglar Keyder. *Economic Growth in Britain and France 1780–1914: Two Paths to the Twentieth Century*. London: Allen & Unwin, 1978.

Oesper, Ralph E. "Priestley, Lavoisier, and Trudaine de Montigny." *Journal of Chemical Education* 13 (1936), 403–412.

Olivier-Martin, François. *L'organisation corporative de l'Ancien Régime*. Paris: Sirey, 1938.

"Ormesson d'Amboile (Henri-François de Paule Lefèvre d')." *Biographie universelle*, 6:306–307. Paris: J. LeRoux, 1849.

Ozanam, Denise. *Claude Baudard de Sainte-James, trésorier général de la Marine et Bureau d'affaires (1738–1787)*. Geneva: Librairie Droz, 1969.

———. "La naissance du Creusot." *Revue d'histoire de la sidérurgie* 4 (1963), 103–118.

Pagès, Georges. *La monarchie d'Ancien Régime en France (de Henri IV à Louis XIV)*. Paris: A. Colin, 1928.

———. "Quelques réflexions sur la centralisation administrative dans l'ancienne France." *Bulletin de la Société d'Histoire Moderne* (1935), 105ff.

———, ed. *Etudes sur l'histoire administrative et sociale de l'Ancien Régime*. Paris: Librairie Félix Alcan, 1938.

Palanque, M. "Le dernier intendant de la généralité d'Auch: Claude-François Bertrand de Boucheporn (1741–1794)." *Bulletin de la Société des Sciences, Lettres et Arts de Pau*, ser. 2, 36 (1908), 272–278.

Paris, Robert. *Histoire de commerce de Marseille*. Vol. 5, *De 1660 à 1789*. Paris: Parlevant, 1975.

Pariset, Ernest. "La Chambre de Commerce de Lyon au dix-huitième siècle: étude faite sur les registres de ses délibérations." *Mémoires de l'Académie des Sciences, Belles-lettres, et Arts de Lyon*, n.s. 24 (1887), 1–177.

———. *Histoire de la fabrique lyonnaise: étude sur le régime social et économique de l'industrie de la soie à Lyon, depuis le XVIe siècle*. Lyon: A. Rey, 1901.

Park, Joseph H., and Esther Glouberman. "The Importance of Chemical Developments in the Textile Industries during the Industrial Revolution." *Journal of Chemical Education* 9 (1932), 1143–1170.

Parker, Harold T. *The Bureau of Commerce in 1781 and Its Policies with Respect to French Industry*. Durham, N.C.: Carolina Academic Press, 1979.

———. "French Administrators and French Scientists during the Old Regime and the Early Years of the Revolution." In *Ideas in History*, edited by Richard Herr and Harold T. Parker, pp. 85–109. Durham: Duke University Press, 1965.

———. "The Transfer of Technology between France and Britain during the Eighteenth Century: Administrative Activity." In *Proceedings (1984) of the Fourteenth Consortium on Revolutionary Europe*, pp. 45–58. Athens, Ga.: Consortium on Revolutionary Europe, 1986.

———. "Two Administrative Bureaus under the Directory and Napoleon." *French Historical Studies* 4 (1965), 150–169.

Partington, James Riddick. *Origins and Development of Applied Chemistry*. London and New York: Longmans, Green, 1935. Reprinted New York: Arno Press, 1975.

Passet, René. *L'industrie dans la généralité de Bordeaux sous l'intendant Tourny: contribution à l'étude de la décadence du système corporatif au milieu du XVIIIe siècle*. Bordeaux: Editions Bière, 1954.

Patault, A. M. "Les origines révolutionnaires de la fonction publique: de l'employé au fonctionnaire." *Revue historique du droit français et étranger* 64 (1986), 389–405.

Payan, Régis. *L'évolution d'un monopole: l'industrie des poudres avant la loi du 13 fructidor An V*. Paris: Les Editions Domat-Mont-Chrestien, F. Loviton & Cie, 1935.

Payen, Jacques. *Capital et machine à vapeur au XVIIIe siècle: les frères Perier et l'introduction en France de la machine à vapeur de Watt*. Paris: Mouton, 1969.

Perez, Liliane. "Invention politique et société en France dans la deuxième moitié du XVIIIe siècle." *Revue d'histoire modern et contemporaine* 37 (1990), 36–63.

Perrin, Carleton E. "Lost Identity: Philippe Frédéric, Baron de Dietrich (1748–1793)." *Isis* 73 (1982), 545–550.

———. "Of Theory Shifts and Industrial Innovations: The Relations of J. A. C. Chaptal and A. L. Lavoisier." *Annals of Science* 43 (1986), 511–542.

———. "Research Traditions, Lavoisier, and the Chemical Revolution." *Osiris* 4 (1988), 53–81.

Perrot, Jean Claude. *Genèse d'une ville moderne: Caen au XVIIIe siècle*. 2 vols. [Thesis, University of Paris, 1974.] Université de Lille III, Service de reproduction des thèses, 1974. Also Ecole des Hautes Etudes en Sciences Sociales, Centre de Recherches Historiques, Civilisations et sociétés, 44. Paris and La Haye: Mouton, 1975.

———. "Recherches sur l'analyse de l'économie urbaine au XVIIIe siècle." *Revue d'histoire économique et sociale* 52 (1974), 350–383.

Petot, Jean. *Histoire de l'administration des ponts et chaussées 1599–1815*. Paris: Marcel Rivière, 1958.

Piccioni, Camille-Vincent. *Les premiers commis des affaires étrangères au XVIIe et au XVIIIe siècles*. Paris: E. de Broccard, 1928.

Pigeire, Jean. *La vie et l'oeuvre de Chaptal, 1756–1832.* Paris: Editions Spès, 1932.

Piquard, M. "Charles-André de Lacoré, intendant de Franche-Comté 1761–1784." *Annales littéraires du Franche Comté* 1 (1946), 7–29.

Place, Dominique de. "Le sort des Ateliers de Vaucanson (1783–1791) d'après un document nouveau." *History and Technology* 1 (1983–84), 79–100, 213–237.

Planel-Arnoux, J. "Premières recherches sur l'administration d'Esmangart, intendant de la généralité de Caen 1775–1783." *Revue historique du droit français et étranger*, ser. 4, 45 (1967), 390–392.

Poussou, Jean Pierre. *Bordeaux et le sud-ouest au XVIIIe siècle: croissance économique et attraction urbaine.* Paris: Ecole des Hautes Etudes en Sciences Sociales; and Jean Touzot, libraire-éditeur, 1983.

Prévost de Levaud, Etienne. *Les théories d'intendant Rouillé d'Orfeuil.* Thèse pour le doctorat, la Faculté de Droit de l'Université de Poitiers. Rouchechouart: Imp. Dupanier Frères, 1909.

Price, Thomas J. "Behavior Modes: Toward a Theory of Decision-Making." *Journal of Politics* 37 (1975), 417–435.

Pris, Claude. "La glace en France au XVIIe et XVIIIe siècles: monopole et liberté d'entreprise dans une industrie de pointe sous l'Ancien Régime." *Revue d'histoire économique et sociale* 55 (1977), 5–23.

———. "La manufacture des glaces de Saint-Gobain avant la révolution industrielle." *Revue d'histoire économique et sociale* 52 (1974), 161–172.

———. *La manufacture royale des glaces de Saint-Gobain: une grande entreprise sous l'Ancien Régime (1665–1830).* 3 vols. Lille: Service de reproduction des thèses, 1975.

Prosser, R. B. *Birmingham Inventors and Inventions.* Wakefield: S. R. Publishers, 1970.

Proust, Jacques. *Diderot et l'Encyclopédie.* Paris: Armand Colin, 1962.

Quénet, Maurice. "Un exemple de consultation dans l'administration monarchique au XVIIIe siècle: les Nantais et leurs députés au Conseil de Commerce." *Annales de Bretagne et des Pays de l'Ouest* 85 (1978), 449–485.

Rackham, Bernard. *A Key to Pottery and Glass.* London and Glasgow: Blackie & Son, 1940.

Raeff, Marc. "The Well-Ordered Police State and the Development of Modernity in Seventeenth- and Eighteenth-Century Europe: An Attempt at a Comparative Approach." *American Historical Review* 80 (1975), 1221–1243.

Rappaport, Rhoda. "G.-F. Rouelle: An Eighteenth-Century Chemist and Teacher." *Chymia* 6 (1960), 68–101.

———. "Government Patronage of Science in Eighteenth-Century France." *History of Science* 8 (1969), 119–136.

———. "Rouelle and Stahl—the Phlogistic Revolution in France." *Chymia* 7 (1961), 73–102.

Reddy, William M. "Organizing Knowledge: The Indirect Impact of the Guilds on Technological Progress in French Textiles, 1750–1789." In *Proceedings (1984) of the Fourteenth Consortium on Revolutionary Europe*, pp. 69–80. Athens, Ga.: Consortium on Revolutionary Europe, 1986.

———. *The Rise of Market Culture: The Textile Trade and French Society, 1750–1900.* London: Cambridge University Press, 1984.

———. "The Spinning Jenny in France: Popular Complaints and Elite Misconceptions on the Eve of the Revolution." In *Proceedings (1981) of the Eleventh Consortium on Revo-*

lutionary Europe, 1750–1850, pp. 51–62. Athens, Ga.: Consortium on Revolutionary Europe, 1981.

———. "The Textile Trade and the Language of the Crowd at Rouen 1752–1871." *Past and Present* 74 (February 1977), 62–89.

Reinhard, Marcel. *Le grand Carnot*. 2 vols. Paris: Hachette, 1950–1952.

Rémond, André. *John Holker: manufacturier et grand fonctionnaire en France au XVIIIe siècle 1719–1786*. Paris: Marcel Rivière, 1946.

Renard, Georges F., and G. Weulersee. *Le travail dans l'Europe moderne*. Paris: F. Alcan, 1920.

Richard, Guy. "De la sidérurgie à la métallurgie de transformation: l'entreprise de Dietrich de Niederbronn de 1685 à 1939." In *Actes du 18e Congrès des Sociétés Savantes (Clermont-Ferrand 1963), section d'histoire moderne et contemporaine*, pp. 505–525. Paris: Imprimerie Nationale, 1964.

———. "Les fonderies de Romilly-sur-Andelle et les débuts de la métallurgie non ferreuse en Haute-Normandie (1782–1850)." In *Actes du 24e Congrès National des Sociétés Savantes (Clermont-Ferrand 1963), section d'histoire moderne et contemporaine*, pp. 451–455. Paris: Imprimerie Nationale, 1964.

———. "La grande métallurgie en Basse-Normandie à la fin du XVIIIe siècle." *Annales de Normandie* 13 (1963), 165–176.

———. "La grande métallurgie en Haute-Normandie à la fin du XVIIIe siècle." *Annales de Normandie* 12 (1962), 263–289.

———. *Noblesse d'affaires au XVIIIe siècle*. Paris: A. Colin, 1974.

Richard, Jules-Marie. *La vie privée dans une province de l'ouest: Laval aux XVIIe et XVIIIe siècles*. Paris: E. Champion, 1922.

Ricommard, Julien. "Les subdélégués des intendants aux XVIIe et XVIIIe siècles." *L'information historique* 4 (1962), 139–148; 5, 190–195; 1 (1963), 1–7.

Rignault, Bernard. "Les forges de Buffon." *Mémoires de la Commission des antiquités du département de la Côte-d'Or* 27 (1970–71), 209–225.

Robinson, Eric. "International Exchange of Men and Machines, 1750–1800, as Seen in the Business Records of Matthew Boulton." *Business History* 1 (1958), 3–15.

———, and Douglas McKie, eds. *Partners in Science: Letters of James Watt and Joseph Black*. Cambridge: Harvard University Press, 1970.

Roche, Daniel. *Le siècle des lumières en province: académies et académiciens provinciaux, 1680–1789*. 2 vols. Paris and The Hague: Mouton, 1978.

Roehl, R. "French Industrialization: A Reconsideration." *Explorations in Economic History* 13 (1976), 233–281.

———. "L'industrialisation française: une remise en cause." *Revue d'histoire économique et sociale* 54 (1976), 406–427.

Roig, Charles. "Théorie et réalité de la décentralisation." *Revue française de science politique* 16 (1966), 445–471.

Rosenau, James N. *The Scientific Study of Foreign Policy*. New York: Nichols, 1980.

Rosenbrand, Leonard N. "Productivity and Labor Discipline in the Montgolfier Paper Mill, 1780–1805." *Journal of Economic History* 45 (1985), 435–444.

Rosselle, Dominique. "La situation des industries textiles du Pas-de-Calais sous l'Ancien Régime et au début du XIXe siècle: première approche." *Revue du Nord* 69 (October–December 1987), 737–750.

Rotours, J. A. des. "Le dernier intendant de la généralité d'Alençon." *Bulletin de la Société Historique et Archéologique de l'Orne* 12 (1893), 503–521.

Rouff, Marcel. *Les mines de charbon en France au XVIIIe siècle, 1744–1791: étude d'histoire économique et sociale*. Paris: F. Rieder, 1922.

Rozy, Henri. *La Chambre de Commerce de Toulouse au XVIIIe siècle: esquisse historique*. Toulouse: Armaing, 1879.

Rudd, Jon D. "A Perception of Hierarchy in Eighteenth-Century France: An Epistolary Etiquette Manual for the Controller General of Finances." *French Historical Studies* 17 (1992), 791–801.

Sadoun-Goupil, Michelle. *Le chimiste Claude-Louis Berthollet, 1784–1822: sa vie, son oeuvre*. Paris: J. Vrin, 1977.

———. "Science pure et science appliquée dans l'oeuvre de Claude-Louis Berthollet." *Revue d'histoire des sciences* 27 (1974), 127–145.

Sagnac, Philippe. *La formation de la société française moderne*. 2 vols. Paris: Presses Universitaires de France, 1945–1946.

Samoyault, M. J.-P. *Les bureaux du Secrétariat d'Etat aux Affaires Etrangères sous Louis XV*. Paris: A. Pedone, 1971.

Saricks, Ambrose. *Pierre Samuel Du Pont de Nemours*. Lawrence: University of Kansas Press, 1965.

Schaeper, Thomas J. *The French Council of Commerce, 1700–1715: A Study of Mercantilism after Colbert*. Columbus: Ohio State University Press, 1983.

Schelle, G[ustave]. *Le Docteur Quesnay*. Paris: Félix Alcan, 1907.

———. *Turgot*. Paris: Félix Alcan, 1909.

———. *Vincent de Gournay*. Paris: Guillaumin, 1897.

Schlechte, Klaus-Dieter. "Vom Reformer zum Konterrevolutionar: zur Tätigkeit Charles Alexander de Calonne 1783 bis 1790." *Zeitschrift für Geschichtswissenschaft* 26 (1978), 1084–1098.

Schmidt, Charles. "Les débuts de l'industrie cotonnière en France 1760–1806." *Revue d'histoire économique et sociale* 6 (1913), 261–295; 7 (1914), 26–55.

Schnakenbourg, C. *Communautés de métiers contre liberté économique à la fin de l'Ancien Régime*. Paris: Presses Universitaires de France, 1976.

Schofield, Robert E. *The Lunar Society of Birmingham: A Social History of Provincial Science and Industry in Eighteenth-Century England*. Oxford: Clarendon Press, 1963.

Scoville, Warren C. *Capitalism and French Glassmaking, 1640–1789*. Berkeley and Los Angeles: University of California Press, 1950.

Sédillot, René. *Deux cent cinquante ans d'industrie en Lorraine: la Maison de Wendel de 1784 à nos jours*. Paris: Riss, 1958.

Sée, Henri. *Histoire économique de la France*. Edited by Robert Schnerb. 2 vols. Paris: Armand Colin, 1939–1942.

———. "Origines de l'industrie capitaliste en France à la fin de l'Ancien Régime." *Revue historique* 144 (1923), 187–200.

———. "Remarques sur la caractère de l'industrie rurale en France et les causes de son extension au XVIIIe siècle." *Revue historique* 142 (1923), 47–53.

Sewell, William H., Jr. *Work and Revolution: The Language of Labor in France from the Old Regime to 1848*. London: Cambridge University Press, 1980.

Shinn, Terry. *L'Ecole Polytechnique: 1794–1914*. Paris: Presses de la Fondation Nationale des Sciences Politiques, 1980.

Simon, Herbert Alexander. *Administrative Behavior: A Study of Decision-Making Processes in Administrative Organisations*. 2nd ed. New York: Macmillan, 1945.

———, Donald W. Smithburg, and Victor A. Thompson. *Public Administration*. New York: Alfred Knopf, 1950.

Singer, Charles, E. J. Holmyard, A. R. Hall, and Trevor L. Williams, eds. *A History of Technology*. Vol. 4, *The Industrial Revolution, c. 1750 to c. 1850*. Oxford: Clarendon Press, 1958.

Smeaton, W. A. "The Contributions of P.-J. Macquer, T. O. Bergman and L. B. Guyton de Morveau to the Reform of Chemical Nomenclature." *Annals of Science* 10 (1954), 87–106.

———. "The Early Years of the Lycée and the Lycée des Arts, I: The Lycée of the rue de Valois." *Annals of Science* 11 (1955), 257–267.

———. "The Early Years of the Lycée and the Lycée des Arts, II: The Lycée des Arts." *Annals of Science* 11 (1955), 309–319.

———. "Fourcroy and the Anti-Phlogiston Theory." *Endeavour* 18 (1959), 70–74.

———. *Fourcroy: Chemist and Revolutionary, 1766–1809*. Cambridge: W. Heffer & Sons, 1962.

———. "Guyton de Morveau and Chemical Affinity." *Ambix* 11 (1963), 55–64.

———. "Guyton de Morveau's Course of Chemistry in the Dijon Academy." *Ambix* 9 (1961), 53–69.

———. "Guyton de Morveau and the Phlogiston Theory." In *Mélanges Alexandre Koyré*, introduction by I. Bernard Cohen and René Taton, 2 vols., 522–540. Paris: Herman, 1964.

———. "L. B. Guyton de Morveau (1737–1816): A Bibliographic Study." *Ambix* 6 (1957), 18–34.

———. "Louis Bernard Guyton de Morveau." *Dictionary of Scientific Biography*, 5:600–604. Edited by Charles Coulston Gillispie. New York: Charles Scribner's Sons, 1972.

———. "Pierre Joseph Macquer." *Dictionary of Scientific Biography*, 8:618–624. Edited by Charles Coulston Gillispie. New York: Charles Scribner's Sons, 1973.

Smith, John Graham. *The Origins and Early Development of the Heavy Chemical Industry in France*. Oxford: Clarendon Press; New York: Oxford University Press, 1979.

Snyder, Richard C., H. W. Brock, and Burton Sapin. *Decision-Making as an Approach to the Study of International Politics*. Princeton: Princeton University, Organizational Behavior Section, 1954.

———, eds. *Foreign Policy Decision-Making: An Approach to the Study of International Politics*. New York: Free Press of Glencoe, 1962.

Sonenscher, Michael. *The Hatters of Eighteenth-Century France*. Berkeley and Los Angeles: University of California Press, 1987.

———. "Journeymen, the Courts, and the French Trades 1781–1791." *Past and Present* 114 (1987), 77–109.

———. *Work and Wages: Natural Law, Politics, and the Eighteenth-Century French Trades*. New York: Cambridge University Press, 1989.

Soudet, Pierre. *L'administration vue par les siens, et par d'autres*. Paris: Berger-Levrault, 1960.

Spurlock, J. "What Price Economic Prosperity: Public Attitudes to Physiocracy in the Reign of Louis XVI." *British Journal of Eighteenth-Century Studies* 9 (1986), 183–196.

Stein, Robert Louis. *The French Sugar Business in the Eighteenth Century*. Baton Rouge: Louisiana State University Press, 1988.

———. "The French Sugar Business in the Eighteenth Century: A Quantitative Study." *Business History* 22 (1980), 3–17.

Surface, George T. *The Story of Sugar*. New York and London: Appleton, 1910.

Tarlé, Eugène. *L'industrie dans les campagnes en France à la fin de l'Ancien Régime*. Paris: E. Cornély, 1910.

Taton, René. *L'oeuvre scientifique de Monge*. Paris: Presses Universitaires de France, 1951.

———, ed. *L'enseignement et diffusion des sciences en France au XVIIIe siècle*. Paris: Hermann, 1964.

———. *Histoire générale des sciences*. Vol. 2, *La science moderne (de 1450 à 1800)*. Paris: Presses Universitaires de France, 1958.

Terson, Henri. *Origines et évolution du Ministère de l'intérieur*. Montpellier: Firmin & Montane, 1913.

Thomson, J. K. J. *Clermont de Lodève, 1633–1789: Fluctuation in the Prosperity of a Languedocian Cloth-Making Town*. New York: Cambridge University Press, 1982.

Thuillier, G. *Témoins de l'administration, de Saint-Just à Marx*. Paris: Berger-Levrault, 1967.

Tinthoin, Robert. "Chaptal créateur de l'industrie chimique de France." In *Fédération Historique de Languedoc Méditerranéen et de Roussillon, XXXme et XXXIme congrès (1956–1957)*, pp. 195–206.

Tocqueville, Alexis Charles Henri Maurice Clérel de. *Oeuvres, papiers et correspondances*. Vol. 2, *L'Ancien Régime et la Révolution*. Edited by J. P. Mayer. Paris: Gallimard, 1952.

Todericiu, Doru. "Balthasar-Georges Sage (1740–1824), chimiste et minéralogiste français fondateur de la première Ecole des Mines (1783)." *Revue d'histoire des sciences* 37 (1984), 29–46.

———. "Chimie appliquée et technologie chimique au milieu du XVIIIe siècle: oeuvre et vie de Jean Hellot, 1685–1766." Doctoral thesis, 3e Cycle, VIe section, 1977, Ecole Pratique des Hautes Etudes, Th 35 II.

Torlais, Jean. *Réaumur: un esprit encyclopédique en dehors de l'Encyclopédie*. Paris: Desclée de Brouwer, 1936.

Trénard, Louis. "La crise sociale lyonnaise à la veille de la Révolution." *Revue d'histoire moderne et contemporaine* 2 (1955), 5–45.

———. *Histoire des Pays-Bas français: Flandre, Artois, Hainaut, Boulonnais, Cambrésis*. Toulouse: Privat, 1972.

———. "Les intendants et leurs enquêtes (d'après des travaux récents)." *L'information historique* 38 (1976), 11–24.

Tresse, René. "Contribution à l'histoire d'une technique agricole: le développement de la fabrication des faux en France de 1785 à 1827 et ses conséquences sur la pratique des moissons." *Annales: économies, sociétés, civilisations* 10, no. 3 (1955), 341–358.

Tulard, J. "Défense et illustration de l'histoire administrative." *Revue administrative* 40 (1987), 422–426.

Turnau, Irena. "La bonneterie en Europe du XVIe et XVIIIe siècle." *Annales: économies, sociétés, civilisations* 26 (1971), 1118–1132.

Vacher de Lapouge, Claude. *Necker économiste*. Paris: Dalloz, 1947.

Vardi, Liana. "The Abolition of the Guilds during the French Revolution." *French Historical Studies* 15 (1988), 704–717.

———. *The Land and the Loom: Rural Industry in the North of France; the Example of Montigny-en-Cambrésis (1600–1800)*. Ottawa: National Library of Canada, 1986.

Vayssière, Pierre. "Un pionnier de la révolution industrielle en Languedoc au XVIIIe siècle: John Holker." *Annales du Midi* 79 (1967), 269–286.

Vidalenc, Jean. "Quelques remarques sur le rôle des Anglais dans la Révolution industrielle en France." *Annales de Normandie* 2 (1958), 273–290.

Vigreux, Pierre. *Turgot (1727–1781): textes choisis et préface*. Paris: Dalloz, 1947.

Waldo, Dwight. *The Administrative State*. New York: Ronald Press, 1948.

Wallon, Henri. *La Chambre de Commerce de la province de Normandie, 1703–1791*. Rouen: Cagniard, 1903.

Weber, Max. "Bureaucracy." In *From Max Weber: Essays in Sociology*, edited and translated by H. H. Gerth and C. Wright Mills. New York: Oxford University Press, 1967.

———. *The Theory of Social and Economic Organization*. Translated by A. M. Henderson and Talcott Parsons. Edited by Talcott Parsons. New York: Free Press, 1968.

Weiss, J. H. *The Making of Technological Man: The Social Origins of French Engineering Education*. Cambridge: MIT Press, 1982.

Weulersse, Georges. *Le mouvement physiocratique en France (de 1756 à 1770)*. 2 vols. Paris: Félix Alcan, 1910.

———. *Les physiocrates*. Paris G. Doin, 1931.

———. *La physiocratie à l'aube de la Révolution, 1781–1792*. Paris: Ecole des Hautes Etudes en Sciences Sociales, 1985.

———. *La physiocratie sous les ministères de Turgot et de Necker (1774–1781)*. Paris: Presses Universitaires de France, 1950.

Whitcomb, Edward A. "Napoleon's Prefects." *American Historical Review* 79 (1974), 1089–1118.

Woronoff, Denis. "La crise de la forêt française pendant la Révolution et l'Empire: l'indicateur sidérurgique." *Cahiers de l'histoire* 24 (1979), 3–18.

———. *L'industrie sidérurgique en France pendant la Révolution et l'Empire*. Paris: Ecole des Hautes Etudes en Sciences Sociales, 1984.

———. "Le monde ouvrier de la sidérurgie ancienne: note sur l'exemple français." *Mouvement social* 97 (1976), 109–119.

———, ed. *Forges et forêts: recherches sur la consommation proto-industrielle de bois*. Paris: Ecole des Hautes Etudes en Sciences Sociales, 1990.

Wrigley, E. A. *Continuity, Chance and Change: The Character of the Industrial Revolution in England*. Cambridge: Cambridge University Press, 1988.

Wybo, Bernard. *Le Conseil de Commerce et le commerce intérieur de la France au XVIIIe siècle*. Paris: Domat-Montchrétien, 1936.

Wykes-Joyce, Max. *7000 Years of Pottery and Porcelain*. London: Peter Owen, 1958.

Young, David Bruce. "Forests, Mines, and Fuel: The Question of Wood and Coal in Eighteenth-Century France." In *Proceedings of the Third Annual Meeting of the Western Society for French History, December 4–6, 1975*, pp. 328–336. College Station, Tex.: Texas A&M University, 1976.

Index

Abbeville, 35, 43, 51–52, 60, 74, 101–102
Académie des Sciences, Arts, et Belles-Lettres of Dijon, 58
Academy of Sciences of Rouen, 53, 79
Acier cémenté, 62–63, 82, 87, 92, 96
Acier fondu, 62–63, 82, 87
Acier naturel, 62–63, 82–83, 92
African slave trade, 45
Agay de Mutigney, François Marie Bruno d', intendant of Picardy (Amiens), 101, 104
Alençon, 17, 44–45
Alkalis, 57
Almanach Royal, 16
Alsace, 17
Alum, 57, 70
Amboise, foundry, 82; hardware manufactory, 82
American War of Independence, 81, 86
Amiens, 34, 51, 101–102, 104
Angoulême, 85; paper factory of Henry Villarmain, 85
Annonay, paper factories of Montgolfier and Johannot, 85
Anzin, coal mines of, 51
Arkwright water frame, 79–80, 86, 91, 92, 96
Armament, of St. Etienne, 83–84
Artois, Charles Philippe, comte d', 50–51, 61, 74
Artois, 17
Ashes, 54, 57
Athénas, Sieur, apothecary and entrepreneur, 58, 76, 77, 78
Auch, 17, 36
Aguesseau de Fresnes, Jean-Baptiste Paulin d', *conseiller d'état*, member of the Bureau of Commerce, 16
Aumale, 45
Auvergne, 17, 25, 36, 42, 100, 104–105
Avignon, 65, 74

Bar iron, 62

Barilla, 57, 69–70
Barrois, 17
Baumé, Anthony, chemist, 58, 61
Bayonne, 99
Béarn, 17, 99
Berry, 56–57
Berthollet, Claude-Louis, chemist, 79
Bertier de Sauvigny, Louis Jean, *conseiller d'état*, member of the Bureau of Commerce, 16
Bigorre, 99
Billet de congé, 27, 29, 38, 46
Binelly, engineer of mines, 82
Birmingham (England), 84
Blankets, 39, 66
Bleaching, 34, 54
Blondel, Antoine Louis, intendant of commerce, 17, 50–52, 90, 93, 104
Boisroger, *inspecteur honoraire*, 30–31
Bolbec, 102
Bologna, 54
Bonneterie, 17, 31, 35, 40, 46
Bordeaux, 17, 25, 52, 60, 84
Boucard, 56–57
Boucher, Sieur, 38
Bouillon, duc de, 100
Boullay, Sieur, fabricant, 103–104
Bourdonnaye de Blossac, Paul Esprit Marie de la, intendant of Poitou (Poitiers), 100–101
Bourges, 17
Bouvier, Demoiselle Eléonore, glass manufacturer, 52
Boyer, glass manufacturer, 63–64, 73–74
Brass, 70
Brest, 32
Bridges and Highways (*Ponts et Chaussées*), 89
Brisson, inspector of manufactures at Lyons, 101
Brittany, 57, 68, 76, 86
Brown, inspector of manufactures of Lower Normandy (Caen), 29–30, 102,

Brown (*continued*)
103
Brunet, inspector of manufactures of Middle Normandy (Alençon), 29, 99, 105
Bruyard, chief clerk of the two Trudaines, 36, 41
Buffon, comte de, 63
Bureau, as an administrative unit, 14
Bureau chief, 14, 16, 17–18
Bureau of Commerce, as a unit, 13, 16, 21, 23, 24, 88–89, 93–95
Bureaux de visite et de marque, 25, 29, 32, 35, 36–37, 39, 40, 42, 99, 100, 101, 102, 103, 104
Burgundy (duchy and county), 17, 24, 52–53, 75–76

Caen, 17
Caisse de Commerce, 17, 100, 103
Caisse d'Escompte, 85
Caisse des étoffes étrangères, in Lyons, 73
Calonne, Charles-Alexandre de, intendant of Flanders and Artois, then Controller General of Finances, 14, 21, 48
Cambrésis, 17
Canada, 66–67
Carcassonne, 86
Carters, 48
Caryu, inspector of manufactures at Bayonne, 99
Cast iron, 62–63, 92
Castres, 100
Castries, secretary of the navy, 81
Cauchy, mathematician, 59
Caze de la Bôve, Gaspard Louis de, intendant of Brittany, 86
Chaix, *préposé* in the Lyonnais and sub-inspector of manufactures at Laval, 44
Chamber of Commerce of Normandy, 60
Chambers of commerce, 18, 25, 49
Chambon-en-forêt, 83
Champagne, 17, 25
Chaptal, Jean Antoine, chemist, 68–70
Charpentier, inventor, 84
Chartres, 29
Chaumont de la Galaizière, Antoine Martin, *conseiller d'état*, member of the Bureau of Commerce, 16
Chemical industry, 54, 57–59, 64–66, 67–70, 74, 76–78, 86, 92, 96

Chemistry, 58, 68
Cherbourg, 77
Claude de Chazerat, Charles Antoine, intendant of Auvergne, 42–43, 100, 104–105
Clermont-de-Lodève, 34
Clozel de la Chabrerie, François Pierre Du, intendant of Tours, 101, 104
Coal (and coke), 54–55, 87, 92, 96
Colbert, 28, 55, 90
Colonia, Pierre Joseph, intendant of commerce, 17, 36–37, 52, 54, 59–60, 65, 75–76, 79, 82, 83–84, 90, 93
Combinations (of workers), 27, 46–47
Compagnie des Poudres, 66, 74, 75
Compagnonnages, 46–47. *See also* Combinations (of workers)
Concept of a balanced economy, 67, 90
Concept of the ethical rightness of a disciplined, orderly, sound administration operating according to law and rational procedures and principles, 44, 49, 64, 89, 90, 94. *See also* Procedures, standard operating
Condorcet, secretary of the Royal Academy of Sciences, 61
Conseil d'en haut, 14
Conseil des dépêches, 14
Conseil royal de commerce, 14
Conseil royal des finances, 14
Controller General, 13, 14, 16, 21, 23, 24, 26, 39, 42, 45, 46–47, 48, 55, 57, 58, 75. *See also* Joly de Fleury; Necker; Ormesson
Controller General, department of the, 13–14, 15
Copper products, 54, 70, 80–81, 87, 91, 96
Coral, manufactured objects of, 70–71
Cornuau, inspector of manufactures at Limoges, 103
Corsica, 14, 65
Cort, Henry, inventor in the iron industry, 93
Cotte, Jules François de, *conseiller d'état*, member of the Bureau of Commerce, 16–17
Cotton (raw), 53
Cottons (industry and cloth), 34, 50, 53, 66–67, 79–80, 86, 91, 92
Creusot, iron and steel complex, 92
Croisic, 77, 78

Cromford, 92
Crommelin, Charles-François Quentin, subinspector of manufactures at Valenciennes, 33–34
Crompton, inventor, 92
Crystal ware, 51, 63, 84–85, 86

D'Archambault, Sieur, manufacturer of lead plate, 84
d'Audouard, Sieur Jean Joseph Gaspard, glass manufacturer, 54–55
D'Auxon, Madame, soap manufacturer, 60–61
Dambourney, chemist, 60, 79
Darby, Abraham, English ironmaster, 92
Darnetal, 102
Dauphiny, 17, 36, 73, 82, 104
De la Boullaye, intendant of the Department of Mines, 63
Delaplace, Jean-Baptiste, inventor in manufacture of iron, 61–63, 81–82
Deputies of commerce, 18, 21, 25, 38, 45, 49, 70–73, 89, 90, 94
Descartes, René, 59, 91
Des Forges, director of waters and forests, 51, 52–53, 60, 74
Desmarest, Nicolas, scientest and industrial expert, 85, 87
Dijon, 52–53, 58, 76, 77
Dufour de Villeneuve, Jean-Baptiste Claude, intendant of Berry, 56–57
Dupré de Saint-Maur, Nicolas, intendant of Bordeaux, 52, 60, 84
Dyeing, 34, 53, 55–56, 60, 69, 79

Earthenware. *See* Faïence
Egypt, 57
Elbeuf, 29, 30–31, 38, 46
Elèves of manufactures, 26, 34, 42
Emigration of French workers, 47–48
Encouragement of industry, general, 49–87; by major industrial sectors: glass, 50–53, 54–55, 56–57, 60, 63–64, 71, 73–74, 84–85; textiles, 50, 53–54, 55–56, 60, 66–67, 71, 79–80, 86; chemicals, 54, 57–59, 64–66, 67–70, 74, 76–78, 86–87; iron and steel, 61–63, 73, 75–76, 81–84, 87; paper, 50, 70, 85, 87
England, 34, 51, 57, 89, 91
English competition, 46, 51, 53, 57, 62, 63–64, 73–74, 79–80, 81, 84–85, 92, 93, 95, 96
English workers (in France), 64, 79–80, 81, 87, 96
Esmangart, Charles François Hyacinthe, intendant of Lower Normandy (Caen), 99
Esnard, Joseph, glass manufacturer, 52
Espionage, industrial, 63–64, 79–80, 86, 96
Essonne, paper factory, 85
Evreux, 45, 53, 100
Exemptions from *taille*, 70; from rules governing admission to guild mastershiip, 84
Expéditionnaire, 14, 18, 93

Faïence, 54
Farmers General, 18, 19, 42–44, 48, 49, 65, 67–68, 71–73, 76–78, 81, 87, 89, 90, 91, 95, 97
Feydeau de Marville, Claude Henry, *conseiller d'état*, member of the Bureau of Commerce, 16
Finishing, 54
Flanders, 17
Flax, 53
Flesselles, Jacques de, intendant of the Lyonnais, 43, 76, 83
Flint glass, 63–64
Flying shuttle, 96
Fontenay-le-Comte, 32, 100–101
Foreign Affairs, Department of, 13, 16, 21, 46–47, 89
Foreign workers, 64, 76, 96
Forest management, 50–51, 74–76, 86
Forêt l'abbaye, 51
Fourcade, *premier commis* of the two Montarans, 41
Fréjard, father and son, glass manufactures, 52–53

Gabelles, 67–68
Garçon de bureau, 14, 18, 93
Gardes-jurés, 25–26, 28, 30–31, 32–33, 35, 36–37, 39, 40, 42, 44–45, 86, 99, 100, 101, 102, 103, 105
Gauss, 59
Gauzes, 54
Généralité, as an administrative unit, 14, 15, 16, 25

INDEX

Geniere, Sieur de la, inspector of manufactures at Castres, 100
Geoffrey, painter, 56
Germany, 34, 57, 80
Givors, 52
Glaesner, Sieur, manufacturer of watches, 76
Glass (industry and product), 50–53, 54–55, 56–57, 60, 63–64, 71, 73–74, 84–85, 86, 96
Glasswort, 57, 69
Godran College and Faculty of Law (Dijon), 58
Gournay, Vincent de, intendant of commerce, 94
Goy, S., inspector of manufactures at Upper Normandy (Rouen), 67, 104
Great Britain. *See* England
Grignon, Chevalier, metallurgical consultant, 63
Guénault, Paris dyer, 65
Guilds, 44–45, 46, 84
Guines, duc de, 63, 74
Guiraud, Sieur, glass manufacturer, 52–53, 60
Gunpowder, 66
Guyton de Morveau, Louis Bernard, 58–59, 64–65, 67–68, 76–78, 86–87, 91

Hainaut, 17
Hardware, 82
Hargreaves's spinning jenny, 79–80, 86, 92, 96
Hayange, 92
Hellot, Jean, chemist, 56
Hemp and hempen products, 32, 53
Holker, John, manufacturer of textiles and chemicals, inspector general of manufactures, 57, 67, 79–80
Holland, 57, 85
Hollenweger, Sieur, inventor, 76–78, 86–87
Hôtel de Mortagne, 59–60, 79, 82, 91
Hue de Miromesnil, keeper of the seals, 45
Huet de Vaudour, inspector of manufactures of Tours, 43–44
Hugh Capet, 13, 95
Huguenots, French *émigrés*, 85

Iberian peninsula, 43, 57
Industrial strategies, 20, 49, 50, 86, 95,
97; for glass, 50–53, 86; for textiles, 50, 53, 86; for chemicals, 50, 57–58, 86–87; for metals, 50, 61–63, 87; for paper, 50, 85, 87
Inspector general of manufactures, 57, 67, 79–80
Inspectors of manufactures, 18–19, 23, 25, 26, 31, 36, 38–39, 41, 42, 49, 55, 90, 94, 95, 103
Instruction of artisans, 59. *See also* Museum, industrial
Intendants (of a *généralité*), 14, 15, 16, 18–20, 21, 23, 25, 28, 29, 31, 48, 49, 56, 89, 90, 94, 99, 103
Intendants of commerce, general, 17, 18–21, 23, 25, 27, 48–49, 89, 93, 97. *See also* Blondel; Colonia; Montaran *père* and *fils*; Tolozan
Intermediate system (between mercantilism and laissez-faire), 24–49, 91, 95, 97
Iron and steel, 61–63, 73, 75–76, 81–84, 87, 92
Italy, 34, 54, 57
Ivoy, 56–57

Jars, Gabriel, inspector general of mines, 82–83, 92
Jewelry, gold, 70
Johannot, paper manufacturer, 85
Joly de Fleury de la Vallette, Jean-François, minister of state and finances, 13, 24, 27–28, 31, 37, 38, 42, 43, 50, 54, 60, 63, 68, 69–70, 73, 74, 75, 76, 83, 99, 100, 102, 103, 104–105
Journeymen, 46
Jubié, inspector of manufactures of Auvergne, 42–43, 100
Juge des manufactures, 13, 42, 45, 104
Jullien, Antoine Jean-Baptiste Alexandre, intendant of Middle Normandy (Alençon), 45
Jullien *dit* Campis, worker in a pin factory, 38

Keeper of the seals, 13, 26, 45, 46–47, 89
Kelp, 57

Labor, 37–38, 46–48, 49, 90. *See also* Combinations (of workers); Journeymen; Master craftsmen; Regulation of workers

INDEX

Labréaux, inventor, 84
La Chaussade, royal manufactory of supplies for naval arsenals, 81–82
LaCoré, Charles André de, intendant of Franche Comté, 75–76
Laigle, 38
Laissez-faire, 24, 35, 91
Lambert, glass manufacturer, 63–64, 73–74
Lambert, Boyer, and Company, 63–64, 73–74
Landes, 60
Languedoc, 17, 25, 28, 34, 36, 37, 39, 40, 41, 42, 43, 44, 47, 65, 69, 85, 86, 91; estates of, 25, 85
Lansel, J. Antoine, subinspector of manufactures, 41
Lapenne, Sieur, manufacturer of chemicals, 65–66, 74
La Rochefort, 32
La Rochelle, 17
La Salle, Philippe de, inventor, 54
La Tour de Glené, Charles Jean-Baptiste Des Galois de, intendant of Provence, 54–55
Lava bottles, 68–69
Laval, 43–44, 97, 98, 103
Lavoisier, Antoine-Laurent, chemist, 58, 66
Lazowsky, Claude, subinspector of manufactures at Elbeuf and Louviers, 30–31, 41
Lead, 70, 84
Leather, 17, 34, 91
Le Camus de Lamare, Louis, copper manufacturer, 81
Le Carpentier, Sieur, receiver of *droit de marque* at Rouen, 100
L'Ecrevisse, M., Dutch carpenter, 85
Le Marchant, inspector of manufactures at St. Simphorien de Lay, 103
Le Noir, lieutenant general of the police of Paris, 54
Lepage, subinspector of manufactures at Aumale, 30
Lepine, near Arpajon, 80
Le Turc, government industrial spy, 79, 86, 91
Levergeois, Jean, weaver, 30
Libour, subinspector of manufactures at Laval, 43–44, 103
Limoges, 103

Limousin, 85
Linens (industry and cloth), 17, 33–34, 39, 43, 53, 91
Liouville, administrator at royal iron works at La Chaussade, 81–82
Lisieux, 44–45, 99–100, 105
Livret, 27, 46
Loire River, 56
Longchamp, 52
Lorraine, 17, 82
Louis XIV, 23
Louis XVI, 13, 14, 24, 50–51, 75, 89
Louviers, 30–31
Lyonnais, 17, 43, 52
Lyons, 34, 36–37, 39, 40, 42, 43, 52, 54, 73, 83, 97, 98, 101

Macquer, Pierre Joseph, chemist, 56, 58–59, 61, 64–65, 67, 73–74, 82, 103
Madder, 55–56
Maître des requêtes, 24
Malherbe, French Benedictine and entrepreneur, 57–59, 64
Manufacture royale, 65–66, 74, 76, 83, 102
Mariaguer, 42
Market, 49, 53, 96
Marseilles, 54, 61, 86
Martin, Jacques, cotton textile manufacturer, 80, 91
Master craftsmen, 29, 31, 33–34, 38, 43–44, 46, 49, 65, 86, 97–98, 99–105
Maur, 101
Melfort, comte de, 56–57
Mercantilism, 24, 54, 90, 96
Merchants, 43–44, 46, 53, 83, 84, 86, 105
Mercier *père*, Rouen merchant, 85
Metallurgy. *See* Copper; Iron and steel; Lead; Tin
Meulan d'Ablois, Marie Pierre Charles, intendant of Montauban, 101
Miller, James Grier, 93
Milne, Jacques, English artisan and French textile manufacturer, 80
Mines, Department of, 63
Monancourt, 45
Montaran (*fils*), Jean-Jacques-Mauville Michau de, intendant of commerce, 17, 22, 31–32, 35–36, 42–44, 54–55, 65, 69–70, 86, 90, 93, 99, 100, 101, 102, 103, 104

156 INDEX

Montaran (*père*), Jacques-Marie-Jérôme Michau de, intendant of commerce, 17, 54, 90, 93
Montauban, 17, 36, 101
Montgolfier, paper manufacturer, 85
Montmarillon, Sieur, glass manufacturer, 52–53, 60
Montpellier, 68, 69, 74; university, 68
Morin, Sieur, merchant of Rouen, 46
Morize, inventor, 53, 79
Morlaix, 86
Moulins, 17
Moyroud, Sieur, ironmaster, 73, 82–83
Museum, industrial, 59–60, 91

Nantes, 76–78
Navy, Department of the, 13, 16, 21, 89
Necker, Jacques, director general of finances, 13, 17, 21, 24, 33–34, 50, 56, 58, 63, 91, 93, 94, 95
Nîmes, 25, 28, 31, 37, 39, 40, 41, 42, 65, 74, 98
Niort, 40
Nitric acid, 65
Nogent-le-Rotrou, 45, 105
Normandy, Lower (Caen), 17, 29–30, 57, 99, 102, 103–104, 105
Normandy, Middle (Alençon), 17, 29, 44–45, 99, 105
Normandy, Upper (Rouen), 17, 30, 53, 67, 84–85, 100, 102, 105

Oak bark, 70
Oils, 34
Olive oil, 57
Oppenheimer, Mayer, 84–85
Orléans, duc d', 74
Orléans, *généralité*, 17, 29; town, 39
Ormesson, Henri François-de Paule Lefèvre d', controller general of finances, 13, 43–44, 48, 75, 76, 77, 78, 83–84, 86

Pajot de Marcheval, Christophe de, intendant of Dauphiny, 73, 82–83, 104
Palle, Clément, ironmaster, 83
Paper (industry and product), 17, 50, 70, 85, 87, 92, 96
Paris, *généralité*, 17, 36, 104–105; city, 17, 58, 61, 74, 84
Parlement of Dijon, 58

Parlement of Paris, 13
Parlement of Provence, 54
Parlement of Rouen, 38
Parlements, 14, 46–47, 89
Partenay de Niort, 32
Passementiers, 28, 46
Peasants, 53
Peat, 34
Pensions (to inventors and scientists), 73, 79
Penthièvre, duc de, 30
Perret, Sieur, "maître coutelier," 82
Perrin de Cipierre, François Claude, intendant of Orléans, 29
Picardy, 17, 25, 34, 35, 50–52, 80, 101
Piedmont, 83
Pierrebénite, 52
Piéton, Sieur, glass manufacturer, 56–57
Pig iron, 62
Plancher-les-Mines, 75
Plate glass, 92, 96. *See also* Royal Plate Glass Company
Poitiers, 66
Poitou, 17, 32–33, 39, 40, 66–67, 100–101
Police, 27, 42, 46, 47, 54, 95, 104
Pontoise, 56
Ponts et chaussées (administration of), 89
Portugal, 57
Potash, 54, 57, 70, 78
Pottier *fils*, Sieur, manufacturer of pins, 38
Premier commis, 15, 17–18, 19, 20, 21, 23, 40–41, 93
Préposés, 25–26, 39, 42, 45, 100, 101, 103, 104, 105
Prévôt des marchands (Lyons), 42
Priqueleur, Sieur, ironmaster, 75
Privileges, 13, 70, 89; exclusive, to manufacture in a locality, 51, 54–55, 56–57, 76–78, 84
Procedures, standard operating, 19–20, 45, 75, 77, 83, 85, 86, 94, 95, 96
Procureurs général (of a parlement), 14, 46–47
Provence, 18, 36, 54–55

Rédacteur, 14, 18, 93
Regulations (industrial): intermediate system, 24, 33–35, 42, 48–49; of quality of product and methods of manufacture, 24–49, 89, 94, 97–98, 99–105; of

workers, 24, 26–27, 29, 37–38, 46–48, 89, 90, 99
Ribbons, colored, 71
Rivey, Sieur, inventor, 73
Robichon, Michel, glass manufacturer, 52
Roland de la Platière, inspector of manufactures of Picardy (Amiens), 33, 34–36, 80, 91, 94, 104; his wife, Manon, assists with publications, 34
Role norms and expectations, 94
Roman Catholic Church, 13, 76
Romilly, 81, 87, 91
Romorantin, 29
Rouen, 17, 36, 46, 53, 54, 57, 60, 67, 81, 85, 91, 100
Roussillon, 17, 36
Royal Academy of Sciences, 19, 58, 59, 61, 85, 103
Royal Household, Department of the, 13
Royal Plate Glass Company, 51

St. Cloud, 63
Saint-Cyr, house of, 75
Sainte-Foy, intendant of Picardy, 51
Saint Etienne, manufactory of muskets, 83–84
Saint-Germain-des-Prés, 57–58, 61
Saint-Gobain, glass factory, 77
Saint-Maixant, 40
Saint-Priest, Jean Emmanuel Guignard de, intendant of Languedoc, 41, 42, 43, 47–48, 65–66, 70, 86, 91, 94
St. Quentin, 101, 102–103, 104
St. Simphorien de Lay, 103
Salt, 54, 58, 76
Saltpeter, 58, 65
Sanche, hardware manufacturer, 82
Saurade de Richard, brothers, paper manufacturers, 85
Science. *See* Chemistry; Royal Academy of Sciences; Scientists
Scientific instruments, 71
Scientists, 19, 23, 53, 54, 55–56, 58, 61, 85, 89, 96, 97
Sedan, 39, 40, 43, 97
Ségur, Maréchal de, minister of war, 48, 83–84
Sens, 80
Silk (industry and cloth), 17, 28, 53, 54, 71, 79, 92, 96
Silk (raw), 53

Simon, Herbert, 20
Smuggling of looms abroad, 48
Soap, 34, 57, 61
Societies of agriculture, 56
Society of Agriculture of Rouen, 53, 79
Soda, 57–58, 69, 70, 76–78, 86–87, 91, 97. *See also* Chaptal; Guyton de Morveau; Hollenweger
Soissons, 17
Somme River, 52
Sonnerat, Sieur, glass manufacturer, 52
Spain, 47, 57, 69. *See also* Iberian peninsula
Spinning, 66, 79–80, 92
Steam engines, 92
Steel. *See* Iron and steel
Stéphanopoli, Sieur Dino, inventor of dyes, 65
Stockings, 17, 31, 35, 40, 46, 66, 79, 103–104
Stoucard, Sieur, manufacturer of copper and tin sheets, 54
Sturgeon, Sieur, manufacturer of earthenware, 54
Subdelegates of intendants of a *généralité*, 15, 18, 20–21, 65–66
Subinspector of manufactures, 21, 25, 34, 42, 90, 94
Subsidies to manufactures, 17, 74, 76, 80
Sugar, 70
Sulfuric acid, 57, 65–66, 70
Switzerland, 57, 76
Syndics, 36–37
Systems analysis, 93–94

Tanning, 34, 70
Tapestries, 70
Tariff, 19, 23, 70–71
Textiles, 24, 50, 53–54. *See also* Cottons; Encouragement to industry (textiles); Industrial strategies (textiles); Linens; Silk; Woolens
Theft (by workers), 48
Thiroux de Crosne, Louis, intendant of Upper Normandy (Rouen), 27–28, 29, 38, 81, 85, 91, 100, 102, 104–105
Thizy, 34
Three Bishoprics (Metz, Toul, Verdun), 17
Tin, 54, 69
Tocqueville, Alexis de, 14

Tolozan, Jean-François, intendant of commerce, 17, 22, 37–38, 40–41, 47–48, 53, 56–57, 60, 63, 76–78, 79, 85, 90, 93
Touraine, 17, 43, 101
Tourlaville, 77
Tours, 104
Transportation, 49, 96
Tribert, inspector of linens and batiste at St. Quentin, 102–103
Trona ("natural soda"), 57
Trudaine, Daniel Charles, director of commerce, 17, 34, 35, 36, 41, 45, 57, 65, 67, 77, 87, 93, 94
Trudaine de Montigny, Jean Charles Philibert, 17, 34, 36, 41, 67, 79–80
Turgot, Anne-Robert-Jacques, intendant of Limoges and controller general of finances, 13, 21, 94
Turin, 83

Utility, concept of, 59, 68, 69, 75
Uzès, 31; bishop of, 31

Valenciennes, 33, 97
Valioud, Etienne Pierre Dormenville, *premier commis*, 13, 41
Vandermonde, Alexandre-Théophile, 54, 59–60, 79, 80, 82, 83, 91

Vaucanson, Jacques de, inventor, 59
Vaugelade, inspector of manufactures of Poitou (Poitiers), 32–33, 40, 66–67
Vergennes, Charles Gravier, comte de, secretary of state for foreign affairs, 54
Vilevault, Louis Guillaume de, intendant of commerce, 18, 43–44
Villard, George, inventor, 59–60
Villarmin, Henry, paper manufacturer, 85
Villeraux, M. de, inquires about *manufactures royales* and seals, 102
Vire, 29–30
Vitriol, oil of. *See* Sulfuric acid

War (the army), Department of, 13, 14–15, 21, 23, 48, 83–84, 89, 97
Watches, 76, 77
Waters and Forests, Administration of, 19, 21, 23, 89
Watt, James, English inventor, 92–93
Weavers, 39, 40, 42, 91
Weaving, 34, 35
Wendel, Ignace de, ironmaster, 92
West Indies, French, 43
Wilkinson, John, English inventor, 92
Wool (raw), 53, 66
Woolens (industry and cloth), 34, 35, 43, 53, 66–67, 86, 91, 99
Wrought iron, 62